WORDS THAT INSPIRED HIM

NORMAN VINCENT PEALE

WORDS THAT INSPIRED HIM

A Lifetime of Favorite
Writings, Poems, and Quotations

Inspirational Press • New York

First Inspirational Press edition published in 1994.

Inspirational Press
A division of BBS Publishing Corporation
386 Park Avenue South
New York, NY 10016

Inspirational Press is a registered trademark of BBS Publishing Corporation.

Published by arrangement with Harper San Francisco, a division of HarperCollins Publishers.

Library of Congress Catalog Card Number: 94-77193

ISBN: 0-88486-100-7

Printed in the United States of America.

Contents

Book I

My Favorite Quotations

Contents

Acknowledgments

I appreciate the efficient work on this
manuscript of my secretaries Sybil Light and
Nancy Dakin and the research of
Donald T. Kauffman.

Introduction

Winston Churchill once said, "It is a good thing to read books of quotations. The quotations when engraved upon the memory give you good thoughts."

And to have "good thoughts" is important, for a person becomes what he thinks. Gautama Buddha told us that. "Mind is everything," he said. "We become what we think."

Charles Edison, one-time governor of New Jersey and son of the famous inventor Thomas A. Edison, was a personal friend of mine; I was with him many times. He loved to talk about his father and told me many stories about him.

It seems that the older Edison thought that the mind is our greatest asset and would often say to his son, "The primary function of the body is to carry the brain." That is not a direct quotation, being simply a remark in conversation, but it may be taken to represent the inventor's thinking. The brain, besides directing motor activity, is, of course, the instrument by which one remembers, considers, evaluates, thinks. And it is through the wonders of the brain that one knows God, the Creator of it all.

William James, sometimes called the father of American psychological science, expressed agreement with these ideas and went even further: "The greatest discovery of my generation is that human beings can alter their lives by altering their attitudes of mind." Professor James's generation lived in what may be called an age of discovery. During that era some of the most notable discoveries of science took place. But the supreme discovery is that we can change our lives by the changing of mental attitudes.

That being true — and that it is true is a generally accepted fact today — then anything that can contribute to a thought process that changes our basic attitudes is of value. I have found over many years that the habit of dropping choice thoughts into consciousness and allowing them to permeate the mental structure results finally in a thought pattern that affects virtually the totality of one's life.

The quotation just cited from William James, for example, was dropped into my thoughts one day long ago as I sat in class at Boston University. It was as if I had been hit by a bolt of lightning. It struck me so forcibly that it vitally affected my total thinking. The truth of it seemed certain. I believed it; I accepted it. From my background, I associated personal change with faith and, in a flash of insight, knew that I could change my life by changing my attitudes of mind. I've been advocating that truth about people ever since.

So the object of this book of quotations is to bring to readers the thoughts I have picked up in a lifetime of reading, as well as others heard in conversation with all sorts of people. All wisdom is not in the past. But, when working with quotations, an old saying often comes to mind: "There is nothing new under the sun." Often today's speakers, writers, and conversationalists may come up with a new formulation of an ancient truth that is fascinating, even exciting. We may expect that these truths may continue to be quoted 100 years from now, perhaps modernized to fit the late twenty-first century.

I have had a lot of pleasure in gathering together these favorite quotations. Incidents in which the quotations have been meaningful to me have come to mind as I collected them for this book. I could actually make another book of stories about those incidents. But for now, just read a few of these quotations at a time and let them "germinate," shall we say, in your consciousness. They may start something. And, when engraved upon the memory, as Churchill said, they will indeed "give you good thoughts."

I hope that you have as much pleasure in reading them as I did when putting them together in this book. And may I add perhaps the greatest quotation of all, though I do not know who first said it: "God bless you."

Norman Vincent Peale

One
Daily Life and Work

As I write this, autumn has returned to the Northeast where I live, and the hills and valleys are bathed in the special light that gives the landscape a crystal clarity.

Vacations are over, and most of us are busy with our work. For some, unfortunately, the daily routine is drudgery; the surveys say that millions of people hate their jobs. But it need not be so! For decades, I have been saying that an enthusiastic, positive outlook can transform any situation, and thousands of individuals testify to the truth of that claim.

It used to be stated—perhaps sometimes with justification—that religion was a matter of "pie in the sky by and by." But real religion is and always has been redemption in the here-and-now as well as a strongly based hope for the hereafter. The realities of faith, hope, and love can make every day an exciting adventure.

I contend that how you do something and the attitude with which you do it are usually even more important than what you do. The other day a friend remarked, "I just had a good, long walk to the post office, and I made an important discovery." When I asked him what he discovered, he said, "During the fall and winter, I try to get as much sun as possible. On my walk today, I could have been in the shade most of the time, but I found it was just as easy to walk on the sunny side of the street."

Often we have no choice about doing things, but we can always choose how to do them. And that, as the following quotations illustrate, can make all the difference in your daily life.

*Wherefore have ye not fulfilled your task?

EXODUS 5:14

The men did the work faithfully.

2 CHRONICLES 34:12

Establish thou the work of our hands upon us.

PSALM 90:17

*All of the quotations in each chapter appear in approximate chronological order by the birthdate of the authors. Anonymous quotations are placed in their estimated chronology.

2

Whatsoever thy hand findeth to do, do it with thy might.

ECCLESIASTES 9:10

He who labors diligently need never despair; for all things are accomplished by diligence and labor.

MENANDER (343–291 B.C.)

The life given us by nature is short, but the memory of a well-spent life is eternal.

MARCUS TULLIUS CICERO (106–43 B.C.)

In adversity remember to keep an even mind.

HORACE (QUINTUS HORATIUS FLACEUS, 65–8 B.C.)

A rolling stone gathers no moss.

PUBLILIUS SYRUS (ca. 42 B.C.)

It is a rough road that leads to the heights of greatness.

LUCIUS ANNAEUS SENECA (4 B.C.–A.D. 65)

Those who aim at great deeds must also suffer
greatly.

PLUTARCH (46–120)

Not slothful in business; fervent in spirit; serving the
Lord.

ROMANS 12:11

Vex not thy spirit at the course of things; they heed
not thy vexation. How ludicrous and outlandish is
astonishment at anything that may happen in life.

MARCUS AURELIUS (121–180)

Art is right reason in the doing of work.

ST. THOMAS AQUINAS (1225–1274)

Diligence is the mother of good luck, and God gives
all things to industry.

BENJAMIN FRANKLIN (1706–1790)

One today is worth two tomorrows; never leave that
till tomorrow which you can do today.

BENJAMIN FRANKLIN (1706–1790)

Never despair, but if you do, work on in despair.

EDMUND BURKE (1729–1797)

If at first you don't succeed, try, try again.

WILLIAM EDWARD HICKSON (1803–1870)

The world's a nettle; disturb it, it stings. Grasp it firmly, it stings not.

EDWARD G. L. BULWER-LYTTON (1803–1873)

The heights by great men reached and kept
Were not attained by sudden flight,
But they, while their companions slept,
Were toiling upward in the night.

HENRY WADSWORTH LONGFELLOW (1807–1882)

Still achieving, still pursuing, learn to labor and to wait.

HENRY WADSWORTH LONGFELLOW (1807–1882)

Men are born to succeed, not to fail.

HENRY DAVID THOREAU (1817–1862)

The greatest use of life is to spend it for something
that will outlast it.

WILLIAM JAMES (1842–1910)

Opportunity is missed by most people because it is
dressed in overalls and looks like work.

THOMAS A. EDISON (1847–1931)

In all human affairs there are *efforts,* and there are
results, and the strength of the effort is the measure
of the result.

JAMES ALLEN (1849–1925)

Turn your stumbling blocks into stepping stones.

ANONYMOUS

Strong people are made by opposition like kites that
go up against the wind.

FRANK HARRIS (1856–1931)

Always take an emergency leisurely.

CHINESE PROVERB

Be strong!
We are not here to play, to dream, to drift;
We have hard work to do and loads to lift;
Shun not the struggle — face it; 'tis God's gift.

MALTBIE D. BABCOCK (1858 – 1901)

We are so outnumbered there's only one thing to do.
We must attack.

SIR ANDREW CUNNINGHAM (1866 – 1963)

Choose your rut carefully; you'll be in it for the next
ten miles.

ROAD SIGN IN UPSTATE NEW YORK

In our day, when a pitcher got into trouble in a
game, instead of taking him out, our manager would
leave him in and tell him to pitch his way out of
trouble.

CY (DENTON TRUE) YOUNG (1867 – 1955)

It is a funny thing about life; if you refuse to accept
anything but the best, you very often get it.

W. SOMERSET MAUGHAM (1874 – 1965)

I have nothing to offer but blood, toil, tears, and sweat.

WINSTON CHURCHILL (1874–1965)

It's the plugging away that will win you the day
So don't be a piker old pard!
Just draw on your grit; it's so easy to quit.
It's the keeping your chin up that's hard.

ROBERT W. SERVICE (1874–1958)

Truth has no special time of its own. Its hour is now-always.

ALBERT SCHWEITZER (1875–1965)

I would never have amounted to anything were it not for adversity. I was forced to come up the hard way.

J.C. PENNEY (1875–1971)

Problems are only opportunities in work clothes.

HENRY J. KAISER (1882–1967)

Grant me the courage not to give up even though I think it is hopeless.

CHESTER W. NIMITZ (1885–1966)

Manual labor to my father was not only good and decent for its own sake, but as he was given to saying, it straightened out one's thoughts.

MARY ELLEN CHASE (1887–1973)

When the rock is hard, we get harder than the rock. When the job is tough, we get tougher than the job.

GEORGE CULLUM, SR. (1895–1983)

There is no sense in the struggle, but there is no choice but to struggle.

ERNIE PYLE (1900–1945)

To every disadvantage there is a corresponding advantage.

W. CLEMENT STONE (1902–   )

We have a problem. "Congratulations." But it's a tough problem. "Then double congratulations."

W. CLEMENT STONE (1902–   )

Strong lives are motivated by dynamic purposes.

KENNETH HILDEBRAND (1906–1979)

When the going gets tough, let the tough get going.

FRANK LEAHY (1908–1973)

I make steel for people but you put steel into people.

STEEL-COMPANY PRESIDENT

Work! Thank God for the swing of it, for the
clamoring, hammering ring of it.

ANGELA MORGAN (?–1957)

10

Two
Enthusiasm and Perseverance

———————■———————

Somewhere out of the past comes a story about three men helping build a cathedral. A passerby, watching one man digging at a wall for the foundation, asked him what he was doing. Between shovels full of earth he grunted, "I'm digging a hole."

A stonemason, asked the same question, answered, "Can't you see I'm making a wall?"

Another laborer was pushing a cart loaded with stones toward the construction site. When he was asked the question, his face lighted up with enthusiasm. He replied, "I'm building a cathedral."

Success at anything requires two vital ingredients: enthusiasm and perseverance. Both can be helped by the broad view that looks beyond temporary difficulties and disappointments to a great goal. What are you doing with your life? Are you putting in time or building something lasting and worthwhile? These are questions we must ask ourselves.

Enthusiasm is the priceless quality that makes everything different. The men and women who achieve the most are invariably inspired by enthusiasm. They approach life, its opportunities, and its problems with this vital characteristic.

Successful individuals also keep at it. Great ideas come to naught unless they are carried to completion. When Glenn Cunningham was seven years old, he was so badly burned in a schoolhouse fire that his doctor said, "I doubt if he'll be able to walk again." But the little boy had been motivated by his father to become a champion runner. He visualized himself winning races. Despite intense pain, he struggled to walk again, then to run, although all he could manage at first was a queer hippety-hop gait. But he kept running until he became the outstanding miler of his time.

As you cultivate enthusiasm and perseverance, more power to you!

He did it with all his heart, and prospered.

2 CHRONICLES 31:21

The people had a mind to work.

NEHEMIAH 4:6

Here am I; send me.

ISAIAH 6:8

A journey of 1,000 miles begins with a single step.

LAO-TZU (FIFTH CENTURY B.C.)

Do not count your chickens before they hatch.

AESOP (620–560 B.C.)

It takes a wise man to recognize a wise man.

XENOPHANES (570–480 B.C.)

When you have faults, do not fear to abandon them.

CONFUCIUS (551–479 B.C.)

God loves to help him who strives to help himself.

AESCHYLUS (525–456 B.C.)

13

Well begun is half done.

ARISTOTLE (384–322 B.C.)

The great man is he who does not lose his child's
heart.

MENCIUS (371–288 B.C.)

Even God lends a hand to honest boldness.

MENANDER (343–291 B.C.)

The drops of rain make a hole in the stone not by
violence but by oft falling.

LUCRETIUS (TITUS LUCRETIUS CARUS, 96–55 B.C.)

Let us go singing as far as we go; the road will be
less tedious.

VIRGIL (PUBLIUS VERGILIUS MARO, 70–19 B.C.)

Better late than never.

LIVY (59 B.C.–A.D. 17)

Having done all, to stand.

EPHESIANS 6:13

This one thing I do, forgetting those things which are behind, and reaching forth unto those things which are before.

PHILIPPIANS 3:13

And whatsoever ye do, do it heartily.

COLOSSIANS 3:23

God helps those who persevere.

THE KORAN

Time is the most valuable thing a man can spend.

LAERTIUS DIOGENES (THIRD CENTURY)

The hammer shatters glass but forges steel.

RUSSIAN PROVERB

Trifles make perfection, but perfection is no trifle.

MICHELANGELO (1475–1564)

Wisely, and slow; they stumble that run fast.

WILLIAM SHAKESPEARE (1564–1616)

15

Foul deeds will rise, though all the earth o'erwhelm them, to men's eyes.

WILLIAM SHAKESPEARE (1564–1616)

He that can have patience can have what he will.

BENJAMIN FRANKLIN (1706–1790)

Austere perseverance, harsh and continuous, may be employed by the least of us and rarely fails of its purpose, for its silent power grows irresistibly greater with time.

JOHANN WOLFGANG VON GOETHE (1749–1832)

You never know what is enough unless you know what is more than enough.

WILLIAM BLAKE (1757–1827)

We must dare, and dare again, and go on daring.

GEORGES JACQUES DANTON (1759–1794)

The best-laid schemes o' mice an' men gang aft a-gley.

ROBERT BURNS (1759–1796)

Circumstances — what are circumstances? I make circumstances.

NAPOLEON BONAPARTE (1769–1821)

Our grand business in life is not to see what lies dimly at a distance, but to do what lies clearly at hand.

THOMAS CARLYLE (1795–1881)

Every noble work is at first impossible.

THOMAS CARLYLE (1795–1881)

Be ashamed to die until you have won some victory for humanity.

HORACE MANN (1796–1859)

Nothing great was ever achieved without enthusiasm.

RALPH WALDO EMERSON (1803–1882)

Keep cool: it will all be over 100 years hence.

RALPH WALDO EMERSON (1803–1882)

17

Everything comes if a man will only wait.

BENJAMIN DISRAELI (1804–1881)

■

We are not creatures of circumstance; we are creators of circumstance.

BENJAMIN DISRAELI (1804–1881)

■

Every production of genius must be the production of enthusiasm.

BENJAMIN DISRAELI (1804–1881)

■

I am in earnest; I will not equivocate; I will not excuse; I will not retreat a single inch; and I will be heard.

WILLIAM LLOYD GARRISON (1805–1879)

■

Perseverance is a great element of success. If you only knock long enough and loud enough at the gate, you are sure to wake up somebody.

HENRY WADSWORTH LONGFELLOW (1807–1882)

■

The great thing in this world is not so much where we are, but in what direction we are moving.

OLIVER WENDELL HOLMES (1809–1894)

To strive, to seek, to find, and not to yield.

ALFRED LORD TENNYSON (1809–1892)

Always bear in mind that your own resolution to success is more important than any other one thing.

ABRAHAM LINCOLN (1809–1865)

Would you have your songs endure? Build on the human heart.

ROBERT BROWNING (1812–1889)

'Tis not what man does which exalts him, but what man would do.

ROBERT BROWNING (1812–1889)

The greatest discovery of my generation is that a human being can alter his life by altering his attitudes of mind.

WILLIAM JAMES (1842–1910)

To improve the golden moment of opportunity, and catch the good that is within our reach, is the great art of life.

WILLIAM JAMES (1842–1910)

19

Men habitually use only a small part of the powers
which they possess and which they might use under
appropriate circumstances.

WILLIAM JAMES (1842–1910)

In any project the important factor is your belief.
Without belief there can be no successful outcome.

WILLIAM JAMES (1842–1910)

He who would be great anywhere must first be great
in his own Philadelphia.

RUSSELL H. CONWELL (1843–1925)

I prefer the folly of enthusiasm to the indifference of
wisdom.

ANATOLE FRANCE (1844–1924)

Whatever you attempt, go at it with spirit. Put some
in!

DAVID STARR JORDAN (1851–1931)

Be strong!
It matters not how deep entrenched the wrong

How hard the battle goes, the day how long
Faint not—fight on! Tomorrow comes the song.

MALTBIE D. BABCOCK (1858–1901)

Destiny is not a matter of chance; it is a matter of
choice. It is not a thing to be waited for; it is a thing
to be achieved.

WILLIAM JENNINGS BRYAN (1860–1925)

A man can succeed at almost anything for which he
has unlimited enthusiasm.

CHARLES M. SCHWAB (1862–1939)

The more things change, the more they remain the
same.

FRENCH PROVERB

The thing always happens that you really believe in;
and the belief in a thing makes it happen.

FRANK LLOYD WRIGHT (1869–1959)

Whatever you do, put romance and enthusiasm into
the life of our children.

MARGARET RAMSEY MACDONALD (1870–1911)

Never, never, never, never give up.

WINSTON CHURCHILL (1874–1965)

■

The real secret of success is enthusiasm. Yes, more
than enthusiasm, I would say excitement. I like to
see men get excited. When they get excited they
make a success of their lives.

WALTER CHRYSLER (1875–1940)

■

God will help you if you try, and you can if you
think you can.

ANNA DELANEY PEALE (1875–1939)

■

If a door slams shut it means that God is pointing to
an open door further on down.

ANNA DELANEY PEALE (1875–1939)

■

Enthusiasm is a kind of faith that has been set afire.

GEORGE MATTHEW ADAMS (1878–1962)

■

The world is moving so fast these days that the man
who says it can't be done is generally interrupted by
someone doing it.

HARRY EMERSON FOSDICK (1878–1968)

22

One can never consent to creep when one feels an
impulse to soar.

HELEN KELLER (1880–1968)

■

My mother said to me, "If you become a soldier
you'll be a general; if you become a monk you'll end
up as the pope." Instead, I became a painter and
wound up as Picasso.

PABLO PICASSO (1881–1973)

■

Somebody said that it couldn't be done
But he with a chuckle replied
That "maybe it couldn't," but he would be one
Who wouldn't say so till he'd tried.

EDGAR A. GUEST (1881–1959)

■

To be happy, drop the words *if only* and substitute
instead the words *next time.*

SMILEY BLANTON, M.D. (1882–1966)

■

Once a decision was made I did not worry about it
afterward.

HARRY S TRUMAN (1884–1972)

The future belongs to those who believe in the
beauty of their dreams.

ELEANOR ROOSEVELT (1884–1962)

Take calculated risks. That is quite different from
being rash.

GEORGE S. PATTON (1885–1945)

Flaming enthusiasm, backed up by horse sense and
persistence, is the quality that most frequently
makes for success.

DALE CARNEGIE (1888–1955)

You can be an ordinary athlete by getting away with
less than your best. But if you want to be a great,
you have to give it all you've got—your everything.

DUKE P. KAHANAMOKU (1890–1968)

I rate enthusiasm even above professional skill.

SIR EDWARD APPLETON (1892–1965)

An enthusiast may bore others, but he has never a
dull moment himself.

JOHN KIERAN (1892–1981)

He was a *how* thinker, not an *if* thinker.

ANONYMOUS

Four steps to achievement: plan purposefully, prepare prayerfully, proceed positively, pursue persistently.

WILLIAM A. WARD (1893–1959)

Act as if it were impossible to fail.

DOROTHEA BRANDE (1893–1948)

Roy has a great asset—20 percent vision. He wears thick glasses with an extra strong lens. So he never sees an obstacle in his path and goes on to success.

JOHN TIGRETT ON PUBLISHER ROY THOMSON (1894–1976)

Hell is the place where one has ceased to hope.

A. J. CRONIN (1896–1981)

There ain't nothing from the outside can lick any of us.

MARGARET MITCHELL (1900–1949), IN *Gone with the Wind*

Man is not the sum of what he has but the totality
of what he does not yet have, of what he might have.

JEAN PAUL SARTRE (1905–1980)

We must dare to think unthinkable thoughts.

JAMES W. FULBRIGHT (1905–   )

Find a need and fill it.

RUTH STAFFORD PEALE (1906–   )

If we really want to live, we'd better start at once to
try.

W.H. AUDEN (1907–1973)

Victory is not won in miles but in inches. Win a
little now, hold your ground, and later win a little
more.

LOUIS L'AMOUR (1908–1988)

We always teach employees to have positive
attitudes toward people and to their work.

RONNIE MORRIS (1911–1989)

Every problem contains the seeds of its own solution.

STANLEY ARNOLD (1925–)

Shoot for the moon. Even if you miss it you will land among the stars.

LES BROWN (1928–)

I want this team to win. I'm obsessed with winning, with discipline, with achieving.

GEORGE STEINBRENNER (1930–)

They never told me I couldn't.

TOM DEMPSEY (1947–)

Don't wait for your ship to come; swim out to it.

ANONYMOUS

Be bold—and mighty forces will come to your aid.

BASIL KING (1859–1928)

Every man is enthusiastic at times. One man has
enthusiasm for thirty minutes, another has it for
thirty days—but it is the man that has it for thirty
years who makes a success in life.

THE CATHOLIC LAYMAN

Every tomorrow has two handles. You can take hold
of the handle of anxiety or the handle of enthusiasm.
Upon your choice so will be the day.

ANONYMOUS

Three
God's Creation

———————■———————

One of the happiest men I ever knew was Bill Stidger, a professor, preacher, and writer. He always seemed to be bubbling over with joy and enthusiasm. I remember having some oyster stew with him in the South Station, Boston, and asking him why he was so full of happiness.

He told me that it was because he practiced the attitude of gratitude. "When I wake up in the morning," he said, "I thank the Lord for a sound night's sleep. I give thanks for my wife and children, for the work I have to do, for my friends and opportunities. I just run over the world in my mind, thanking him for the wonderful things in it."

I guarantee that no one can be dull or blasé with such an attitude. And what marvelous things there are for which to be grateful in God's great Creation! My wife, Ruth, and I like to travel. I experience a kind of rebirth every time I think about some of the fascinating places we have visited: Japan with its vibrant aliveness; the green island of Formosa lying in the azure sea; the Philippines and the golden sunlight there; the profound serenity of the great forests of Australia; the breathtaking grandeur of the Swiss mountains; the lovable charm of England; and the beautiful vastness of America, from New England to the Deep South, the Grand Canyon, Alaska, and the matchless Hawaiian Islands.

But above all I am thankful for people like you, the reader of this book, for you are a creation of God unequaled anywhere in the universe. God never made anyone else exactly like you, and he never will again. Thank him for yourself and then for all the rest of his glorious handiwork.

And God saw every thing that he had made, and, behold, it was very good.

GENESIS 1:31

The earth is the Lord's, and the fulness thereof.

PSALM 24:1

The earth is full of the goodness of the Lord.

PSALM 33:5

30

O Lord, how manifold are thy works! in wisdom hast
thou made them all.

PSALM 104:24

We are his workmanship.

EPHESIANS 2:10

Thou has created all things, and for thy pleasure they
are and were created.

REVELATION 4:11

April hath put a spirit of youth in every thing.

WILLIAM SHAKESPEARE (1564–1616)

Night's candles are burnt out, and jocund day
Stands tiptoe on the misty mountain tops.

WILLIAM SHAKESPEARE (1564–1616)

The sky is the daily bread of the eyes.

RALPH WALDO EMERSON (1803–1882)

31

The splendor falls on castle walls
And snowy summits old in story
The long light shakes across the lakes
And the wild cataract leaps in glory.

ALFRED LORD TENNYSON (1809–1892)

The gathering orange stain
Upon the edge of yonder western peak
Reflects the sunsets of a thousand years.

ANONYMOUS

I must go down to the seas again,
To the lonely sea and the sky,
And all I ask is a tall ship and a star
To steer her by.

JOHN MASEFIELD (1878–1967)

A sense of curiosity is nature's original school of
education.

SMILEY BLANTON, M.D. (1882–1966)

32

Poems are made by fools like me,
But only God can make a tree.

JOYCE KILMER (1886–1918)

It's a beautiful day for it.

DAILY COMMENT OF WILBUR CROSS (1862–1948)

Syracuse weather consists of eleven months of
winter and one month of poor sleighing.

SAYING IN SYRACUSE, NEW YORK (CA. 1920)

Spring is God's way of saying, "One more time!"

ROBERT ORBEN (1927–   )

Four
Faith

———■———

One of my favorite places is the little Swiss village of Burgenstock, near Lucerne. It is such a charming mixture of farms, cottages, shops, and hotels that it captures the essence of Swiss beauty and efficiency.

Burgenstock is pervaded by the spirit of a remarkable man named Friedrich Frey, who developed it. Born a peasant, Frey became an important figure in the Swiss power industry and then one of the greatest hotelkeepers in the world. His son Fritz once surprised me with the statement that his father's greatness arose out of a youthful sickness that required him to spend a year in the hospital. When I asked Fritz how that experience led to greatness, he said, "During that year my father read the Bible six times."

From that, Fritz said, his father developed such a faith that, if he were to walk a ridge with steep precipices on both sides, he would do it absolutely without fear: "He was never afraid of anything after the time he poured the Bible down inside himself."

For me, faith is another word for positive thinking. When real faith grips you, you develop a mind-set that looks for the best in everything, refuses to give up, finds a way around (or through) every obstacle, and presses on to victory. Such faith is the consequence of "pouring down inside yourself" the great truths of the Bible and thus being triumphant in human experience.

The quotations in this section, as you make them a vital part of your thoughts and actions, will help you to live positively and triumphantly.

God is our refuge and strength, a very present help in trouble.

PSALM 46:1

Be still, and know that I am God.

PSALM 46:10

Let us hear the conclusion of the whole matter: Fear God, and keep his commandments: for this is the whole duty of man.

ECCLESIASTES 12:13

Where your treasure is, there will your heart be also.

MATTHEW 6:21

If ye have faith as a grain of mustard seed . . .
nothing shall be impossible unto you.

MATTHEW 17:20

All things are possible to him that believeth.

MARK 9:23

The things which are impossible with men are
possible with God.

LUKE 18:27

I am come that they might have life, and that they
might have it more abundantly.

JOHN 10:10

If it were not so, I would have told you.

JOHN 14:2

If God be for us, who can be against us?

ROMANS 8:31

Eye hath not seen, nor ear heard, neither have
entered into the heart of man, the things which God
hath prepared for them that love him.

1 CORINTHIANS 2:9

Faith is the substance of things hoped for, the
evidence of things not seen.

HEBREWS 11:1

Men willingly believe what they wish.

JULIUS CAESAR (102−44 B.C.)

The one thing worth living for is to keep one's soul
pure.

MARCUS AURELIUS (121−180)

For the multitude of worldly friends profiteth not,
nor may strong helpers anything avail, nor wise
counselors give profitable counsel, nor the cunning of
doctors give consolation, nor riches deliver in time of
need, nor a secret place defend, if Thou, Lord, do not
assist, help, comfort, counsel, inform, and defend.

THOMAS À KEMPIS (1380−1471)

Great and wonderful are thy works, Almighty God.

MOUNTAINTOP PLAQUE, SWITZERLAND

A mighty fortress is our God,
A bulwark never failing;
Our helper he amid the flood
Of mortal ills prevailing.

MARTIN LUTHER (1483–1546)

Let nothing disturb you, let nothing frighten you:
everything passes away except God; God alone is
sufficient.

ST. THERESA (1515–1582)

Two things fill the mind with ever increasing
wonder and awe . . . the starry heavens above me and
the moral law within me.

IMMANUEL KANT (1724–1804)

The writers against religion, whilst they oppose
every system, are wisely careful never to set up any
of their own.

EDMUND BURKE (1729–1797)

God moves in a mysterious way
His wonders to perform;
He plants his footsteps in the sea
And rides upon the storm.

WILLIAM COWPER (1731–1800)

What the inner voice says will not disappoint the
hoping soul.

JOHANN CHRISTOPH FRIEDRICH VON SCHILLER (1759–1805)

In God we trust.

MOTTO ON U.S. CURRENCY

Truth, crushed to earth, shall rise again;
The eternal years of God are hers;
But Error, wounded, writhes in pain,
And dies among his worshipers.

WILLIAM CULLEN BRYANT (1794–1878)

Before me, even as behind,
God is, and all is well.

JOHN GREENLEAF WHITTIER (1807–1892)

God asks no man whether he will accept life. This is
not the choice. You must take it. The only question
is how.

HENRY WARD BEECHER (1813–1887)

God gives us always strength enough, and sense
enough, for every thing he wants us to do.

JOHN RUSKIN (1819–1900)

Fear knocked at the door.
Faith answered.
No one was there.

OLD SAYING

The light of God surrounds me,
The love of God enfolds me,
The power of God protects me,
The Presence of God watches over me,
Wherever I am, God is.

PRAYER CARD

Ten minutes spent in Christ's society every day, aye
two minutes, will make the whole day different.

HENRY DRUMMOND (1851–1897)

41

Every day affirm: I am never alone. I can do my job
well. With God's help I can succeed. I am a positive
thinker and believer.

JOHN GLOSSINGER (1868–?)

Always remember and never forget it: Jesus Christ
can make men and women what they can be.

CHARLES CLIFFORD PEALE (1870–1955)

Every morning I spend fifteen minutes filling my
mind full of God; and so there's no room left for
worry thoughts.

HOWARD CHANDLER CHRISTY (1873–1952)

It may be that each individual consciousness is a
brain cell in a universal mind.

SIR JAMES JEANS (1877–1946)

I am full-fed and yet I hunger. What means this
deeper hunger in my heart?

ALFRED NOYES (1880–1958)

We have only to believe, then little by little we shall
see the universal horror unbend and then smile upon
us.

PIERRE TEILHARD DE CHARDIN (1881–1955)

The first and finest lesson that parents can teach
their children is faith and courage.

SMILEY BLANTON, M.D. (1882–1966)

A power greater than any human being helped make
this decision.

HERBERT J. STIEFEL (1917–   )

Boys, this is only a game. But it's like life in that you
will be dealt some bad hands. Take each hand, good
or bad, and don't whine and complain but play it out.
If you're men enough to do that, God will help and
you will come out well.

DWIGHT D. EISENHOWER (1890–1969), QUOTING HIS MOTHER

The soul can split the sky in two, and let the face of
God shine through.

EDNA ST. VINCENT MILLAY (1892–1950)

We have grasped the mystery of the atom and
rejected the Sermon on the Mount.

OMAR N. BRADLEY (1893–1986)

I learned really to practice mustard seed faith, and
positive thinking, and remarkable things happened.

SIR JOHN WALTON (1904–   )

Think of only three things—your God, your family,
and the Green Bay Packers—in that order.

VINCE LOMBARDI (1913–1970), TO HIS TEAM

Now you just believe. That is all you have to do; just
believe.

ADVICE FROM AN OLD OHIO FARMER

The Bible tells us that a sparrow does not fall
without God's notice. I know he will help us meet
our responsibilities through his guidance.

MICHAEL CARDONE, SR. (1917–   )

Given willpower enough and brains enough and faith
enough, almost anything can be done.

ANONYMOUS ENGINEER

44

Five
Prayer

There are three principal ways to get what we need: by work, by thought, and by prayer. Most people work hard, and some utilize the power of thought. But prayer is greatly neglected. And this is unfortunate, for the most powerful energy one can generate is prayer energy.

How does a person acquire this energy? The first step is simply to pray. As a young man, I was interested in public speaking and listened to some of the greatest orators of my time. Once, after a particularly rousing masterpiece of elocution, I asked the speaker how one could become proficient in that art. His answer was, "By speaking." He explained: "Learn by doing. Speak every time you get a chance. Keep doing it. Practice constantly, seeking to improve your ability."

The best way to learn anything is by doing.

If you want to utilize the matchless power of prayer, begin praying immediately and continue at every opportunity. I have observed from a number of inquiries that the average person probably spends about five minutes a day in prayer. That is one half of 1 percent of one's waking hours. Back in the days of Prohibition in the United States, half of 1 percent of alcohol was declared by act of Congress to be nonintoxicating. That percentage is also nonintoxicating in religion! If you want to experience the heady energy of prayer, practice it more often.

The physician Alexis Carrel, a spiritual pioneer, advised praying everywhere: in the street, the office, the shop, the school. You can transform spare moments by praying for your needs, for those around you, for your friends and loved ones, for everyone and everything you can think of. Then believe that your prayers will be answered. They will be. And prayer is always answered in one of three ways: no, yes, or wait awhile.

What things soever ye desire, when ye pray, believe that ye receive them, and ye shall have them.

MARK 11:24

Ye have not, because ye ask not.

JAMES 4:2

Lord, I shall be very busy this day. I may forget thee,
but do not thou forget me.

SIR JACOB ASTLEY (ELEVENTH CENTURY)

My words fly up, my thoughts stay below;
Words without thoughts never to heaven go.

WILLIAM SHAKESPEARE (1564–1616)

Work as if you were to live 100 years; pray as if you
were to die tomorrow.

BENJAMIN FRANKLIN (1706–1790)

I who still pray at morning and at eve
Thrice in my life perhaps have truly prayed,
Thrice stirred below conscious self
Have felt that perfect disenthrallment which is God.

JAMES RUSSELL LOWELL (1819–1891)

Prayer is a cry of distress, a demand for help, a hymn
of love.

ALEXIS CARREL (1873–1944)

Prayer, like radium, is a luminous and self-generating form of energy.

ALEXIS CARREL (1873–1944)

When we pray we link ourselves with an inexhaustible motive power.

ALEXIS CARREL (1873–1944)

When I have a problem I pray about it, and what comes to mind and stays there I assume to be my answer. And this has been right so often that I know it is God's answer.

J. L. KRAFT (1874–1953)

God listens to our weeping when the occasion itself is beyond our knowledge but still within his love and power.

DANIEL A. POLING (1884–1968)

Prayer may not change things for you, but it for sure changes you for things.

SAMUEL M. SHOEMAKER (1893–1963)

Prayer begins where human capacity ends.

MARIAN ANDERSON (1902–   )

There are three answers to prayer: yes, no, and wait awhile. It must be recognized that no is an answer.

RUTH STAFFORD PEALE (1906–   )

Visualize, "prayerize," "actionize," and your wishes will come true.

CHARLES L. ALLEN (1913–   )

Six
Relationships

———————■———————

We hear so much about relationships today that one might get the idea that this is a twentieth-century concept. Actually, the importance of good relationships has been known throughout history.

The great Rabbi Hillel (30 B.C.–A.D. 10) was once asked if he could sum up the Jewish law while standing on one foot. He answered: "Do not unto others that which you would not have them do unto you. That is the entire Torah; the rest is commentary." And the ancient law codes of Babylon and China revolve primarily around just and fair relationships.

But our relationships with other people remain today one of our greatest problems. The president of a large company once told me that the most important thing in his business was the relationships among the employees.

During one of Billy Graham's evangelistic crusades in London, the British newspapers quoted some cutting remarks about him by a well-known clergyman of that country. It was reported that when someone began telling Billy about this, he said: "God bless that man. If I were in his place, I'd probably feel the same way about me." Such an attitude ensures personal peace of mind as well as the love and respect of other people.

Mahatma Gandhi spent his whole life helping his fellow citizens achieve their independence. What it took George Washington seven years of bloody war to accomplish, Gandhi did over more than thirty years by the power of quiet, loving nonresistance.

Jesus made it clear that the most important thing in the world is our relationship to God and to others. When we achieve that, everything good will follow.

Hatred stirreth up strifes: but love covereth all sins.

PROVERBS 10:12

A bad neighbor is a misfortune, as much as a good one is a great blessing.

HESIOD (EIGHTH CENTURY B.C.)

Once harm has been done, even a fool understands it.

HOMER (1200–850 B.C.)

What you do not want done to yourself, do not do to others.

CONFUCIUS (551–479 B.C.)

It is in the character of very few men to honor without envy a friend who has prospered.

AESCHYLUS (525–456 B.C.)

A lie never lives to be old.

SOCRATES (469–399 B.C.)

We secure our friends not by accepting favors but by doing them.

THUCYDIDES (460–400 B.C.)

We should behave to our friends as we would wish our friends to behave to us.

ARISTOTLE (384–322 B.C.)

The shifts of fortune test the reliability of friends.

MARCUS TULLIUS CICERO (106–43 B.C.)

Once a word has been allowed to escape, it cannot be
recalled.

HORACE (QUINTUS HORATIUS FLACCUS, 65–8 B.C.)

Grant that we may not so much seek to be
understood as to understand.

ST. FRANCIS OF ASSISI (1182–1266)

This above all: to thine own self be true;
And it must follow, as the night the day,
Thou canst not then be false to any man.

WILLIAM SHAKESPEARE (1564–1616)

Teach me, my God and King, in all things thee to
see, and what I do in any thing, to do it as for thee.

GEORGE HERBERT (1593–1633)

Do all the good you can,
By all the means you can,
In all the ways you can,
In all the places you can,
At all the times you can,

To all the people you can,
As long as ever you can.

JOHN WESLEY (1703–1791)

Trust not him with your secrets, who left alone in
your room, turns over your papers.

JOHANN KASPAR LAVATER (1741–1801)

Common-looking people are the best in the world:
that is the reason the Lord makes so many of them.

ABRAHAM LINCOLN (1809–1865)

To look up and not down,
To look forward and not back,
To look out and not in, and
To lend a hand.

EDWARD EVERETT HALE (1822–1909)

Nothing is ever lost by courtesy. It is the cheapest of
pleasures, costs nothing, and conveys much. It
pleases him who gives and receives and thus, like
mercy, is twice blessed.

ERASTUS WIMAN (1834–1904)

There is no happiness in having or in getting, but
only in giving.

HENRY DRUMMOND (1851–1897)

Too many people do not care what happens as long
as it does not happen to them.

WILLIAM HOWARD TAFT (1857–1930)

Example is not the main thing in influencing others.
It is the only thing.

ALBERT SCHWEITZER (1875–1965)

You give but little when you give of your
possessions. It is when you give of yourself that you
truly give.

KAHLIL GIBRAN (1883–1931)

Conscience is the perfect interpreter of life.

KARL BARTH (1886–1968)

Do things for others and you'll find your
self-consciousness evaporating like morning dew on a
Missouri cornfield in July.

DALE CARNEGIE (1888–1955)

56

You can make more friends in two months by becoming more interested in other people than you can in two years by trying to get people interested in you.

DALE CARNEGIE (1888–1955)

There can be no daily democracy without daily citizenship.

RALPH NADER (1934–   )

Seven
Self

---■---

Although most of us probably attribute our problems to other people or to bad luck or to the circumstances around us, the truth is that we create our own success or failure. The road to successful, positive living begins with an analysis of ourselves and depends ultimately on how we think of ourselves.

Years ago I wrote: "Without a humble but reasonable confidence in your own powers you cannot succeed. But with sound self-confidence you can succeed. A sense of inferiority and inadequacy interferes with the attainment of your hopes, but self-confidence leads to self-realization and successful achievement" (*The Power of Positive Thinking*). Now, more than ever, I am convinced that this is true.

How do you build confidence in yourself? Take your mind off the things that seem to be against you. Thinking about negative factors simply builds them up into a power they need not have. Instead, mentally affirm and reaffirm and visualize your assets—the love of God your Father, the ability of your mind and talents, the goodwill of your friends and family, your physical health, your strengths, your future, your possibilities. Stamp indelibly on your mind a picture of yourself succeeding. Make an accurate estimate of your ability, then raise it 10 percent. Affirm that God is with you. Put yourself in his hands and believe that you are now receiving power from him for all your needs.

Read the statements that follow and make them part of yourself. You will learn how to better control your thought processes and, ultimately, your destiny.

Thou shalt love thy neighbor as thyself.

LEVITICUS 19:18

■

There is a spirit in man: and the inspiration of the Almighty giveth them understanding.

JOB 32:8

■

He restoreth my soul.

PSALM 23:3

Bless the Lord, O my soul: and all that is within me,
bless his holy name.

PSALM 103:1

I am fearfully and wonderfully made.

PSALM 139:14

Say to them that are of a fearful heart, Be strong, fear
not.

ISAIAH 35:4

We would often be sorry if our wishes were gratified.

AESOP (620–560 B.C.)

The destiny of man is in his own soul.

HERODOTUS (FIFTH CENTURY B.C.)

Life is to be in relations.

LAO-TZU (FIFTH CENTURY B.C.)

Numberless are the world's wonders but none more
wonderful than man.

SOPHOCLES (496–406 B.C.)

Often when looking at a mass of things for sale, he would say to himself, "How many things I have no need of."

SOCRATES (469–399 B.C.)

The life which is unexamined is not worth living.

PLATO (427–347 B.C.)

Nothing is easier than self-deceit.

DEMOSTHENES (384–322 B. C.)

Sincerity is the way to heaven.

MENCIUS (371–288 B.C.)

Yield not to evil, but attack all the more boldly.

VIRGIL (PUBLIUS VERGILIUS MARO, 70–19 B.C.)

A good reputation is more valuable than money.

PUBLILIUS SYRUS (CA. 42 B.C.)

You can tell the character of every man when you see how he receives praise.

LUCIUS ANNAEUS SENECA (4 B.C.–A.D. 65)

By their fruits ye shall know them.

MATTHEW 7:20

What shall it profit a man, if he shall gain the whole world, and lose his own soul?

MARK 8:36

If ye know these things, happy are ye if ye do them.

JOHN 13:17

Put on the new man, which after God is created in righteousness and true holiness.

EPHESIANS 4:24

I can do all things through Christ which strengtheneth me.

PHILIPPIANS 4:13

With man most of his misfortunes are occasioned by man.

PLINY THE ELDER (23–79)

63

The first rule is to keep an untroubled spirit. The
second is to look things in the face and know them
for what they are.

MARCUS AURELIUS (121–180)

Man must be arched and buttressed from within, else
the temple wavers to the dust.

MARCUS AURELIUS (121–180)

Our life is what our thoughts make of it.

MARCUS AURELIUS (121–180)

To live each day as though one's last, never flustered,
never apathetic, never attitudinizing—here is the
perfection of character.

MARCUS AURELIUS (121–180)

A cheerful look makes a dish a feast.

AURELIUS CLEMENS PRUDENTIUS (346–410)

To go against one's conscience is neither safe nor
right. Here I stand. I cannot do otherwise.

MARTIN LUTHER (1483–1546)

He got the better of himself, and that's the best kind
of victory one can wish for.

MIGUEL DE CERVANTES (1546–1611)

A man of words and not of deeds is like a garden full
of weeds.

ANONYMOUS

The fault, dear Brutus, is not in our stars
But in ourselves that we are underlings.

WILLIAM SHAKESPEARE (1564–1616)

Assume a virtue, if you have it not.

WILLIAM SHAKESPEARE (1564–1616)

His life was gentle, and the elements
So mixed in him that might stand up and say
To all the world, "This was a man!"

WILLIAM SHAKESPEARE (1564–1616)

Every man's work, whether it be literature, or music,
or pictures, or architecture, or anything else, is
always a portrait of himself.

SAMUEL BUTLER (1612–1680)

I do all my actions in the sight of God, who must
judge of them, and to whom I have consecrated them
all.

BLAISE PASCAL (1623–1662)

Do not weep; do not wax indignant. Understand.

BARUCH SPINOZA (1632–1677)

Cheerfulness keeps up a kind of daylight in the
mind, and fills it with a steady and perpetual
serenity.

JOSEPH ADDISON (1672–1719)

Genius is nothing but a greater aptitude for patience.

BENJAMIN FRANKLIN (1706–1790)

Dost thou love life? Then do not squander time, for
that's the stuff life is made of.

BENJAMIN FRANKLIN (1706–1790)

I agree that there is a natural aristocracy among men.
The grounds of this are virtue and talents.

THOMAS JEFFERSON (1743–1826)

As soon as you trust yourself, you will know how to
live.

JOHANN WOLFGANG VON GOETHE (1749–1832)

He who has a firm will molds the world to himself.

JOHANN WOLFGANG VON GOETHE (1749–1832)

Let us not forget that a man can never get away from
himself.

JOHANN WOLFGANG VON GOETHE (1749–1832)

Talent develops itself in solitude; character in the
stream of life.

JOHANN WOLFGANG VON GOETHE (1749–1832)

One ought every day at least to hear a little song,
read a good poem, see a fine picture, and, if it were
possible, to speak a few reasonable words.

JOHANN WOLFGANG VON GOETHE (1749–1832)

67

The good things of life are not to be had singly but
come to us with a mixture.

CHARLES LAMB (1775–1834)

To live content with small means; to seek elegance
rather than luxury, and refinement rather than
fashion; to be worthy, not respectable, and wealthy,
not rich; to study hard, think quietly, talk gently, act
frankly; to listen to the stars and birds, to babes and
sages, with open heart; to bear on cheerfully, do all
bravely, awaiting occasions, worry never; in a word
to, like the spiritual, unbidden and unconscious,
grow up through the common.

WILLIAM ELLERY CHANNING (1780–1842)

Give me a man who sings at his work.

THOMAS CARLYLE (1795–1881)

Alas! the fearful unbelief is unbelief in yourself.

THOMAS CARLYLE (1795–1881)

Silence is the element in which great things fashion
themselves together.

THOMAS CARLYLE (1795–1881)

Nothing can bring you peace but yourself.

RALPH WALDO EMERSON (1803–1882)

A man is a method, a progressive arrangement; a selecting principle, gathering his like unto him wherever he goes. What you are comes to you.

RALPH WALDO EMERSON (1803–1882)

Nature arms each man with some faculty which enables him to do easily some feat impossible to any other.

RALPH WALDO EMERSON (1803–1882)

Self-trust is the first secret of success.

RALPH WALDO EMERSON (1803–1882)

A man is what he thinks about all day long.

RALPH WALDO EMERSON (1803–1882)

The world belongs to the energetic.

RALPH WALDO EMERSON (1803–1882)

Make the most of yourself for that is all there is to you.

RALPH WALDO EMERSON (1803–1882)

The secret to success in life is for a man to be ready for his opportunity when it comes.

BENJAMIN DISRAELI (1804–1881)

In character, in manner, in style, in all things, the supreme excellence is simplicity.

HENRY WADSWORTH LONGFELLOW (1807–1882)

Self-reverence, self-knowledge, self-control. These three alone lead life to sovereign power.

ALFRED LORD TENNYSON (1809–1892)

Grateful for the blessing lent of simple tastes and mind content!

OLIVER WENDELL HOLMES (1809–1894)

What a man thinks of himself, that it is which determines or rather indicates his fate.

HENRY DAVID THOREAU (1817–1862)

70

Blessed is the man who, having nothing to say,
abstains from giving in words evidence of the fact.

GEORGE ELIOT (MARY ANN EVANS, 1819–1880)

Mishaps are like knives, that either serve us or cut
us, as we grasp them by the blade or the handle.

JAMES RUSSELL LOWELL (1819–1891)

Tell yourself in your secret reveries, I was made to
handle affairs.

ANDREW CARNEGIE (1835–1919)

Men habitually use only a small part of the power
they possess and which they might use under
appropriate circumstances.

WILLIAM JAMES (1842–1910)

If you want a quality, act as if you already had it. Try
the "as if" technique.

WILLIAM JAMES (1842–1910)

I am the master of my fate; I am the captain of my
soul.

WILLIAM ERNEST HENLEY (1849–1903)

71

A man is literally what he thinks.

JAMES ALLEN (1849–1925)

Sit loosely in the saddle of life.

ROBERT LOUIS STEVENSON (1850–1894)

A man can stand a lot as long as he can stand himself.

AXEL MUNTHE (1857–1949)

All the resources we need are in the mind.

THEODORE ROOSEVELT, JR. (1858–1919)

The bigger they come, the harder they fall.

BOB FITZSIMMONS (1862–1917)

We have forty million reasons for failure but not a single excuse.

RUDYARD KIPLING (1865–1936)

You are beaten to earth? Well, well, what's that?
Come up with a smiling face,

It's nothing against you to fall down flat
But to lie there—that's disgrace.

EDMUND VANCE COOKE (1866–1932)

I dare you to be the strongest boy in this class.

WILLIAM H. DANFORTH (1870–1955), QUOTING A TEACHER

We are what we believe we are.

BENJAMIN N. CARDOZO (1870–1938)

When I decided to go into politics I weighed the cost:
I would get criticism. But I went ahead. So when the
virulent criticism came I wasn't surprised. I was
better able to handle it.

HERBERT HOOVER (1874–1964)

Speech is silver; silence is golden.

SWISS PROVERB

Knock the *t* off the *can't*.

GEORGE REEVES (1876–1925)

We're all born under the same sky, but we don't all
have the same horizon.

KONRAD ADENAUER (1876–1967)

Don't ever say, "I can't." All you need is God and
gumption. You can if you think 'tis you.

A. HARRY MOORE (1879–1952), QUOTING HIS MOTHER

Three outstanding qualities make for success:
judgment, industry, health. And the greatest of these
is judgment.

WILLIAM MAXWELL AITKEN, LORD BEAVERBROOK (1879–1964)

Our life is at all times and before all else the
consciousness of what we can do.

JOSÉ ORTEGA Y GASSET (1883–1955)

Rancor is an outpouring of a feeling of inferiority.

JOSÉ ORTEGA Y GASSET (1883–1955)

It isn't life that matters; it's the courage you bring to
it.

HUGH WALPOLE (1884–1941)

74

Never build a case against yourself.

ROBERT ROWBOTTOM (1887–1973)

If you have to keep reminding yourself of a thing,
perhaps it isn't so.

CHRISTOPHER MORLEY (1890–1957)

Adversity causes some men to break; others to break
records.

WILLIAM A. WARD (1921–   )

Keep strong if possible; in any case keep cool.

SIR BASIL LIDDELL HART (1895–1970)

Our self-image strongly held essentially determines
what we become.

MAXWELL MALTZ (1899–1975)

When people are bored it is primarily with their own
selves that they are bored.

ERIC HOFFER (1902–1983)

To every disadvantage there is a corresponding advantage.

W. CLEMENT STONE (1902–   )

The longest journey is the journey inward.

DAG HAMMARSKJÖLD (1905–1961)

I am somebody. I am me. I like being me. And I need nobody to make me somebody.

LOUIS L'AMOUR (1908–1988)

A man can lose sight of everything else when he's bent on revenge, and it ain't worth it.

LOUIS L'AMOUR (1908–1988)

Nothing in life is more exciting and rewarding than the sudden flash of insight that leaves you a changed person—not only changed, but for the better.

ARTHUR GORDON (1912–   )

Most people don't plan to fail; they fail to plan.

JOHN L. BECKLEY (1925–   )

76

We have left undone those things which we ought to have done; and we have done those things which we ought not to have done.

THE BOOK OF COMMON PRAYER

Eight
Physical Health

———■———

A few years ago, I clipped out a newspaper story about James A. Hard, who lived to the age of one hundred and eleven. One way this man cooperated with the forces of health and longevity, according to the paper, was by taking everything in stride. His friends said he was always happy. He never let himself get overly excited or upset, and he kept control of his life.

At the age of ninety, Mr. Hard had a cataract on one eye. His granddaughter said, "We were going to arrange to have an operation, but Grandpa beat us to it. All by himself, he went to a physician's office where he made the doctor perform the operation. Right after, he came home by himself in a cab. That was nothing but grit and courage."

Emotional tranquility, refusal to worry, the attitude of happiness, zest for life, keeping control, having grit and courage—these are important factors in physical health and long life.

Dr. Bernie S. Siegel of New Haven, Connecticut, believes, as many other physicians do today, that there is a close connection between health and mental attitudes. He sometimes asks his patients, "Why do you need this disease?" When they change their outlook, he reports, their health problems often end.

To practice the basic principles of good health, visualize yourself as sound, healthy and filled with the vitality and boundless life of your Creator. Look upon yourself as the unique individual that you are. Get in harmony with the creative, life-giving, health-maintaining forces of the universe. Affirm peace, wholeness, and good health—and they will be yours.

I am the Lord that healeth thee.

EXODUS 15:26

The Lord will take away from thee all sickness.

DEUTERONOMY 7:15

The Lord is the strength of my life.

PSALM 27:1

The tongue of the wise is health.

PROVERBS 12:18

A merry heart doeth good like a medicine.

PROVERBS 17:22

If a man insisted always on being serious, and never
allowed himself a bit of fun and relaxation, he would
go mad or become unstable without knowing it.

HERODOTUS (FIFTH CENTURY B.C.)

Those whom God wishes to destroy he first makes
mad.

EURIPIDES (485–406 B.C.)

Beloved, I wish above all things that thou mayest
prosper and be in health, even as thy soul prospereth.

3 JOHN 2

I am searching for that which every man seeks —
peace and rest.

DANTE ALIGHIERI (1265–1321)

A well-spent day brings happy sleep.

LEONARDO DA VINCI (1452–1519)

Most of man's trouble comes from his inability to be still.

BLAISE PASCAL (1623–1662)

Strange how a good dinner reconciles everybody.

SAMUEL PEPYS (1633–1703)

The best doctors in the world are Doctor Diet, Doctor Quiet, and Dr. Merryman.

JONATHAN SWIFT (1667–1745)

Early to bed and early to rise, Makes a man healthy, wealthy, and wise.

BENJAMIN FRANKLIN (1706–1790)

Do not worry, eat three square meals a day, say your prayers, be courteous to your creditors, keep your digestion good, exercise, go slow and easy.

ABRAHAM LINCOLN (1809–1865)

At the heart of a cyclone tearing the sky is a place of central calm.

EDWIN MARKHAM (1852–1940)

■

If you have arthritis, calmly say, "Okay, I have arthritis and this is the way arthritis is." Take pain, like people, as it comes and you can better master it.

CHARLES CLIFFORD PEALE (1870–1955)

■

The reason worry kills more people than work is that more people worry than work.

ROBERT FROST (1874–1963)

■

Practice easing your way along. Don't get het up or in a dither. Do your best; take it as it comes. You can handle anything if you think you can. Just keep your cool and your sense of humor.

SMILEY BLANTON, M.D. (1882–1966)

■

Faith is necessary for physical as well as spiritual well-being.

SMILEY BLANTON, M.D. (1882–1966)

I don't know why we are in such a hurry to get up
when we fall down. You might think we would lie
there and rest awhile.

MAX EASTMAN (1883–1969)

Hate and fear can poison the body as surely as any
toxic chemicals.

JOSEPH KRIMSKY, M.D. (1883–?)

I come to the office each morning and stay for long
hours doing what has to be done to the best of my
ability. And when you've done the best you can, you
can't do any better. So when I go to sleep I turn
everything over to the Lord and forget it.

HARRY S TRUMAN (1884–1972)

We little realize the number of human diseases that
are begun or affected by worry.

WALTER CLEMENT ALVAREZ, M.D. (1884–1978)

I have found that if you love life, life will love you
back.

ARTHUR RUBINSTEIN (1887–1982)

Internal balance is health and internal unbalance is sickness.

CLARENCE COOK LITTLE, M.D. (1888–1971)

To get the body in tone, get the mind in tune.

ZACHARY T. BERCOVITZ, M.D. (1895–1984)

Some patients I see are actually draining into their bodies the diseased thoughts of their minds.

ZACHARY T. BERCOVITZ, M.D. (1895–1984)

Worry affects the circulation, the heart, the glands, the whole nervous system, and profoundly affects heart action.

CHARLES W. MAYO, M.D. (1898–1968)

Most of the time we think we're sick it's all in the mind.

THOMAS WOLFE (1900–1938)

The best and most efficient pharmacy is within your own system.

ROBERT C. PEALE, M.D. (1900–1970)

I have become convinced that there is a definite
relationship between medical science and religious
faith and that God has given us both as weapons
against disease.

ROBERT C. PEALE, M.D. (1900–1970)

If you go long enough without a bath even the fleas
will let you alone.

ERNIE PYLE (1900–1945)

Many of my patients could have healthy hearts by
just practicing the therapy of their religion.

LOUIS F. BISHOP, M.D. (1901–1986)

I said to that high-strung patient, "Practice the peace
of God which passes all understanding and you will
be well."

LOUIS F. BISHOP, M.D. (1901–1986)

This is the age
Of the half-read page
And the quick hash
And the mad dash
The bright night

With the nerves tight
The plane hop
With the brief stop
The lamp tan
In a short span
The Big Shot
In a good spot
And the brain strain
And the heart pain
And the catnaps
Till the spring snaps
And the fun's done.

VIRGINIA BRASIER (1910–   )

Bacteria and other microorganisms find it easier to
infect people who worry and fret.

LEO RANGELL (1913–   )

Have you that gray sickness—half awake, half
asleep—half alive, half dead?

ADVERTISEMENT CAPTION

I told the doctors that God was my partner and I
believed he would help me walk again.

JANE WITHERS (1927–   ), WHEN PARALYZED

You can become strongest in your weakest place.

ANONYMOUS CONTEMPORARY

A clean engine always delivers power.

GAS STATION SIGN

Nine
Mental Health

---■---

At the bottom of the Great Depression of the 1930s I did a lot of counseling, trying to help many troubled people. As I attempted to meet the flood of need, I became aware of the role of unhealthy thought patterns in so many human problems. But I also realized my limitations in psychiatric knowledge, and I began searching for assistance in this important area.

In 1935, I met Dr. Smiley Blanton, one of the finest people I have ever known, skilled in spiritual as well as psychiatric wisdom and sensitivity. After I had told him of my search, Dr. Blanton surprised me by asking, "Do you believe in prayer?" When I assured him that I did, he said, "So do I," explaining that he had been praying for years that he would meet a pastor with whom he could work as a partner, uniting pastoral care with psychological science.

We formed such a team. At first, he counseled me about my problem cases. But he himself became increasingly involved, eventually bringing in young student psychiatrists to work with him. This work finally grew into the Institutes of Religion and Health, which now provide superior accredited training in pastoral counseling. Out of the institutes have developed more than a hundred pastoral counseling centers across the United States.

There is no doubt in my mind that mental and spiritual health are the foundation of physical health, harmonious relationships, and a happy and successful life. The quotations in this book may be thought of as prescriptions. Take one or more a day for increased courage and self-confidence.

The thing which I greatly feared is come upon me.

JOB 3:25

■

He healeth the broken in heart, and bindeth up their wounds.

PSALM 147:3

Thou wilt keep him in perfect peace, whose mind is
stayed on thee.

ISAIAH 26:3

Speech is like the cloth of Arras opened and spread
abroad, whereas in thought it lies in packs.

THEMISTOCLES (527–460 B.C.)

The greatest griefs are those we cause ourselves.

SOPHOCLES (496–406 B.C.)

There are two sides to every question.

PROTAGORAS (485–410 B.C.)

The mind is never right but when it is at peace
within itself.

LUCIUS ANNAEUS SENECA (4 B.C.–A.D. 65)

And be not conformed to this world: but be ye
transformed by the renewing of your mind.

ROMANS 12:2

Now the God of hope fill you with all joy and peace
in believing, that ye may abound in hope.

ROMANS 15:13

Ⅲ

The peace of God, which passeth all understanding,
shall keep your hearts and minds through Christ
Jesus.

PHILIPPIANS 4:7

Ⅲ

For God hath not given us the spirit of fear; but of
power, and of love, and of a sound mind.

2 TIMOTHY 1:7

Ⅲ

Intellectual passion drives out sensuality.

LEONARDO DA VINCI (1452–1519)

Ⅲ

Canst thou not minister to a mind diseased . . .
Raze out the written troubles of the brain? . . .
Therein the patient
Must minister to himself.

WILLIAM SHAKESPEARE (1564–1616)

The mind is its own place, and in itself can make a
heaven of hell, a hell of heaven.

JOHN MILTON (1608–1674)

Great men are they who see that the spiritual is
stronger than any material force; that thoughts rule
the world.

RALPH WALDO EMERSON (1803–1882)

Do the thing you fear and the death of fear is certain.

RALPH WALDO EMERSON (1803–1882)

Nothing is so much to be feared as fear.

HENRY DAVID THOREAU (1817–1862)

Let us be of good cheer, however, remembering that
the misfortunes hardest to bear are those which
never come.

JAMES RUSSELL LOWELL (1819–1891)

There is no more miserable human being than one in
whom nothing is habitual but indecision.

WILLIAM JAMES (1842–1910)

93

A great many people think they are thinking when
they are merely rearranging their prejudices.

WILLIAM JAMES (1842–1910)

Quiet minds cannot be perplexed or frightened but go
on in fortune or misfortune at their own private pace
like the ticking of a clock during a thunderstorm.

ROBERT LOUIS STEVENSON (1850–1894)

Laugh, and the world laughs with you; weep, and
you weep alone.

ELLA WHEELER WILCOX (1850–1919)

Some other faculty than the intellect is necessary for
the apprehension of reality.

HENRI BERGSON (1859–1941)

The only thing we have to fear is fear itself.

FRANKLIN DELANO ROOSEVELT (1882–1945)

Anxiety is the great modern plague. But faith can
cure it.

SMILEY BLANTON, M.D. (1882–1966)

94

Every day give yourself a good mental shampoo.

SARA JORDAN, M.D. (1884–1959)

If you want to conquer fear, don't sit at home and think about it. Go out and get busy.

DALE CARNEGIE (1888–1955)

I know only that what is moral is what you feel good after and what is immoral is what you feel bad after.

ERNEST HEMINGWAY (1899–1961)

Positive thinking is the key to success in business, education, pro football, anything that you can mention. I go out there thinking that I am going to complete every pass.

RON JAWORSKI (1951–   )

Ten
Pain and Suffering

———————◾———————

P ain and suffering have wracked humanity throughout history. Evidence of arthritis has been discovered in the earliest skeletons of the past.

My friend Lloyd Ogilvie, distinguished pastor of the First Presbyterian Church of Hollywood, California, once said that he had learned several important lessons from personally experiencing pain and suffering. He found he grew the most spiritually during those ordeals. Another lesson was that, on looking back on such an experience afterward, he discovered it had deepened his trust in God. As a result, says Dr. Ogilvie, he is now able to thank God in advance for the prospect of such trials, praying, in effect, "Lord, thank you for the good that is going to happen in and through me as a result of what I am about to experience."

No one welcomes pain. But, rightly faced, it can bring about great good. And we can triumph over it. The day before the January 1988 Superbowl football game, Doug Williams, quarterback for the Washington Redskins, had to endure hours of dental surgery. During the game, his knee was injured. But he led the Redskins to victory in spite of his problems, breaking one record after another. No wonder he was named most valuable player that year!

When pain strikes, we often ask the wrong questions, such as, Why me? The right questions are, What can I learn from this? What can I do about it? What can I accomplish in spite of it?

Bring pain or suffering to the One who suffered for us on a cross and you will find "what a friend we have in Jesus."

Weeping may endure for a night, but joy cometh in the morning.

PSALM 30:5

The pain of the mind is worse than the pain of the body.

PUBLILIUS SYRUS (CA. 42 B.C.)

They brought unto him all sick people that were
taken with diverse diseases and torments . . . and he
healed them.

MATTHEW 4:24

For our light affliction, which is but for a moment,
worketh for us a far more exceeding and eternal
weight of glory.

2 CORINTHIANS 4:17

He said unto me, My grace is sufficient for thee: for
my strength is made perfect in weakness.

2 CORINTHIANS 12:9

Is any among you afflicted? Let him pray.

JAMES 5:13

The God of all grace . . . after that ye have suffered a
while, make you perfect, stablish, strengthen, settle
you.

1 PETER 5:10

And God shall wipe away all tears from their eyes;
and there shall be no more death, neither sorrow, nor
crying, neither shall there be any more pain: for the
former things are passed away.

REVELATION 21:4

When pain is to be borne, a little courage helps more
than much knowledge, a little human sympathy
more than much courage, and the least tincture of
the love of God more than all.

C. S. LEWIS (1898–1963)

In times like these, it helps to recall that there have
always been times like these.

PAUL HARVEY (1918–   )

It takes more distress and poison to kill someone
who has peace of mind and loves life.

BERNIE S. SIEGEL, M.D. (1928–   )

Diseases can be our spiritual flat tires — disruptions
in our lives that seem to be disasters at the time but
end by redirecting our lives in a meaningful way.

BERNIE S. SIEGEL, M.D. (1928–   )

100

One cannot get through life without pain. . . . What
we can do is choose how to use the pain life presents
to us.

BERNIE S. SIEGEL, M.D. (1928–   )

Eleven
Healing

———————■———————

While I was completing this book I met a friend whose son has been plagued by severe emotional problems. "Last Sunday," my friend said, "my son asked me to go to a church that helps him feel better. As soon as I went in, I looked around with interest because there were so many young people present. Some of them were playing drums and guitars and other instruments. The music had a fast beat that I don't usually associate with church. But it was lively, and nearly everyone present was singing and either clapping or raising their hands.

"During a prayer," my friend went on, "the pastor said, 'Lord, we renounce defeat. We renounce poverty. We renounce sickness. We claim health and prosperity and victory in the name of Jesus.' Then the pastor announced some answers to prayer, and people clapped. A woman stood up and said that she wanted to thank those who had been praying about the growth on her kidney. The preceding Tuesday, she said, she had got the results of a CAT scan; the growth had disappeared.

"I guess I'm fussy," my friend concluded, "because some of that isn't my cup of tea. But I wish more churches had that kind of faith and enthusiasm and positive outlook. If they did, there would probably be a lot more people in church."

The encouraging thing is that many churches today seem to be discovering anew the power of positive faith and the reality of healing. Many sick people came to Jesus long ago, and the Gospels tell us "he healed them all." Whether through the science of medicine or the force of faith, God is still healing spirits, minds, and bodies.

I am the Lord that healeth thee.

EXODUS 15:26

I shall yet praise him, who is the health of my countenance, and my God.

PSALM 42:11

I will cure them, and will reveal unto them the abundance of peace and truth.

JEREMIAH 33:6

The first petition that we are to make to Almighty
God is for a good conscience, the next for health of
mind, and then of body.

LUCIUS ANNAEUS SENECA (4 B.C.—A.D. 65)

To wish to be well is a part of becoming well.

LUCIUS ANNAEUS SENECA (4 B.C.—A.D. 65)

Thy faith hath made thee whole.

MATTHEW 9:22

He ordained twelve . . . to have power to heal
sicknesses, and to cast out devils.

MARK 3:14—15

The power of the Lord was present to heal them.

LUKE 5:17

In that same hour he cured many of their infirmities.

LUKE 7:21

Jesus Christ maketh thee whole.

ACTS 9:34

105

And the leaves of the tree were for the healing of the nations.

REVELATION 22:2

Humanity . . . created sick, commanded to be sound.

SIR FULKE GREVILLE (1554–1628)

What wound did ever heal but by degrees?

WILLIAM SHAKESPEARE (1564–1616)

Sleep that knits up the ravell'd sleave of care,
The death of each day's life, sore labor's bath,
Balm of hurt minds, great nature's second course,
Chief nourisher in life's feast.

WILLIAM SHAKESPEARE (1564–1616)

He healeth those that are broken in heart: and giveth medicine to heal their sickness.

THE BOOK OF COMMON PRAYER

Health and cheerfulness mutually beget each other.

JOSEPH ADDISON (1672–1719)

How sweet the name of Jesus sounds
In a believer's ear!
It soothes his sorrows, heals his wounds,
And drives away his fear.

EDWARD PERRONET (1721–1792)

Jesus speaks, and speaks to thee . . .
I deliver'd thee when bound,
And, when bleeding, heal'd thy wound;
Sought thee wand'ring, set thee right,
Turn'd thy darkness into light.

WILLIAM COWPER (1731–1800)

Sometimes a light surprises
The Christian while he sings;
It is the Lord who rises
With healing in his wings.

WILLIAM COWPER (1731–1800)

Our Creator has given us five senses to help us survive threats from the external world, and a sixth sense, our healing system, to help us survive internal threats.

BERNIE S. SIEGEL, M.D. (1928–   )

Feelings are chemical and can kill or cure.

BERNIE S. SIEGEL, M.D. (1928–   )

Twelve
Community

---■---

The ancient words, "It is not good that the man should be alone" (*Genesis 2:18*), apply to more than love and marriage. Modern science is replete with evidence that it is good for human beings to live in community, to relate constructively to others in various ways, from local groups to patriotic endeavors and worldwide ventures in brotherhood and sisterhood.

While I was an active pastor, I supported ecumenical efforts and councils of churches. At one gathering of the New York City Council of Churches, of which I was once president, I remarked that if no such organization existed, someone would have had to invent it, so important is its work. I have long been active in Rotary and similar organizations where there is not only camaraderie but participation in projects of goodwill.

And I am an enthusiastic citizen of the United States of America. This country's great heritage of freedom comes from the mingling of two mighty streams. One stream is that of classical antiquity. The great thinkers of ancient Greece held that the human mind is sacred and that no one must enslave it. The other stream is that of the Judeo-Christian heritage, which upholds the infinite worth and the right to freedom of every individual.

It is very interesting that this ideal of freedom is now being sought, and often celebrated, in almost every country on earth. For the idea of community cannot be satisfied until it embraces the whole world. The ancient prophets and mystics had a noble vision of worldwide human kinship and peace. As we reach out positively to others, each one of us can bring that vision closer to reality.

To do justice and judgment is more acceptable to the
Lord than sacrifice.

PROVERBS 21:3

If thine enemy be hungry, give him bread to eat; and
if he be thirsty, give him water to drink.

PROVERBS 25:21

Where there is no vision, the people perish: but he
that keepeth the law, happy is he.

PROVERBS 29:18

Learn to do well; seek judgment, relieve the
oppressed, judge the fatherless, plead for the widow.

ISAIAH 1:17

They shall beat their swords into plowshares, and
their swords into pruninghooks: nation shall not lift
up sword against nation, neither shall they learn war
any more.

ISAIAH 2:4

Oh, what times! Oh, what standards!

MARCUS TULLIUS CICERO (106–43 B.C.)

Who, then, is free? The wise man who can govern
himself.

HORACE (QUINTUS HORATIUS FLACCUS, 65–8 B.C.)

I found Rome a city of bricks, and left it a city of
marble.

AUGUSTUS CAESAR (63 B.C.–A.D. 14)

111

Blessed are the peacemakers.

MATTHEW 5:9

All they that take the sword shall perish with the
sword.

MATTHEW 26:52

Pure religion and undefiled before God and the
Father is this, to visit the fatherless and widows in
their affliction, and to keep himself unspotted from
the world.

JAMES 1:27

Play the man, Master Ridley; we shall this day light
such a candle, by God's grace, in England, as I trust
shall never be put out.

HUGH LATIMER (1485–1555)

Heaven is above all yet; there sits a judge
That no king can corrupt.

WILLIAM SHAKESPEARE (1564–1616)

112

Nothing emboldens sin so much as mercy.

WILLIAM SHAKESPEARE (1564–1616)

I pray heaven to bestow the best of all blessings on
this house and all that hereafter shall inhabit it. May
none but honest and wise men ever rule under this
roof.

JOHN ADAMS (1725–1826), INSCRIPTION IN WHITE HOUSE

Rebellion to tyrants is obedience to God.

THOMAS JEFFERSON (1743–1826)

The God who gave us life gave us liberty at the same
time.

THOMAS JEFFERSON (1743–1826)

Man's inhumanity to man makes countless
thousands mourn.

ROBERT BURNS (1759–1796)

Whither is fled the visionary gleam
Where is it now, the glory and the dream?

WILLIAM WORDSWORTH (1770–1850)

Breathes there the man, with soul so dead,
Who never to himself hath said,
This is my own, my native land!

SIR WALTER SCOTT (1771–1832)

Greater than the tread of mighty armies is an idea
whose time has come.

VICTOR HUGO (1802–1885)

This will remain the land of the free only so long as
it is the land of the brave.

ELMER DAVIS (1890–1958)

Either war is obsolete or men are.

R. BUCKMINSTER FULLER (1895–1983)

I decline to accept the end of man.

WILLIAM FAULKNER (1897–1962)

Those who corrupt the public mind are just as evil as
those who steal from the public purse.

ADLAI STEVENSON (1900–1965)

114

Learning isn't a means to an end; it is an end in itself.

ROBERT A. HEINLEIN (1907–   )

Unfortunately, many Americans live on the outskirts of hope—some because of their poverty, some because of their color, and all too many because of both. Our task is to help replace their despair with opportunity.

LYNDON BAINES JOHNSON (1908–1973)

We are confronted primarily with a moral issue. It is as old as the Scriptures and is as clear as the American Constitution.

JOHN F. KENNEDY (1917–1963)

Education's purpose is to replace an empty mind with an open one.

MALCOLM S. FORBES (1919–1990)

115

Injustice anywhere is a threat to justice everywhere.

MARTIN LUTHER KING, JR. (1929–1968)

We shall overcome, we shall overcome
We shall overcome someday
Oh, deep in my heart, I do believe
We shall overcome someday.

CIVIL RIGHTS SONG

Thirteen
Love and Family

———————————■———————————

Family trees are interesting. My mother's father, Andrew DeLaney, was born in Ballynakill, Ireland. But as a lad he stowed away on a ship bound for America, where he married blue-eyed Margaret Potts and became an industrious Ohioan. My mother, Anna DeLaney, had a face matched by the beauty of her character. A hard worker, she took a happy delight in life and possessed the gift of infectious laughter.

The Peales came from England; my great grandfather Thomas Peale was one of the early settlers of Lynchburg, Ohio. His sons Samuel and Wilson Peale operated a dry-goods store. My father, Charles Clifford Peale, was trained as a physician and, after practicing medicine for some time, became a full-time minister. As both an M.D. and a D.D., Father sometimes punned whimsically that he was a "pair-o'-docs." Father was one of the first men to demonstrate the partnership of spiritual with physical health.

My wife Ruth's parents were Canadians. Her father, Frank Burton Stafford, was a minister, one of the finest men I have ever known. Her mother, Loretta Crosby Stafford, combined a saintly character with strength and firmness.

The dynamic qualities of enthusiasm, excitement, energy, and faith run like golden cords through the lives of the Staffords, the Peales, the Crosbys, and the DeLaneys. And they manifest themselves in each of our children—Margaret, John, and Elizabeth—and their spouses and children. How fortunate I am to be part of such a splendid family.

Families, like individuals, are unique. Cherish your family connections. They are one of God's greatest ways of demonstrating his love and fellowship.

A friend loveth at all times, and a brother is born for adversity.

PROVERBS 17:17

His banner over me was love.

SONG OF SOLOMON 2:4

118

Many waters cannot quench love, neither can the
floods drown it.

SONG OF SOLOMON 8:7

One's best asset is a sympathetic spouse.

EURIPIDES (485–406 B.C.)

Absence makes the heart grow fonder.

SEXTUS AURELIUS PROPERTIUS (54 B.C.–A.D. 2)

Love yields to business. If you seek a way out of
love, be busy; you'll be safe then.

OVID (43 B.C.–A.D. 18)

By this shall all men know that ye are my disciples,
if ye have love one to another.

JOHN 13:35

Love worketh no ill to his neighbor: therefore love is
the fulfilling of the law.

ROMANS 13:10

119

The fruit of the Spirit is love.

GALATIANS 5:22

If any provide not for his own, and specially for those
of his own house, he hath denied the faith, and is
worse than an infidel.

1 TIMOTHY 5:8

Beloved, let us love one another: for love is of God;
and every one that loveth is born of God.

1 JOHN 4:7

Who has never tasted what is bitter does not know
what is sweet.

GERMAN PROVERB

I speak Spanish to God, Italian to women, French to
men, and German to my horse.

CHARLES V OF FRANCE (1337–1380)

There is no more lovely, friendly, and charming
relationship, communion, or company than a good
marriage.

MARTIN LUTHER (1483–1546)

The heart has reasons which the reason cannot
understand.

BLAISE PASCAL (1623–1662)

There are three faithful friends—an old wife, an old
dog, and ready money.

BENJAMIN FRANKLIN (1706–1790)

Mid pleasures and palaces though we may roam,
Be it ever so humble, there's no place like home.

JOHN HOWARD PAYNE (1791–1852)

'Tis better to have loved and lost
Than never to have loved at all.

ALFRED LORD TENNYSON (1809–1892)

Love is a gentle courtesy.

ANONYMOUS

Her voice is full of money.

ANONYMOUS

121

It is better not to live than not to love.

HENRY DRUMMOND (1851–1897)

Holy Matrimony; which is an honorable estate,
instituted of God in the time of innocency, signifying
unto us the mystical union that is betwixt Christ
and his Church.

THE BOOK OF COMMON PRAYER

The holy estate of matrimony . . . to have and to
hold from this day forward, for better for worse, for
richer for poorer, in sickness and in health, to love
and to cherish, till death do us part.

THE BOOK OF COMMON PRAYER

Fourteen
Aging

The process of aging is often thought of as a slow, sad descent into the grave. I suppose I am fortunate in having been exposed all my life to dynamic men and women who lived to a vigorous old age and whose passing from this life seemed not a defeat but a celebration. My parents, my wife's parents, and many of our ancestors lived considerably beyond the traditional "threescore years and ten." And I have often been impressed by people who displayed uncommon energy and good health into their seventies, eighties, and nineties.

One such person was William H. Danforth, head of the Ralston Purina Company, who, as a sickly child, accepted his teacher's dare to become the healthiest boy in his class. He not only did so but inspired thousands of others to be their best both physically and spiritually with his book *I Dare You*. In his "old age," Danforth was an amazing example of tireless energy. So was the vaudeville entertainer Mort Cheshire, who still played the "bones" vigorously at the age of one hundred and two.

Nearly forty years ago, I wrote in *The Power of Positive Thinking*, "The longer I live the more I am convinced that neither age nor circumstance need to deprive us of energy and vitality." I still find that true. Although I have retired from my church, I occupy my working hours with *Guideposts* magazine, the Foundation for Christian Living, speaking, and writing books and articles. I go to bed as early as possible every night, usually sleep soundly and rise early. I try to eat sensibly, exercise regularly, and avoid bad habits of all kinds.

I mentally repudiate physical, mental, or spiritual decline or disability. I trust in the living God. And I recommend the same to anyone who desires a long and healthy life.

And Moses was a hundred and twenty years old
when he died: his eye was not dim, nor his natural
force abated.

DEUTERONOMY 34:7

The Lord blessed the latter end of Job more than the
beginning.

JOB 42:12

124

So teach us to number our days, that we may apply
our hearts unto wisdom.

PSALM 90:12

They shall still bring forth fruit in old age.

PSALM 92:14

The hoary head is a crown of glory.

PROVERBS 16:31

Your old men shall dream dreams.

JOEL 2:28

It is always in season for old men to learn.

AESCHYLUS (525–456 B. C.)

He who is of a calm and happy nature will hardly
feel the pressure of age.

PLATO (427–347 B.C.)

Give me a young man in whom there is something
of the old, and an old man in whom there is
something of the young. Guided so, a man may grow
old in body but never in mind.

MARCUS TULLIUS CICERO (106–43 B.C.)

Perhaps someday it will be pleasant to remember
even this.

VIRGIL (PUBLIUS VERGILIUS MARO, 70–19 B.C.)

The years as they pass plunder us of one thing after
another.

HORACE (QUINTUS HORATIUS FLACCUS, 65–8 B.C.)

A man's life is what his thoughts make of it.

MARCUS AURELIUS (121–180)

All is well that ends well.

JOHN HEYWOOD (1497–1580)

The proof of the pudding is in the eating.

MIGUEL DE CERVANTES (1546–1611)

Man wants but little here below, nor wants that
little long.

OLIVER GOLDSMITH (1728–1774)

We grow gray in our spirit long before we grow gray
in our hair.

CHARLES LAMB (1775–1834)

When I go down to the grave I can say I have
finished my day's work. But I cannot say I have
finished my life. My day's work will begin again the
next morning.

VICTOR HUGO (1802–1885)

We do not count a man's years until he has nothing
else to count.

RALPH WALDO EMERSON (1803–1882)

For of all sad words of tongues or pen
The saddest are these: It might have been.

JOHN GREENLEAF WHITTIER (1807–1892)

Time's wheel runs back or stops: Potter and clay
endure.

ROBERT BROWNING (1812–1889)

None are so old as those who have outlived
enthusiasm.

HENRY DAVID THOREAU (1817–1862)

To know how to grow old is the master-work of
wisdom, and one of the most difficult chapters in the
great art of living.

HENRI FREDERIC AMIEL (1821–1881)

If wrinkles must be written upon our brows, let
them not be written upon the heart. The spirit
should not grow old.

JAMES A. GARFIELD (1831–1881)

When life was like a story, holding neither sob nor sigh
In the golden olden glory of the days gone by.

JAMES WHITCOMB RILEY (1849–1916)

Little by little the time goes by,
Short if you sing it, long if you sigh.

ANONYMOUS

We may let go all things which we cannot carry into
the eternal life.

ANNA R. BROWN LINDSAY (1864–1948)

I dare you to be healthy, live a long time, and never
think old age.

WILLIAM H. DANFORTH (1870–1955)

It is wonderful to be young, but it is equally
desirable to be mature and rich in experience.

BERNARD BARUCH (1870–1965)

I am not interested in the past. I am interested in the
future, for that is where I expect to spend the rest of
my life.

CHARLES F. KETTERING (1876–1958)

129

Live your life and forget your age.

FRANK BERING (1877–1965)

■

If you wait for the perfect moment when all is safe
and assured, it may never arrive. Mountains will not
be climbed, races won, or lasting happiness achieved.

MAURICE CHEVALIER (1888–1972)

■

Never think any oldish thoughts. It's oldish thoughts
that make a person old.

JAMES A. FARLEY (1888–1976)

■

Every business organization should have a
vice-president in charge of constant renewal.

DWAYNE ORTON (1903–1971)

■

Don't look back. Something may be gaining on you.

SATCHEL PAIGE (1906–1982)

■

If you carry your childhood with you, you never
become older.

ABRAHAM SUTZKEVER (1913–   )

130

To those who shall sit here rejoicing, and to those
who shall sit here lamenting—greeting and
sympathy. So have we done in our time.

BENCH INSCRIPTION, CORNELL UNIVERSITY

The future is something which everyone reaches at
the rate of sixty minutes an hour, whatever he does,
whoever he is.

C. S. LEWIS (1898–1963)

Fifteen
Death and Beyond

What we call death comes eventually to every one of us. And the loss of a loved one is usually a heartrending experience.

Early in my ministry, I noticed a black wreath on a door in my city parish. It was the Christmas season. I did not know anyone at the address, but I knocked on the door and discovered that a little girl had died. When I saw that beautiful child in her casket, I wanted to hold the parents in my arms and weep with them. I could hardly find words to express my feelings. But the bereaved father and mother must have felt my grief, for what I did say seemed to give them some comfort.

One of my lifelong convictions is that death, far from being the end, is but the door to an existence larger and more glorious than any human conception. Years ago, my wife, Ruth, and I took a helicopter ride above the Swiss Alps. Leaving the heliport at Zermatt, we flew up a green

valley and doubled back over the little toy village far below. Then we soared past the peaks of Gornergrat and
Stockhorn and over a vast gleaming glacier.

But suddenly the glacier came to an abrupt end. We
hung suspended over what seemed to be *nothing*. We were
at least eleven thousand feet high—and it seemed as
though there was only an empty void below. Later Ruth
wrote about that flight, "Perhaps dying is like that: an
outward rush into the unknown where there is nothing
recognizable, nothing to cling to, and yet you are sus-
tained and supported over the great void just as you were
over the comfortable and familiar terrain."

Helen Steiner Rice once wrote, "The end of the road
is but a bend in the road." I believe that is true of life and
death. At the end of God's world there is his endless world
beyond.

Naked came I out of my mother's womb, and naked
shall I return thither: the Lord gave, and the Lord
hath taken away; blessed be the name of the Lord.

JOB 1:21

I know that my Redeemer liveth.

JOB 19:25

134

Though I walk through the valley of the shadow of
death, I will fear no evil: for thou art with me.

PSALM 23:4

Pale death with impartial tread beats at the poor
man's cottage door and at the palaces of kings.

HORACE (QUINTUS HORATIUS FLACCUS, 65–8 B.C.)

Peace I leave with you, my peace I give unto you:
not as the world giveth, give I unto you.

JOHN 14:27

Our Saviour Jesus Christ, who hath abolished death,
and hath brought life and immortality to light
through the gospel.

2 TIMOTHY 1:10

Blessed are the dead who die in the Lord from
henceforth: Yea, saith the Spirit, that they may rest
from their labors.

REVELATION 14:13

There shall be no more death.

REVELATION 21:4

As a well-spent day brings happy sleep, so life well
used brings happy death.

LEONARDO DA VINCI (1452–1519)

To be or not to be, that is the question.

WILLIAM SHAKESPEARE (1564–1616)

No man is an island, entire of itself; every man is a
piece of the continent, a part of the main. If a clod be
washed away by the sea, Europe is the less, as well
as if a promontory were, as well as if a manor of thy
friend's or of thine own were. Any man's death
diminishes me because I am involved in mankind;
and therefore never send to know for whom the bell
tolls; it tolls for thee.

JOHN DONNE (1572–1631)

It is so soon that I am done for
I wonder what I was begun for.

TOMBSTONE INSCRIPTION, CHELTENHAM

Hide me, O my Savior, hide,
Till the storm of life be past;

Safe into the haven guide,
O receive my soul at last.

CHARLES WESLEY (1707–1788)

It is well. I die hard but I am not afraid to go.

GEORGE WASHINGTON (1732–1799)

We do not believe in immortality because we can
prove it, but we try to prove it because we cannot
help believing it.

HARRIET MARTINEAU (1802–1876)

Now I lay me down to sleep.
I pray thee, Lord, my soul to keep.
If I should die before I wake,
I pray thee, Lord, my soul to take
And this I ask for Jesus' sake.

ANONYMOUS

I know not where his islands lift
Their fronded palms in air;
I only know I cannot drift
Beyond his love and care.

JOHN GREENLEAF WHITTIER (1807–1892)

137

Yet Love will dream, and Faith will trust
(Since he knows our need is just),
That somehow, somewhere, meet we must.
— Life is ever lord of Death
And Love can never lose its own.

JOHN GREENLEAF WHITTIER (1807–1892)

O Christ, that it were possible
For one short hour to see
The souls we loved, that they may tell us
What and where they be.

ALFRED LORD TENNYSON (1809–1892)

Thou wilt not leave us in the dust.
Thou madest man, he knows not why;
He thinks he was not made to die.
Thou hast made him; thou art just.

ALFRED LORD TENNYSON (1809–1892)

We are citizens of eternity.

FEODOR DOSTOEVSKI (1821–1881)

138

In the night of death hope sees a star and listening
love can hear the rustle of a wing.

ROBERT INGERSOLL (1833–1899)

When a man dies, if he can pass enthusiasm along to
his children, he has left them an estate of
incalculable value.

THOMAS A. EDISON (1847–1931)

Think of him still as the same, I say,
He is not dead; he is just—away.

JAMES WHITCOMB RILEY (1849–1916)

When the one Great Scorer comes to write against
your name, he marks not that you won or lost, but
how you played the game.

GRANTLAND RICE (1880–1954)

Who may regret what was, since it has made Himself
himself?

JOHN FREEMAN (1881–1929)

In the heart of London City,
'Mid the dwellings of the poor,
These bright, golden words were uttered,
"I have Christ! What want I more?"
Spoken by a lonely woman,
Dying on a garret floor,
Having not one earthly comfort—
"I have Christ! What want I more?"

ANONYMOUS

Book II

My Christmas Treasury

Acknowledgments

The editor and publisher gratefully acknowledge permission to use copyrighted material in this volume. While every effort has been made to secure permissions, if we have failed to acknowledge copyrighted material, we apologize and will make suitable acknowledgment in any future edition.

American Bible Society for "The Birth of Jesus" from the *Contemporary English Version,* copyright © American Bible Society 1991 and used by permission.

The K. S. Giniger Company, Inc., for "Christmas Is for the Whole World" by Pope John XXIII, from *Prayers and Devotions from Pope John XXIII,* copyright © 1967, 1966 by The K. S. Giniger Company, Inc.

Guideposts Associates, Inc., Carmel, NY 10512, for "The Glory of Christmas" by Laverne Riley O'Brien and "A Christmas List" by Marilyn Morgan Helleberg, reprinted from *The Treasures of Christmas: The Guideposts Family Christmas Book,* copyright © 1982 by Guideposts Associates, Inc.; "A Long Walk" by Gerald Horton Bath and "The

Contents

III. Poems and Songs 186

IV. Christmas Stories 214

V. *Christmas Thoughts* 288

Introduction

As I write this, people are worried about the myriad of problems that afflict our world today, and there is no question but that they are very serious problems. Yet everywhere I go, people have smiling faces and happy voices. Streets and shop windows are gaily decorated. The world seems full of familiar music, and there is excitement in the air. Why?

Christmas is coming. Unhappiness seems to be driven from our minds at this season, along with cynicism and gloomy negativism. A strange and wonderful phenomenon is at work; merriment and gaiety fill the air, and a heavenly chorus resounds in our hearts: "Behold, I bring you tidings of great joy" (Luke 2:10).

With the joy of Christmas there also come fond memories of the Bible passages always read to us at this time of year, of the carols and hymns that we have known all our lives and that now fill the air, of the poems and stories bringing us the Christmas spirit.

This little book attempts to collect in one volume some of my own Christmas favorites. Some of them may also be yours; others may be new to you. But they all carry the Bible message of joy, because the

Bible is the happiest book ever written. Jesus told us, "Be of good cheer; I have overcome the world" (John 16:33)—meaning that we, too, can overcome the world. "These things have I spoken unto you . . . that your joy might be full" (John 15:11). And again, "Rejoice," and to make sure that we understand, he repeated, "and again I say, Rejoice" (Philippians 4:4).

I truly believe that if we keep telling the Christmas story, singing the Christmas songs, and living the Christmas spirit, we can bring joy and happiness and peace to this world. I hope that these selections will help you do this.

Merry Christmas to you! May the glory that we celebrate in this Christmas season fill your life forever and ever.

Norman Vincent Peale

I.

The World's Most
Loved Narrative

*W*HAT A WONDERFUL story it is, the Christmas story. Only God could have thought of it. Here the greatest storytellers of the ages have found their art outmatched. And that story has done more to soften and change humanity than all the stories ever told, all the sermons ever preached, and all the moralisms ever promulgated.

As St. Matthew tells it in the second chapter of his Gospel, it is the story of a star in the east that was observed by some wise scholars. They followed that star for many months, over deserts and mountains and seas, until it came to rest over a little town in a little country. That town was called Bethlehem. There they found an inn, but it was crowded, so they were put in the stable.

The scholars (or wise men or magi, as they were sometimes called) found with them in that stable a young couple with a young baby boy. They who had journeyed so far for so long, following a star, instinctively knew that the baby was immensely important, that he was actually the Son of God. They realized that God, who had tried to win the hearts of men and women in other ways, had finally laid a baby on the doorstep of the world. That baby's crying and cooing were to win the world's heart.

The wise men, representing the intellectuals of the world of that time, fell to their knees before him, recognizing that he, when grown, would be the supreme intellect of all time.

There were some shepherds in a nearby field keeping watch over their flocks by night. Overhead, that chilly night, stretched the star-studded sky. Suddenly the shepherds were startled: a heavenly choir appeared, singing about peace and announcing the birth of the prince of peace. When the shepherds, representing the working people of the world, were told about the birth of the Savior, they said, "Let us now go even unto Bethlehem, and see this thing which is come to pass, which the Lord hath made known unto us" (Luke 2:15, KJV).

And they found the stable and fell to their knees and worshiped God's Son, who had come to earth in the same manner as all men and women—from the heavenly Father, their Creator.

Jesus had come to remind all people that the heavenly Father loved them and to teach them how to live and return ultimately to the Father's House.

In Luke's version of this immortal story (in the second chapter of his Gospel)—a favorite in the King James Version of the

Bible with older people who have loved it since childhood—he features the shepherds; while Matthew, in his first chapter, tells essentially the same story featuring the wise men.

The Birth of Jesus

And it came to pass in those days, that there went out a decree from Caesar Augustus, that all the world should be taxed. (And this taxing was first made when Cyrenius was governor of Syria.) And all went to be taxed, every one into his own city. And Joseph also went up from Galilee, out of the city of Nazareth, into Judea, unto the city of David, which is called Bethlehem, (because he was of the house and lineage of David,) to be taxed with Mary his espoused wife, being great with child.

And so it was, that, while they were there, the days were accomplished that she should be delivered. And she brought forth her first-born son, and wrapped him in swaddling clothes, and laid him in a manger; because there was no room for them in the inn.

And there were in the same country shepherds abiding in the field, keeping watch over their flock by night. And, lo, the angel of the Lord came upon them, and the glory of the Lord shone round about them; and they were sore afraid. And the angel said unto them, Fear not: for, behold, I bring you good tidings of great joy, which shall be to all people. For unto you is born this day in the city of David a Saviour, which is Christ the Lord. And this shall be a sign unto you; Ye shall find the babe wrapped in swaddling clothes, lying in a manger.

And suddenly there was with the angel a multitude of the heavenly host praising God, and saying, Glory to God in the highest, and on earth peace, good will toward men.

And it came to pass, as the angels were gone away from them into heaven, the shepherds said one to another, Let us now go even unto Bethlehem, and see this thing which is come to pass, which the Lord hath made known unto us. And they came with haste, and found Mary and Joseph, and the babe lying in a manger.

And when they had seen it, they made known abroad the saying which was told them concerning this child. And all they that heard it wondered at those things which were told them by the shepherds.

But Mary kept all these things, and pondered them in her heart.

And the shepherds returned, glorifying and praising God for all the things there they had heard and seen, as it was told unto them.

Luke 2:1–20, (KJV)

Now when Jesus was born in Bethlehem of Judea in the days of Herod the king, behold, there came wise men from the east to Jerusalem, saying, Where is he that is born King of the Jews? for we have seen his star in the east, and are come to worship him.

When Herod the king had heard these things, he was troubled, and all Jerusalem with him. And when he had gathered all the chief priests and scribes of the people together, he demanded of them where Christ should be born.

And they said unto him, In Bethlehem of Judea: for thus it is written by the prophet. And thou Bethlehem, in the land of Juda, art not the least among the princes of Juda; for out of thee shall come a Governor, that shall rule my people Israel.

Then Herod, when he had privily called the wise men, inquired of them diligently what time the star appeared. And he sent them to Bethlehem, and said, Go and search diligently for the young child; and when ye have found him, bring me word again, that I may come and worship him also.

When they had heard the king, they departed; and, lo, the star, which they saw in the east, went before them, till it came and stood over where the young child was. When they saw the star, they rejoiced with exceeding great joy. And when they were come into the house, they saw the young child with Mary his mother, and fell down, and worshipped him: and when they had opened their treasures, they presented unto him gifts; gold, and frankincense, and myrrh.

And being warned of God in a dream that they should not return to Herod, they departed into their own country another way.

Matthew 2:1–12, (KJV)

To repeat this same beloved story in the English language of the present day, here is a modern translation for young readers and their families called the Contemporary English Version. It is translated directly from the Greek original and is not based on any other English translation. The New Testament was made available by the American Bible Society the same year as this book, and the complete Bible is scheduled for publication at a later date.

The Birth of Jesus

This is how Jesus Christ was born. A young woman named Mary was engaged to Joseph from King David's family. But before they were married, she learned that she was going to have a baby by God's Holy Spirit. Joseph was a good man and did not want to embarrass Mary in front of everyone. So he decided to quietly call off the wedding.

While Joseph was thinking about this, an angel from the Lord came to him in a dream. The angel said, "Joseph, the baby that Mary will have is from the Holy Spirit. Go ahead and marry her. Then after her baby is born, name him Jesus, because he will save his people from their sins."

So God's promise came true, just as the prophet had said, "A virgin will have a baby boy, and he will be called Immanuel," which means "God is with us."

About that time Emperor Augustus gave orders for the names of all the people to be listed in record books. These first records were made when Quirinius was governor of Syria.

Everyone had to go to their own hometown to be listed. So Joseph had to leave Nazareth in Galilee and go to Bethlehem in Judea. Long ago Bethlehem had been King David's hometown, and Joseph went there because he was from David's family.

Mary was engaged to Joseph and traveled with him to Bethlehem. She was soon going to have a baby, and while they were there, she gave birth to her first-born son. She dressed him in baby clothes and laid him in a feed box, because there was no room for them in the inn.

Matthew 1:18–23; Luke 2:1–7, (CEV)

That night in the fields near Bethlehem some shepherds were guarding their sheep. All at once an angel came down to them from the Lord, and the brightness of the Lord's glory flashed around them. The shepherds were frightened. But the angel said, "Don't be afraid! I have good news for you, which will make everyone happy. This very day in King David's hometown a Savior was born for you. He is Christ the

Lord. You will know who he is, because you will find him dressed in baby clothes and lying in a feed box."

Suddenly many other angels came down from heaven and joined in praising God. They said:

> "Praise to God in heaven!
> Peace on earth to everyone
> who pleases God."

After the angels had left and gone back to heaven, the shepherds said to each other, "Let's go to Bethlehem and see what the Lord has told us about." They hurried off and found Mary and Joseph, and they saw the baby lying in the feed box.

When the shepherds saw Jesus, they told his parents what the angel had said about him. Everyone listened and was surprised. But Mary kept thinking about all this and wondered what it meant.

As the shepherds returned to their sheep, they were praising God and saying wonderful things about him. Everything they had seen and heard was just as the angel had said.

Luke 2:8–20, (CEV)

When Jesus was born in the village of Bethlehem in Judea, Herod was king. During this time some wise men from the east came to Jerusalem and said, "Where is the child born to be king of the Jews? We saw his star in the east and have come to worship him."

When King Herod heard about this, he was worried, and so was everyone else in Jerusalem. Herod brought together all the chief priests and the teachers of the Law of Moses and asked them, "Where will the Messiah be born?"

They told him, "He will be born in Bethlehem, just as the prophet wrote,

> 'Bethlehem in the land of Judea,
> you are very important among the towns of Judea.
> From your town will come a leader,
> who will be like a shepherd for my people Israel.' "

Herod secretly called in the wise men and asked them when they had first seen the star. He tod them, "Go to Bethlehem and search carefully for the child. As soon as you find him, let me know. I want to go and worship him, too."

The wise men listened to what the king said and then left. And the star they had seen in the east went on ahead of them until it stopped over the place where the child was. They were thrilled and excited to see the star.

When the men went into the house and saw the child with Mary, his mother, they kneeled down and worshiped him. They took out their gifts of gold, frankincense, and myrrh and gave them to him. Later they were warned in a dream not to return to Herod, and they went back home by another road.

Matthew 2:1–12, (CEV)

II.
Hymns and Carols

*F*OR MOST OF US, the music we hear on the radio, through television, in our churches, and even on the streets at Christmas time is very familiar. We have known these carols and hymns since childhood. The tunes are well known, but we cannot always remember all the words. Yet the words carry a message that goes back a very long time.

"O Come, All Ye Faithful," for example, is the Latin hymn *"Adeste Fideles";* "God Bless the Master of This House" is an old, traditional English carol. And when I was a boy growing up in Cincinnati, which had a large German population, I used to hear the old German Christmas songs, such as *"Stille Nacht,"* which we know as "Silent Night," and *"O Tannenbaum,"* or "O Christmas Tree."

But whatever the original language—Latin, German, or English—the memories these tunes and their words bring back help us keep the joy and freshness and romance and glory of life. They carry the spirit of Jesus, and this brings back deep sentiments and fills us with zest for life.

The old Wanamaker department store, which stood for many years at the corner of Broadway and 9th Street in New York City, was established by John Wanamaker, a Philadelphian who was also a great Christian. In both his Philadelphia and New York stores there was a great wide staircase leading to a balcony, from which a large choir gave a sacred concert every afternoon during the days leading up to Christmas. At the close, the choir led the vast crowd (which invariably assembled) in Christmas carols.

In one Christmas season during the Great Depression of the early 1930s, I met a businessman I knew on the street in New York. He had experienced hard times. "Merry Christmas," I said.

"Now, Norman," he said to me glumly, "what is there to be merry about?"

"Well, Jack," I responded, "God lives and our country will recover. Besides, it's Christmas."

A few days later, I happened to be in Wanamaker's store when the magnificent organ and choir burst into that stirring hymn "O Come, All Ye Faithful." Several thousand people joined in, in one of the most inspiring moments I can recall. Suddenly I saw my friend Jack, with a reverent look on his uplifted countenance. He was singing enthusiastically. I bumped into him at the door later. He had tears in his eyes. All he said was,

"Sure, we'll get through our troubles. Better days are coming."
With a wave of his hand, he was lost in the crowd. Christmas had
given Jack a new lease on life.

Sing these hymns. And if you can't sing, read them.

Come, Thou Long-Expected Jesus

Come, thou long-expected Jesus,
    Born to set thy people free;
From our fears and sins release us,
    Let us find our rest in thee.

Israel's strength and consolation,
    Hope of all the earth thou art;
Dear desire of every nation,
    Joy of every longing heart.

Born thy people to deliver,
    Born a child, and yet a king,
Born to reign in us for ever,
    Now thy gracious kingdom bring.

By thine own eternal Spirit
    Rule in all our hearts alone:
By thine all-sufficient merit
    Raise us to thy glorious throne. Amen.

Charles Wesley, 1744

Adeste Fideles

O come, all ye faithful,
Joyful and triumphant,
O come ye, O come ye to Bethlehem;
Come and behold him,
Born the King of angels;

Refrain
O come, let us adore him,
O come, let us adore him,
O come, let us adore him,
Christ the Lord.

God of God,
Light of Light,
Lo! he abhors not the Virgin's womb:
Very God,
Begotten, not created;
(Refrain)

Sing, choirs of angels,
Sing in exultation,
Sing, all ye citizens of heav'n above;
Glory to God, all glory
In the highest;
(Refrain)

See how the shepherds,
Summoned to his cradle,
Leaving their flocks, draw nigh to gaze;
We too will thither
Bend our joyful footsteps;
(Refrain)

Child, for us sinners,
Poor and in the manger,
We would embrace thee, with love and awe;
Who would not love thee,
Loving us so dearly?
(Refrain)

Yea, Lord, we greet thee,
Born this happy morning;
Jesus, to thee be glory giv'n;
Word of the Father,
Now in flesh appearing;
(Refrain)

Latin carol, 18th century

While Shepherds Watched

While shepherds watch'd their flocks by night,
    All seated on the ground,
The angel of the Lord came down,
    And glory shone around.
"Fear not," said he, for mighty dread
    Had seized their troubled mind;
"Glad tidings of great joy I bring
    To you and all mankind.

"To you, in David's town, this day
    Is born of David's line
The Saviour, who is Christ the Lord;
    And this shall be the sign:
The heav'nly Babe you there shall find
    To human view displayed,
All meanly wrapped in swathing bands,
    And in a manger laid."

Thus spake the seraph, and forthwith
    Appeared a shining throng
Of angels praising God, who thus
    Addressed their joyful song:
"All glory be to God on high
    And on the earth be peace;
Good will henceforth from heav'n to men
    Begin and never cease."

Nahum Tate, 1700

Silent Night

Father Joseph Mohr sat alone working on the sermon he would de-liver at St. Nicholas Church in Oberndorf in the Austrian Alps on Christmas Eve, 1818. He was refreshing his mind with the first Christmas story—"And this shall be a sign unto you: you shall find the babe . . ."—when a woman knocked at his door and asked him to come and bless the wife and just-born child of a poor charcoal-maker high up in the mountains.

The village priest felt a strange exaltation when he arrived at the poor couple's crude hut and found the happy young mother proudly holding her sleeping child. He recalled with a start the words he had been reading when summoned to this primitive bedside: "You shall find the babe."

*When midnight mass was over and the last parishioner had called out a cheerful "*Gute Nacht!*" the priest was still struck with wonder by the charming coincidence of his summons to the bedside in that mountain shack and the Bethlehem mystery celebrated a few hours later. He began to put his thoughts down on paper, and the words became verse. By dawn he had a poem, which he took to Franz Xavier Gruber, a neighboring Arnsdorf music teacher, who on Christmas Day composed the music for "Silent Night." The carol soon became popular in Austria and Germany as "Song from Heaven."*

> Silent Night! Holy Night!
> All is calm, all is bright.
> Round yon virgin mother and child!
> Holy Infant so tender and mild,
> Sleep in heavenly peace, sleep in heavenly peace.

Silent Night! Holy Night!
Shepherds quake at the sight!
Glories stream from heaven afar,
Heaven'ly hosts sing Alleluia,
Christ the Saviour is born! Christ the Saviour is born!

Silent Night! Holy Night!
Son of God, love's pure light;
Radiant beams from Thy holy face,
With the dawn of redeeming grace,
Jesus Lord, at Thy birth, Jesus Lord, at Thy birth.

Joseph Mohr, 1818

Hark! the Herald Angels Sing

Hark! the herald angels sing,
   "Glory to the newborn King;
Peace on earth, and mercy mild;
   God and sinners reconciled."

Joyful, all ye nations, rise,
    Join the triumph of the skies;
With the angelic hosts proclaim,
    "Christ is born in Bethlehem."

Refrain
Hark, the herald angels sing,
    "Glory to the newborn King."

Christ, by highest heaven adored;
    Christ, the everlasting Lord:
Late in time behold Him come,
    Offspring of a virgin's womb.
Veiled in flesh the God-head see,
    Hail the incarnate Deity!
Pleased as man with men to appear,
    Jesus our Immanuel here.
(Refrain)

Hail the heavenborn Prince of Peace!
    Hail the Sun of righteousness!

Light and life to all He brings,
    Risen with healing in His wings:
Mild He lays His glory by,
    Born that man no more may die;
Born to raise the sons of earth;
    Born to give them second birth.
(Refrain)

Come, Desire of nations come!
    Fix in us Thy humble home:
Rise, the woman's conquering seed,
    Bruise in us the serpent's head;
Adam's likeness now efface,
    Stamp Thine image in its place:
Second Adam from above,
    Reinstate us in Thy love.
(Refrain)

Charles Wesley, 1739

Noel

It came upon the midnight clear,
    That glorious song of old,
From angels bending near the earth
    To touch their harps of gold:
"Peace on the earth, good will to men,
    From heav'n's all-gracious King."
The world in solemn stillness lay
    To hear the angels sing.

Still through the cloven skies they come
    With peaceful wings unfurled,
And still their heav'nly music floats
    O'er all the weary world;
Above its sad and lowly plains
    They bend on hov'ring wing,
And ever o'er its Babel-sounds
    The blessed angels sing.

Yet with the woes of sin and strife
    The world has suffered long;
Beneath the heav'nly strain have rolled
    Two thousand years of wrong;
And man, at war with man, hears not
    The tidings which they bring;
O hush the noise, ye men of strife,
    And hear the angels sing!

O ye, beneath life's crushing load,
    Whose forms are bending low,
Who toil along the climbing way
    With painful steps and slow,
Look now! for glad and golden hours
    Come swiftly on the wing;
O rest beside the weary road
    And hear the angels sing!

For lo! the days are hast'ning on,
    By prophets seen of old,

When with the ever-circling years
   Shall come the time foretold,
When peace shall over all the earth
   Its ancient splendors fling,
And the whole world give back the song
   Which now the angels sing.

                Edmund Hamilton Sears, 1846

God Rest You Merry, Gentlemen

God rest you merry, gentlemen,
   Let nothing you dismay,
Remember Christ our Saviour
   Was born on Christmas Day;
To save us all from Satan's power
   When we were gone astray.

Refrain
O tidings of comfort and joy,
    comfort and joy;
O tidings of comfort and joy!

From God our heav'nly Father
    A blessed angel came;
And unto certain shepherds
    Brought tidings of the same;
How that in Bethlehem was born
    The Son of God by name.
(Refrain)

"Fear not, then," said the angel,
    "Let nothing you affright;
This day is born a Saviour
    Of a pure virgin bright,
To free all those who trust in him
    From Satan's power and might."
(Refrain)

Now to the Lord sing praises,
    All you within this place,
And with true love and brotherhood
    Each other now embrace;
This holy tide of Christmas
    Doth bring redeeming grace.
(Refrain)

London carol, 18th century

O Christmas Tree

O Christmas tree, O Christmas tree,
How lovely are your branches.
In summer sun, in winter snow,
A dress of green you always show.
O Christmas tree, O Christmas tree,
How lovely are your branches.

O Christmas tree, O Christmas tree,
With happiness we greet you.
When decked with candles once a year,
You fill our hearts with yuletide cheer.
O Christmas tree, O Christmas tree,
With happiness we greet you.

Traditional German carol

O Little Town of Bethlehem

O little town of Bethlehem,
How still we see thee lie!
Above thy deep and dreamless sleep
The silent stars go by;
Yet in thy dark streets shineth
The everlasting Light;
The hopes and fears of all the years
Are met in thee tonight.

For Christ is born of Mary,
    And gathered all above,
While mortals sleep, the angels keep
    Their watch of wond'ring love.
O morning stars, together
    Proclaim the holy birth!
And praises sing to God the King,
    And peace to men on earth.

How silently, how silently,
    The wondrous gift is giv'n!
So God imparts to human hearts
    The blessings of his heav'n.
No ear may hear his coming,
    But in this world of sin,
Where meek souls will receive him still
    The dear Christ enters in.

Where children pure and happy
    Pray to the blessed Child,
Where misery cries out to thee,
    Son of the mother mild;
Where charity stands watching
    And faith holds wide the door,
The dark night wakes, the glory breaks,
    And Christmas comes once more.

O holy Child of Bethlehem!
    Descend to us, we pray;
Cast out our sin and enter in,
    Be born in us today.
We hear the Christmas angels
    The great glad tidings tell;
O come to us, abide with us,
    Our Lord Emmanuel! Amen.

Phillips Brooks, 1867

Christmas Carol

God bless the master of this house,
    Likewise the mistress too:
And all the little children
    That round the table go.
Love and joy come to you,
    And to your wassail too,
And God bless you and send you
    A Happy New Year.

Traditional English carol

*One of America's most popular poets was inspired by Christmas music
to write:*

Christmas

I hear along our street
Pass the minstrel throngs;
Hark! they play so sweet,

On their hautboys, Christmas songs!
  Let us by the fire
  Ever higher
Sing them till the night expire!

  In December ring
  Every day the chimes;
  Loud the gleemen sing
In the street their merry rhymes.
  Let us by the fire
  Ever higher
Sing them till the night expire!

  Shepherds at the grange,
  Where the Babe was born,
  Sang, with many a change,

Christmas carols until morn.
Let us by the fire
Ever higher
Sing them till the night expire!

Henry Wadsworth Longfellow, 1847

III.
Poems and Songs

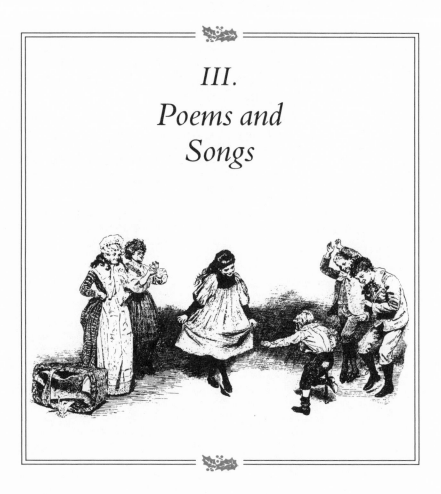

*W*HEN I WAS growing up, children were made to take elocution lessons, in the course of which they had to memorize poems. (Not all of the verses, to be sure, could be dignified by the name poetry.) These poems would then be recited, with appropriate gestures, to admiring audiences of family and relatives. This custom seems to have vanished, but for those of us who survived the experience, the lines of poetry we learned then remain with us still.

Because family gatherings at Christmas were favorite occasions for such recitations, many of the verses dealt with Christmas, and two of those favorites are here: Eugene Field's "Jest 'Fore Christmas" and Clement C. Moore's "A Visit from St. Nicholas," popularly known as "The Night Before Christmas."

"Jingle Bells," of course, continues to be the all-time favorite Christmas song, and no herd of red-nosed reindeer or longings for a white Christmas can displace it.

Memories of songs and poems such as these can keep Christmases past fresh within you and help you feel young again in spirit, even though you may be adding up your years.

Eugene Field was a Chicago newspaper columnist. Three of his poems, "Little Boy Blue," "Wynken, Blynken, and Nod," and this one were recited in almost every household when I was a boy.

Jest 'Fore Christmas

Father calls me William, sister calls me Will,
Mother calls me Willie, but the fellers call me Bill!
Mighty glad I ain't a girl—ruther be a boy,
Without them sashes, curls, an' things that's worn by Fauntleroy!
Love to chawnk green apples an' go swimmin' in the lake—
Hate to take the castor-ile they give for belly-ache!
'Most all the time, the whole year round, there ain't no flies on me,
But jest 'fore Christmas I'm as good as I kin be!

Got a yeller dog named Sport, sic him on a cat;
First thing she knows she doesn't know where she is at!
Got a clipper sled, an' when us kids goes out to slide,
'Long comes the grocery cart, an' we all hook a ride!
But sometimes when the grocery man is worrited an' cross,

He reaches at us with his whip, an' larrups up his hoss,
An' then I laff and holler, "Oh, ye never teched me!"
But jest 'fore Christmas I'm as good as I kin be!

Gran'ma says she hopes that when I git to be a man,
I'll be a missionarer like her oldest brother, Dan,
As was et up by the cannibuls that lives in Ceylon's Isle,
Where every prospeck pleases, an' only man is vile!

189

But Gran'ma she has never been to see a Wild West show,
Not read the Life of Daniel Boone, or else I guess she'd know
That Buff'lo Bill an' cowboys is good enough for me!
Excep' just 'fore Christmas when I'm good as I kin be!

And then old Sport he hangs around, so solemn-like an' still
His eyes they seem a'sayin': "What's the matter, little Bill?"
The old cat sneaks down off her perch an' wonders what's become

190

Of them two enemies of hern that used to make things hum!
But I am so perlite an' tend to earnestly to biz,
That mother says to father: "How improved our Willie is!"
But father, havin' been a boy hisself, suspicions me
When, jest 'fore Christmas I'm as good as I kin be!

For Christmas, with its lots an' lots of candles, cakes, an' toys,
Was made, they says, for proper kids an' not for naughty boys;
So wash yer face an' bresh yer hair, an' mind yer *p*'s and *q*'s,
An' don't bust out yer pantaloons, an' don't wear out yer shoes;
Say "Yessum" to the ladies, an' "Yessir" to the men,
An' when they's company, don't pass yer plate for pie again;
But, thinkin' of the things yer'd like to see upon that tree,
Jest 'fore Christmas be as good as yer kin be!

Eugene Field, 1892

A Christmas Song

Everywhere, everywhere, Christmas to-night!
Christmas in lands of fir tree and pine;
Christmas in lands of palm tree and vine;
Christmas where snow peaks stand solemn and white;
Christmas where cornfields lie sunny and bright:
    Everywhere, everywhere, Christmas to-night!

Christmas where children are hopeful and gay;
Christmas where old men are patient and gray;
Christmas where peace, like a dove in its flight,
Broods o'er brave men in the thick of the fight:
    Everywhere, everywhere, Christmas to-night!

Then let every heart keep its Christmas within,
Christ's pity for sorrow, Christ's hatred for sin,
Christ's care for the weakest, Christ's courage for right,
Christ's dread of the darkness, Christ's love of the light,
    Everywhere, everywhere, Christmas to-night!

Phillips Brooks, 1879

Jingle Bells

Dashing thro' the snow in a one-horse open sleigh,
O'er the fields we go, laughing all the way;
Bells on bob-tail ring, making spirits bright;
What fun it is to ride and sing a sleighing song tonight!

Refrain
Jingle bells! Jingle bells! Jingle all the way!
Oh! what fun it is to ride in a one-horse open sleigh!

A day or two ago I thought I'd take a ride,
And soon Miss Fanny Bright was seated by my side;
The horse was lean and lank, misfortune seemed his lot,
He got into a drifted bank, and we, we got upsot.
(Refrain)

Now the ground is white, go it while you're young,
Take the girls tonight, and sing this sleighing song;
Just get a bob-tailed nag, two-forty for his speed,
Then hitch him to an open sleigh, and crack! you'll take the lead.
(Refrain)

John Pierpont, 1827

A Visit from St. Nicholas

'Twas the night before Christmas, when all through the house
Not a creature was stirring, not even a mouse;
The stockings were hung by the chimney with care,
In hopes that St. Nicholas soon would be there.
The children were nestled all snug in their beds,
While visions of sugar-plums danced in their heads;
And mamma in her kerchief, and I in my cap,
Had just settled our brains for a long winter's nap;
When out on the lawn there arose such a clatter,

I sprang from my bed to see what was the matter.
Away to the window I flew like a flash,
Tore open the shutters and threw up the sash.
The moon on the breast of the new-fallen snow
Gave the luster of midday to objects below,
When, what to my wondering eyes should appear,
But a miniature sleigh and eight tiny reindeer,

With a little old driver, so lively and quick,
I knew in a moment it must be St. Nick.
More rapid than eagles his coursers they came,
And he whistled, and shouted, and called them by name:
"Now, Dasher! now, Dancer! now, Prancer and Vixen!
On Comet! on, Cupid! on, Donder and Blitzen!
To the top of the porch, to the top of the wall!
Now, dash away! dash away! dash away all!"
As dry leaves that before the wild hurricane fly,
When they meet with an obstacle, mount to the sky,
So up to the house-top the coursers they flew,
With the sleigh full of toys, and St. Nicholas, too.
And then, in a twinkling, I heard on the roof
The prancing and pawing of each little hoof.
As I drew in my head, and was turning around,
Down the chimney St. Nicholas came with a bound.
He was dressed all in fur, from his head to his foot,
And his clothes were all tarnished with ashes and soot;
A bundle of toys he had flung on his back,
And he looked like a peddler just opening his pack.
His eyes—how they twinkled! his dimples, how merry!

His cheeks were like roses, his nose like a cherry.
His droll little mouth was drawn up like a bow,
And the beard of his chin was as white as the snow.
The stump of a pipe he held tight in his teeth,
And the smoke it encircled his head like a wreath.
He had a broad face and a little round belly
That shook, when he laughed, like a bowlful of jelly.
He was chubby and plump, a right jolly old elf,
And I laughed when I saw him, in spite of myself.
A wink of his eye and a twist of his head
Soon gave me to know I had nothing to dread.
He spoke not a word, but went straight to his work,
And filled all the stockings; then turned with a jerk,
And laying his finger aside of his nose,
And giving a nod, up the chimney he rose.
He sprang to his sleigh, to his team gave a whistle,
And away they all flew like the down of a thistle.
But I heard him exclaim, ere he drove out of sight,
"Happy Christmas to all, and to all a good-night!"

Clement C. Moore, 1823

Christmas Bells

I heard the bells on Christmas Day
Their old, familiar carols play,
    And wild and sweet
    The words repeat
Of peace on earth, good-will to men!

And thought how, as the day had come,
The belfries of all Christendom
    had rolled along
    The unbroken song
Of peace on earth, good-will to men!

Till, ringing, singing on its way,
The world revolved from night to day,
    A voice, a chime,
    A chant sublime
Of peace on earth, good-will to men!

Then from each black, accursed mouth
The cannon thundered in the South,
    And with the sound
    The carols drowned
Of peace on earth, good-will to men!

It was as if an earthquake rent
The hearth-stones of a continent
    And made forlorn
    The households born
Of peace on earth, good-will to men!

And in despair I bowed my head;
"There is no peace on earth," I said;
    "For hate is strong,
    And mocks the song
Of peace on earth, good-will to men!"

Then pealed the bells more loud and deep:
"God is not dead; nor doth He sleep!
    The Wrong shall fail,

The Right prevail,
With peace on earth, good-will to men!"

Henry Wadsworth Longfellow, 1861

Somehow

Somehow not only for Christmas
But all the long year through,
The joy that you give to others
Is the joy that comes back to you.
And the more you spend in blessing
The poor and lonely and sad,
The more of your heart's possessing
Returns to make you glad.

John Greenleaf Whittier, 1866

Christmas Day and Every Day

Star high,
Baby low:
'Twixt the two
Wise men go;
Find the baby,
Grasp the star—
Heirs of all things
Near and far!

George MacDonald, 1855

The Three Ships

As I went up the mountain-side
The sea below me glitter'd wide,
And, Eastward, far away, I spied
    On Christmas Day, on Christmas Day,
The three great ships that take the tide
    On Christmas Day in the morning.

Ye have heard the song, how these must ply
From the harbours of home to the ports o' the sky!
Do ye dream none knoweth the whither and why
 On Christmas Day, on Christmas Day,
The three great ships go sailing by
 On Christmas Day in the morning?

Yet, as I live, I never knew
That ever a song could ring so true,
Till I saw them break thro' a haze of blue
 On Christmas Day, on Christmas Day;
And the marvellous ancient flags they flew
 On Christmas Day in the morning!

From the heights above the belfried town
I saw that the sails were patched and brown,
But the flags were a-flame with a great renown
 On Christmas Day, on Christmas Day,
And on every mast was a golden crown
 On Christmas Day in the morning.

Most marvellous ancient ships were these!
Were their prows a-plunge to the Chersonese,
For the pomp of Rome, of the glory of Greece,
    On Christmas Day, on Christmas Day?
Were they out on a quest for the Golden Fleece
    On Christmas Day in the morning?

The sun and the wind they told me there
How goodly a load the three ships bear,
For the first is gold and the second is myrrh
    On Christmas Day, on Christmas Day;
And the third is frankincense most rare,
    On Christmas Day in the morning.

They have mixed their shrouds with the golden sky,
They have faded away where the last dreams die . . .
Ah yet, will ye watch, when the mist lifts high
    On Christmas Day, on Christmas Day?

Will ye see three ships come sailing by
   On Christmas Day in the morning?

Alfred Noyes, 1907

I have personal memories of poet Edwin Markham in his latter years, a white-haired genial giant. Some thought he looked like Santa Claus. During a never-to-be-forgotten evening with him, I asked which of his poems he valued the most. He answered, "How can you choose between your own children?" He added that these four lines called "Outwitted" might have more lasting qualities than some of his others, because love itself lasts.

He drew a circle that shut me out—
Heretic, rebel, a thing to flout.
But Love and I had the wit to win:
We drew a circle that took him in!

He was a lovable man. I often used the following poem by him in my Christmas sermons at Marble Collegiate Church.

Before the Cathedral in grandeur rose
At Ingelburg where the Danube goes
Before its forest of silver spires
Went airily up the clouds and fires;
Before the oak had ready a beam,
While yet the arch was stone and dream—
There where the altar was later laid,
Conrad, the cobbler, plied his trade.

. . . .

It happened one day at the year's white end,
Two neighbors called on their old-time friend;
And they found the shop, so meager and mean,
Made gay with a hundred boughs of green.
Conrad was stitching with face ashine,
But suddenly stopped as he twitched a twine:
"Old friends, good news! At dawn today,
As the cocks were scaring the night away,

The Lord appeared in a dream to me,
And said, 'I am coming your Guest to be!'
So I've been busy with feet astir,
Strewing the floor with branches of fir.
The wall is washed and the shelf is shined,
And over the rafter the holly twined.
He comes today, and the table is spread
With milk and honey and wheaten bread."

His friends went home; and his face grew still
As he watched for the shadow across the sill.
He lived all the moments o'er and o'er
When the Lord should enter the lowly door—
The knock, the call, the latch pulled up,
The lighted face, the offered cup.
He would wash the feet where the spikes had been,
He would kiss the hands where the nails went in,
And then at last would sit with Him
And break the bread as the day grew dim.

While the cobbler mused there passed his pane
A beggar drenched by the driving rain.
He called him in from the stony street
And gave him shoes for his bruised feet.
The beggar went and there came a crone,
Her face with wrinkles of sorrow sown.
A bundle of fagots bowed her back,
And she was spent with the wrench and rack.
He gave her his loaf and steadied her load
As she took her way on the weary road.
Then to his door came a little child,
Lost and afraid in the world so wild,
In the big, dark world. Catching it up,
He gave it the milk in the waiting cup,
And let it come to its mother's arms,
Out of the reach of the world's alarms.

The day went down in the crimson west
And with it the hope of the blessed Guest,
And Conrad sighed as the world turned gray:
"Why is it, Lord, that your feet delay?

Did You forget that this was the day?"
Then soft in the silence a Voice he heard:
"Lift up your heart, for I kept my word.
Three times I came to your friendly door;
Three times my shadow was on your floor.
I was the beggar with the bruised feet;
I was the woman you gave to eat;
I was the child on the homeless street!"

Edwin Markham, 1899

A Christmas List

"Ask," He said, "and you shall receive."
When you're nine years old, your heart can believe.
"Give me a doll that drinks and sleeps."
I asked, but oh, I didn't receive.

"Ask," He said, "and you shall receive."
I was young and in love, it was Christmas Eve.
"Give me the heart of that special boy."
I asked, but oh, I didn't receive.

"Ask," He said, "and you shall receive."
Money was scarce but I tried to believe.
"Give us enough for the gifts on our list."
I asked, but oh, I didn't receive.

"Ask," He said, "and you shall receive."
Sorting my values, I began to perceive.
"Give me Your Son. Let Him shine through me."
I asked, and lo, I began to receive . . .

More than I'd ever dared to believe—
Treasures unmeasured, blessings undreamed,
All I'd asked or hoped to achieve.
"Ask," He said, "and you shall receive."

Marilyn Morgan Helleberg, 1982

The Glory of Christmas

Give thanks to the baby asleep in the hay,
For it's Jesus who gave us our first Christmas Day.
A king in disguise, God sent Him to men,
Revealed to our hearts, He comes again.

Lord of the galaxies as well as our earth,
A hymn of the Universe celebrates His birth.
He gives us His Spirit, His kingdom's within,
His peace can be ours by believing in Him.

His truth is a flame that ignites young souls,
He is comfort to men for whom the bell tolls,
He restores an image both marred and grown dim,
He's a constant wonder to those who love Him.

As we wrap up our presents to give them away,
We do this because of that first Christmas Day,

When the Lord of all glory and beauty and wealth
Came to earth as a Baby to give us Himself.

Laverne Riley O'Brien, 1982

The Love That Lives

Every child on earth is holy,
Every crib is a manger lowly,
Every home is a stable dim,
Every kind word is a hymn,
Every star is God's own gem,
And every town is Bethlehem,
For Christ is born and born again,
When His love lives in hearts of men.

W. D. Dorrity, 1909

211

The Priceless Gift of Christmas
Is meant just for the heart
And we receive it only
When we become a part
Of the kingdom and the glory
Which is ours to freely take.
For God sent the Holy Christ Child
At Christmas for our sake,
So man might come to know Him
And feel His Presence near
And see the many miracles.
And this Priceless Gift of Christmas
Is within the reach of all,
The rich, the poor, the young and old
The greatest and the small.

So take His Priceless Gift of Love,
Reach out and you receive,
And the only payment that God asks
Is just that you believe.

Helen Steiner Rice, 1970

IV.
Christmas
Stories

COUNTLESS STORIES with Christmas as their theme have been published, and selecting from among them is difficult. Although Harriet Beecher Stowe is well remembered for *Uncle Tom's Cabin,* her "Christmas; Or, The Good Fairy," with its sentimental note, may be new to you. On the other hand, it is Henry Van Dyke's two Christmas stories that have kept his reputation alive. O. Henry's "Gift of the Magi" continues to be performed as a play in many cities each Christmas, as well as on television. And Charles Dickens's "A Christmas Carol" remains an all-time favorite. Franklin Delano Roosevelt, whether spending Christmas at Hyde Park or in the White House, used to gather his family around him each Christmas Eve and read the Dickens story to them. Unfortunately, space allows me to include here only its last three paragraphs.

Each of these selections has, as do all Christmas stories, a moral best expressed in the last words of Van Dyke's "The First Christmas Tree": "Good-will, henceforth, from heaven to men begin and never cease."

When you think of Charles Dickens's Scrooge, do you recall his being mean and miserable and miserly? Why not remember him as Dickens left him in the closing paragraphs of "A Christmas Carol"?

From "A Christmas Carol"

"A merry Christmas, Bob!" said Scrooge, with an earnestness that could not be mistaken, as he clapped him on the back. "A merrier Christmas, Bob, my good fellow, than I have given you for many a year! I'll raise your salary, and endeavor to assist your struggling family, and we will discuss your affairs this very afternoon, over a Christmas bowl of smoking bishop, Bob! Make up the fires, and buy another coal-scuttle before you dot another *i*, Bob Cratchit!"

Scrooge was better than his word. He did it all, and infinitely more; and to Tiny Tim, who did NOT die, he was a second father. He became as good a friend, as good a master, and as good a man, as the good old city knew, or any other good old city, town, or borough, in the good old world. Some people laughed to see the alteration in him, but he let them laugh, and little heeded them; for he was wise enough to know that nothing ever happened on this globe, for good, at which some people did not have their fill of laughter in the outset; and knowing that such as these would be blind anyway, he thought it quite as well that they should wrinkle up their eyes in grins, as have the malady in less attractive forms. His own heart laughed: and that was quite enough for him.

He had no further intercourse with Spirits, but lived upon the Total Abstinence Principle, ever afterwards; and it was always said of him, that he knew how to keep Christmas well, if any man alive possessed the knowledge. May that be truly said of us, and all of us! And so, as Tiny Tim observed, God Bless Us, Every One!

Charles Dickens, 1843

Christmas; Or, The Good Fairy

"Oh, dear! Christmas is coming in a fortnight, and I have got to think up presents for everybody!" said young Ellen Stuart, as she leaned languidly back in her chair. "Dear me, it's so tedious! Everybody has got everything that can be thought of."

"Oh, no," said her confidential adviser, Miss Lester, in a soothing tone. "You have means of buying everything you can fancy; and when every shop and store is glittering with all manner of splendors, you cannot surely be at a loss."

"Well, now, just listen. To begin with, there's mamma. What can I get for her? I have thought of ever so many things. She has three card cases, four gold thimbles, two or three gold chains, two writing desks of different patterns; and then as to rings, brooches, boxes, and all other things, I should think she might be sick of the sight of them. I am sure I am," said she, languidly gazing on her white and jeweled fingers.

This view of the case seemed rather puzzling to the adviser, and there was silence for a few minutes, when Ellen, yawning, resumed: "And then there's cousins Jane and Mary; I suppose they will be coming down on me with a whole load of presents; and Mrs. B. will send me something—she did last year; and then there's cousins William and Tom—I must get them something; and I would like to do it well enough, if I only knew what to get."

"Well," said Eleanor's aunt, who had been sitting quietly rattling her knitting needles during this speech, "it's a pity that you had not such a subject to practice on as I was when I was a girl. Presents did not fly about in those days as they do now. I remember, when I was ten years old, my father gave me a most marvelously ugly sugar dog for a Christmas gift, and I was perfectly delighted with it, the very idea of a present was so new to us."

"Dear aunt, how delighted I should be if I had any such fresh, unsophisticated body to get presents for! But to get and get for people that have more than they know what to do with now; to add pictures, books, and gilding when the center tables are loaded with them now, and rings and jewels when they are a perfect drug! I wish myself that I were not sick, and sated, and tired with having everything in the world given me."

"Well, Eleanor," said her aunt, "if you really do want unsophisticated subjects to practice on, I can put you in the way of it. I can show you more than one family to whom you might seem to be a very good fairy, and where such gifts as you could give with all ease would seem like a magic dream."

"Why, that would really be worth while, aunt."

"Look over in that back alley," said her aunt. "You see those buildings?"

"That miserable row of shanties? Yes."

"Well, I have several acquaintances there who have never been tired of Christmas gifts or gifts of any other kind. I assure you, you could make quite a sensation over there."

"Well, who is there? Let us know."

"Do you remember Owen, that used to make your shoes?"

"Yes, I remember something about him."

"Well, he has fallen into a consumption, and cannot work any-more; and he, and his wife, and three little children live in one of the rooms."

"How do they get along?"

"His wife takes in sewing sometimes, and sometimes goes out washing. Poor Owen! I was over there yesterday; he looks thin and wasted, and his wife was saying that he was parched with constant fever, and had very little appetite. She had, with great self-denial, and by restricting herself almost of necessary food, got him two or three oranges; and the poor fellow seemed so eager after them."

"Poor fellow!" said Eleanor, involuntarily.

"Now," said her aunt, "suppose Owen's wife should get up on Christmas morning and find at the door a couple dozen of oranges, and some of those nice white grapes, such as you had at your party last week; don't you think it would make a sensation?"

"Why, yes, I think very likely it might; but who else, aunt? You spoke of a great many."

"Well, on the lower floor there is a neat little room, that is always kept perfectly trim and tidy; it belongs to a young couple who have nothing beyond the husband's day wages to live on. They are, never-theless, as cheerful and chipper as a couple of wrens; and she is up and down half a dozen times a day, to help poor Mrs. Owen. She has a baby of her own about five months old, and of course does all the cooking, washing, and ironing for herself and husband; and yet, when Mrs. Owen goes out to wash, she takes her baby, and keeps it whole days for her."

"I'm sure she deserves that the good fairies should smile on her," said Eleanor; "one baby exhausts my stock of virtues very rapidly."

"But you ought to see her baby," said Aunt E.; "so plump, so rosy, and good-natured, and always clean as a lily. This baby is a sort of household shrine; nothing is too sacred or too good for it; and I believe the little thrifty woman feels only one temptation to be extravagant, and that is to get some ornaments to adorn this little divinity."

"Why, did she ever tell you so?"

"No; but one day, when I was coming down stairs, the door of their room was partly open, and I saw a peddler there with open box. John, the husband, was standing with a little purple cap on his hand, which he was regarding with mystified, admiring air, as if he didn't quite comprehend it, and trim little Mary gazing at it with longing eyes.

" 'I think we might get it,' said John.

" 'Oh, no,' said she, regretfully; 'yet I wish we could, it's so pretty!' "

"Say no more, aunt. I see the good fairy must pop a cap into the window on Christmas morning. Indeed, it shall be done. How they will wonder where it came from, and talk about it for months to come!"

"Well, then," continued her aunt, "in the next street to ours there is a miserable building, that looks as if it were just going to topple over; and away up in the third story, in a little room just under the eaves, live two poor, lonely old women. They are both nearly on to ninety. I was in there day before yesterday. One of them is constantly confined to her bed with rheumatism; the other, weak and feeble, with failing sight and trembling hands, totters about, her only helper; and they are entirely dependent on charity."

"Can't they do anything? Can't they knit?" said Eleanor.

"You are young and strong, Eleanor, and have quick eyes and nimble fingers; how long would it take you to knit a pair of stockings?"

"I?" said Eleanor. "What an idea! I never tried, but I think I could get a pair done in a week, perhaps."

"And if somebody gave you twenty-five cents for them, and out of this you had to get food, and pay room rent, and buy coal for your fire, and oil for your lamp—"

"Stop, aunt, for pity's sake!"

"Well, I will stop; but they can't: they must pay so much every month for that miserable shell they live in, or be turned into the street. The meal and flour that some kind person sends goes off for them just as it does for others, and they must get more or starve; and coal is now scarce and high priced."

"O aunt, I'm quite convinced, I'm sure; don't run me down and annihilate me with all these terrible realities. What shall I do to play good fairy to these old women?"

"If you will give me full power, Eleanor, I will put up a basket to be sent to them that will give them something to remember all winter."

"Oh, certainly I will. Let me see if I can't think of something myself."

"Well, Eleanor, suppose, then, some fifty or sixty years hence, if you were old, and if your father, and mother, and aunts, and uncles, now so thick around you, lay cold and silent in so many graves—you have somehow got away off to a strange city, where you were never known—you live in a miserable garret, where snow blows at night through the cracks, and the fire is very apt to go out in the old cracked stove—you sit crouching over the dying embers the evening before Christmas—nobody to speak to you, nobody to care for you, except another poor soul who lies moaning in the bed. Now, what would you like to have sent you?"

"Oh aunt, what a dismal picture!"

"And yet, Ella, all poor, forsaken old women are made of young girls, who expected it in their youth as little as you do, perhaps."

"Say no more, aunt. I'll buy—let me see—a comfortable warm shawl for each of these poor women; and I'll send them—let me see—oh, some tea—nothing goes down with old women like tea; and I'll make John wheel some coal over to them; and, aunt, it would not be a very bad thought to send them a new stove. I remember, the other day, when mamma was pricing stoves, I saw some such nice ones for two or three dollars."

"For a new hand, Ella, you work up the idea very well," said her aunt.

"But how much ought I to give, for any one case, to these women, say?"

"How much did you give last year for any single Christmas present?"

"Why, six or seven dollars for some; those elegant souvenirs were seven dollars; that ring I gave Mrs. B. was twenty."

"And do you suppose Mrs. B. was any happier for it?"

"No, really, I don't think she cared much about it; but I had to give her something, because she had sent me something the year before, and I did not want to send a paltry present to one in her circumstances."

"Then, Ella, give the same to any poor, distressed, suffering creature who really needs it, and see in how many forms of good such a sum will appear. That one hard, cold, glittering ring, that now cheers nobody, and means nothing, that you give because you must, and she takes because she must, might, if broken up into smaller sums, send real warm and heartfelt gladness through many a cold and cheerless dwelling, through many an aching heart."

"You are getting to be an orator, aunt; but don't you approve of Christmas presents, among friends and equals?"

"Yes, indeed," said her aunt, fondly stroking her head. "I have had some Christmas presents that did me a world of good—a little book mark, for instance, that a certain niece of mine worked for me, with wonderful secrecy, three years ago, when she was not a young lady with a purse full of money—that book mark was a true Christmas present; and my young couple across the way are plotting a profound surprise to each other on Christmas morning. John has contrived, by an hour of extra work every night, to lay by enough to get Mary a new calico dress; and she, poor soul, has bargained away the only thing in the jewelry line she ever possessed, to be laid out on a new hat for him.

"I know, too, a washerwoman who has a poor lame boy—a patient, gentle little fellow—who has lain quietly for weeks and months in his little crib, and his mother is going to give him a splendid Christmas present."

"What is it, pray?"

"A whole orange! Don't laugh. She will pay ten whole cents for it; for it shall be none of your common oranges, but a picked one of the very best going! She has put by the money, a cent at a time, for a whole month; and nobody knows which will be happiest in it, Willie or his mother. These are such Christmas presents as I like to think of—gifts coming from love, and tending to produce love; these are the appropriate gifts of the day."

"But don't you think that it's right for those who *have* money to give expensive presents, supposing always, as you say, they are given from real affection?"

"Sometimes, undoubtedly. The Saviour did not condemn her who broke an alabaster box of ointment—very precious—simply as a proof of love, even although the suggestion was made, 'This might have been sold for three hundred pence, and given to the poor.' I have thought he would regard with sympathy the fond efforts which human love sometimes makes to express itself by gifts, the rarest and most costly. How I rejoiced with all my heart, when Charles Elton gave his poor mother that splendid Chinese shawl and gold watch! because I knew they came from the very fullness of his heart to a mother that he could not do too much for—a mother that has done and suffered everything for him. In some such cases, when resources are ample, a costly gift seems to have a graceful appropriateness; but I cannot approve of it if it exhausts all the means of doing for the poor; it is better, then, to give a simple offering, and to do something for those who really need it."

Eleanor looked thoughtful; her aunt laid down her knitting, and said, in a tone of gentle seriousness, "Whose birth does Christmas commemorate, Ella?"

"Our Saviour's, certainly, aunt."

"Yes," said her aunt. "And when and how was he born? In a stable! laid in a manger; thus born, that in all ages he might be known as the brother and friend of the poor. And surely, it seems but appropriate to commemorate his birthday by an especial remembrance of the lowly, the poor, the outcast, and distressed; and if Christ should come back to our city on a Christmas day, where should we think it most appropriate to his character to find him? Would he be carrying splendid gifts to splendid dwellings, or would he be gliding about in the cheerless haunts of the desolate, the poor, the forsaken, and the sorrowful?"

And here the conversation ended.

"What sort of Christmas presents is Ella buying?" said Cousin Tom, as the servant handed in a portentous-looking package, which had been just run in at the door.

"Let's open it," said saucy Will. "Upon my word, two great gray blanket shawls! These must be for you and me, Tom! And what's this? A great bolt of cotton flannel and gray yarn stockings!"

The door bell rang again, and the servant brought in another bulky parcel, and deposited it on the marble-topped centre table.

"What's here?" said Will, cutting the cord. "Whew! a perfect nest of packages! Oolong tea! oranges! grapes! white sugar! Bless me, Ella must be going to housekeeping!"

"Or going crazy!" said Tom; "and on my word," said he, looking out of the window, "there's a drayman ringing at our door, with a stove, with a teakettle set in the top of it!"

"Ella's cook stove, of course," said Will; and just at this moment the young lady entered, with her purse hanging gracefully over her hand.

"Now, boys, you are too bad!" she exclaimed, as each of the mischievous youngsters was gravely marching up and down, attired in a gray shawl.

"Didn't you get them for us? We thought you did," said both.

"Ella, I want some of that cotton flannel, to make me a pair of pantaloons," said Tom.

"I say, Ella," said Will, "when are you going to housekeeping? Your cooking stove is standing down in the street; 'pon my word, John is loading some coal on the dray with it."

"Ella, isn't that going to be sent to my office?" said Tom; "do you know I do so languish for a new stove with a teakettle in the top, to heat a fellow's shaving-water!"

Just then, another ring at the door, and the grinning servant handed in a small brown paper parcel for Miss Ella. Tom made a dive at it, and tearing off the brown paper, discovered a jaunty little purple velvet cap, with silver tassels.

"My smoking cap, as I live!" said he; "only I shall have to wear it on my thumb, instead of my head—too small entirely," said he, shaking his head gravely.

"Come, you saucy boys," said Aunt E., entering briskly. "What are you teasing Ella for?"

"Why, do you see this lot of things, aunt! What in the world is Ella going to do with them?"

"Oh, I know!"

"You know! Then I can guess, aunt, it is some of your charitable works. You are going to make a juvenile Lady Bountiful of El, eh?"

Ella, who had colored to the roots of her hair at the exposé of her very unfashionable Christmas preparations, now took heart, and bestowed a very gentle and salutary little cuff on the saucy head that still wore the purple cap, and then hastened to gather up her various purchases.

"Laugh away," said she, gayly; "and a good many others will laugh, too, over these things. I got them to make people laugh—people that are not in the habit of laughing!"

"Well, well, I see into it," said Will; "and I tell you I think right well of the idea, too. There are worlds of money wasted, at this time of the year, in getting things that nobody wants, and nobody cares for after they are got; and I am glad, for my part, that you are going to get up a variety in this line; in fact, I should like to give you one of these stray leaves to help on," said he, dropping a ten dollar note into her paper. "I like to encourage girls to think of something besides breastpins and sugar candy."

But our story spins on too long. If anybody wants to see the results of Ella's first attempts at *good fairyism,* they can call at the doors of two or three old buildings on Christmas morning, and they shall hear all about it.

Harriet Beecher Stowe, 1869

The Story of the Other Wise Man

THE SIGN IN THE SKY

In the days when Augustus Caesar was master of many kings and Herod reigned in Jerusalem, there lived in the city of Ecbatana, among the mountains of Persia, a certain man named Artaban, the Median. His house stood close to the outermost of the seven walls which encircled the royal treasury. From his roof he could look over the rising battlements of black and white and crimson and blue and red and silver and gold, to the hill where the summer palace of the Parthian emperors glittered like a jewel in a sevenfold crown.

Around the dwelling of Artaban spread a fair garden, a tangle of flowers and fruit trees, watered by a score of streams descending from the slopes of Mount Orontes, and made musical by innumerable birds. But all color was lost in the soft and odorous darkness of the late September night, and all sounds were hushed in the deep charm of its silence, save the plashing of water, like a voice half sobbing and half laughing under the shadows. High above the trees a dim glow of light shone through the curtained arches of the upper chamber, where the master of the house was holding council with his friends.

He stood by the doorway to greet his guests—a tall, dark man of about forty years, with brilliant eyes set near together under his broad brow, and firm lines graven around his fine, thin lips; the brow of a dreamer and the mouth of a soldier, a man of sensitive feeling but inflexible will—one of those who, in whatever age they may live, are born for inward conflict and a life of quest.

His robe was of pure white wool, thrown over a tunic of silk; and a white, pointed cap, with long lapels at the sides, rested on his flowing black hair. It was the dress of the ancient priesthood of the Magi, called the fire-worshipers.

"Welcome!" he said, in his low, pleasant voice, as one after another entered the room—"welcome, Abdus; peace be with you, Rhadaspes and Tigranes, and with you; my father, Abgarus. You are all welcome, and this house grows bright with the joy of your presence."

There were nine of the men, differing widely in age, but alike in the richness of their dress of many-colored silks and in the massive golden collars around their necks, marking them as Parthian nobles, and in the winged circles of gold resting upon their breasts, the sign of the followers of Zoroaster.

They took their places around a small black altar at the end of the room, where a tiny flame was burning. Artaban, standing beside it, and waving a barsom of thin tamarisk branches above the fire, fed it with dry sticks of pine and fragrant oils. Then he began the ancient chant of the Yasna, and the voices of his companions joined in the beautiful hymn to Ahura-Mazda:

> We worship the Spirit Divine,
> all wisdom and goodness possessing,
> Surrounded by Holy Immortals,
> the givers of bounty and blessing,
> We joy in the works of His hands,
> His truth and His power confessing.
>
> We praise all the things that are pure,
> for these are His only Creation;
> The thoughts that are true, and the words
> and deeds that have won approbation;
> These are supported by Him
> and for these we make adoration.
>
> Hear us, O Mazda! Thou livest
> in truth and in heavenly gladness;
> Cleanse us from falsehood, and keep us
> from evil and bondage to badness;
> Pour out the light and the joy of Thy life
> on our darkness and sadness.

Shine on our gardens and fields,
Shine on our working and weaving;
Shine on the whole race of man,
Believing and unbelieving;
Shine on us now through the night,
Shine on us now in Thy might,
The flame of our holy love
and the song of our worship receiving.

The fire rose with the chant, throbbing as if it were made of musical flame, until it cast a bright illumination through the whole apartment, revealing its simplicity and splendor.

The floor was laid with tiles of dark blue veined with white; pilasters of twisted silver stood out against the blue walls; the clear-story of round-arched windows above them was hung with azure silk; the vaulted ceiling was a pavement of sapphires, like the body of heaven in its clearness, sown with silver stars. From the four corners of the roof hung four golden magic-wheels, called the tongues of the gods. At the eastern end, behind the altar, there were two dark-red pillars of porphyry; above them a lintel of the same stone, on which was carved the figure of a winged archer, with his arrow set to the string and his bow drawn.

The doorway between the pillars, which opened upon the terrace of the roof, was covered with a heavy curtain of the color of a ripe pomegranate, embroidered with innumerable golden rays shooting upward from the floor. In effect the room was like a quiet, starry night, all azure and silver, flushed in the east with rosy promise of the dawn. It was, as the house of a man should be, an expression of the character and spirit of the master.

He turned to his friends when the song was ended, and invited them to be seated on the divan at the western end of the room.

"You have come tonight," said he, looking around the circle, "at my call, as the faithful scholars of Zoroaster, to renew your worship and rekindle your faith in the God of Purity, even as this fire has been rekindled on the altar. We worship not the fire, but Him of whom it is the chosen symbol, because it is the purest of all created things. It speaks to us of one who is Light and Truth. Is it not so, my father?"

"It is well said, my son," answered the venerable Abgarus. "The enlightened are never idolaters. They lift the veil of the form and go in to the shrine of the reality, and the new light and truth are coming to them continually through the old symbols."

"Hear me, then, my father and my friends," said Artaban, very quietly, "while I tell you of the new light and truth that have come to me through the most ancient of all signs. We have searched the secrets of nature together, and studied the healing virtues of water and fire and the plants. We have read also the books of prophecy in which the future is dimly foretold in words that are hard to understand. But the highest of all learning is the knowledge of the stars. To trace their courses is to untangle the threads of the mystery of life from the beginning to the end. If we could follow them perfectly, nothing would be hidden from us. But is not our knowledge of them still incomplete? Are there not many stars still beyond our horizon—lights that are known only to the dwellers in the far southland, among the spice-trees and Punt and the gold-mines of Ophir?"

There was a murmur of assent among the listeners.

"The stars," said Tigranes, "are the thoughts of the Eternal. They are numberless. But the thoughts of man can be counted, like the years of his life. The wisdom of the Magi is the greatest of all wisdoms on earth, because it knows its own ignorance. And that is the secret of power. We keep men always looking and waiting for a new sunrise. But we ourselves know that the darkness is equal to the light, and that the conflict between them will never be ended."

"That does not satisfy me," answered Artaban, "for, if the waiting must be endless, if there could be no fulfillment of it, then it would not be wisdom to look and wait. We should become like those new teachers of the Greeks, who say that there is no truth, and that the only wise men are those who spend their lives in discovering and exposing the lies that have been believed in the world. But the new sunrise will certainly dawn in the appointed time. Do not our own books tell us that this will come to pass, and that men will see the brightness of a great light?"

"That is true," said the voice of Abgarus; "every faithful disciple of Zoroaster knows the prophecy of the Avesta and carries the word in his heart. 'In that day Sosiosh the Victorious shall arise out of the number of the prophets in the east country. Around him shall shine a mighty brightness, and he shall make life everlasting, incorruptible, and immortal, and the dead shall rise again.'"

"This is a dark saying," said Tigranes, "and it may be that we shall never understand it. It is better to consider the things that are near at hand, and to increase the influence of the Magi in their own country, rather than to look for one who may be a stranger, and to whom we must resign our power."

The others seemed to approve these words. There was a silent feeling of agreement manifest among them; their looks responded with that indefinable expression which always follows when a speaker has uttered the thought that has been slumbering in the hearts of his listeners. But Artaban turned to Abgarus with a glow on his face, and said:

"My father, I have kept this prophecy in the secret place of my soul. Religion without a great hope would be like an altar without a living fire. And now the flame has burned more brightly, and by the light of it I have read other words which also have come from the fountain of Truth, and speak yet more clearly of the rising of the Victorious One in his brightness."

He drew from the breast of his tunic two small rolls of fine linen, with writing upon them, and unfolded them carefully upon his knee.

"In the years that are lost in the past, long before our fathers came into the land of Babylon, there were wise men in Chaldea, from whom the first of the Magi learned the secret of the heavens. And of these Balaam, the son Beor, was one of the mightiest. Hear the words of his prophecy: 'There shall come a star out of Jacob, and a scepter shall arise out of Israel.'"

The lips of Tigranes drew downward with contempt, as he said:

"Judah was a captive by the waters of Babylon, and the sons of Jacob were in bondage to our kings. The tribes of Israel are scattered through the mountains like lost sheep, and from the remnant that dwells in Judea under the yoke of Rome neither star nor sceptre shall arise."

"And yet," answered Artaban, "it was the Hebrew Daniel, the mighty searcher of dreams, the counsellor of kings, the wise Belteshazzar, who was most honored and beloved of our great King Cyrus. A prophet of sure things and a reader of the thoughts of God, Daniel proved himself to our people. And these are the words that he wrote." (Artaban read from the second roll:) " 'Know, therefore, and understand that from the going forth of the commandment to restore Jerusalem, unto the Anointed One, the Prince, the time shall be seven and three-score and two weeks.' "

"But, my son," said Abgarus, doubtfully, "these are mystical numbers. Who can interpret them, or who can find the key that shall unlock their meaning?"

Artaban answered, "It has been shown to me and to my three companions among the Magi—Caspar, Melchior, and Balthazar. We have searched the ancient tables of Chaldea and computed the time. It falls in this year. We have studied the sky, and in the spring of the year we saw two of the greatest stars draw near together in the sign of the Fish, which is the house of the Hebrews. We also saw a new star there, which shone for one night and then vanished. Now again the two great planets are meeting. This night is their conjunction. My three brothers are watching at the ancient Temple of the Seven Spheres, at Borsippa, in Babylonia, and I am watching here. If the star shines again, they will wait ten days for me at the temple, and then we will set out together for Jerusalem, to see and worship the promised one who shall be born King of Israel. I believe the sign will come. I have made ready for the journey. I have sold my house and my possessions, and brought these three jewels—a sapphire, a ruby, and a pearl—to carry them as tribute to the King. And I ask you to go with me on the pilgrimage, that we may have joy together in finding the Prince who is worthy to be served."

While he was speaking he thrust his hand into the inmost fold of his girdle and drew out three great gems—one blue as a fragment of the night sky, one redder than a ray of sunrise, and one as pure as the peak of a snow mountain at twilight—and laid them out on the outspread linen scrolls before him.

But his friends looked on with strange and alien eyes. A veil of doubt and mistrust came over their faces, like a fog creeping up from the marshes to hide the hills. They glanced at each other with looks of wonder and pity, as those who have listened to incredible sayings, the story of a wild vision, or the proposal of an impossible enterprise.

At last Tigranes said: "Artaban, this is a vain dream. It comes from too much looking upon the stars and the cherishing of lofty thoughts. It would be wiser to spend the time in gathering money for the new fire-temple at Chala. No king will ever rise from the broken race of Israel, and no end will ever come to the eternal strife of light and darkness. He who looks for it is a chaser of shadows. Farewell."

And another said: "Artaban, I have no knowledge of these things, and my office as guardian of the royal treasure binds me here. The quest is not for me. But if thou must follow it, fare thee well."

And another said: "In my house there sleeps a new bride, and I cannot leave her nor take her with me on this strange journey. This quest is not for me. But may thy steps be prospered wherever thou goest. So, farewell."

And another said: "I am ill and unfit for hardship, but there is a man among my servants whom I will send with thee when thou goest, to bring me word how thou farest."

But Abgarus, the oldest and the one who loved Artaban the best, lingered after the others had gone, and said, gravely: "My son, it may be that the light of truth is in this sign that has appeared in the skies, and then it will surely lead to the Prince and the mighty brightness. Or it may be that it is only a shadow of the light, as Tigranes has said, and then he who follows it will have only a long pilgrimage and an empty search. But it is better to follow even the shadow of the best than to remain content with the worst. And those who would see wonderful things must often be ready to travel alone. I am too old for this journey, but my heart shall be a companion of the pilgrimage day and night, and I shall know the end of thy quest. Go in peace."

So one by one they went out of the azure chamber with its silver stars, and Artaban was left in solitude.

He gathered up the jewels and replaced them in his girdle. For a long time he stood and watched the flame that flickered and sank upon the altar. Then he crossed the hall, lifted the heavy curtain, and passed out between the dull red pillars of porphyry to the terrace on the roof.

The shiver that thrills through the earth ere she rouses from her night sleep had already begun, and the cool wind that heralds the daybreak was drawing downward from the lofty, snow-traced ravines of Mount Orontes. Birds, half-awakened, crept and chirped among the rustling leaves, and the smell of ripened grapes came in brief wafts from the arbors.

Far over the eastern plain a white mist stretched like a lake. But where the distant peak of Zagros serrated the western horizon the sky was clear. Jupiter and Saturn rolled together like drops of lambent flame about to blend in one.

As Artaban watched them, behold, an azure spark was born out of the darkness beneath, rounding itself with purple splendors to a crimson sphere, and spiring upward through rays of saffron and orange into a point of white radiance. Tiny and infinitely remote, yet perfect in every part, it pulsated in the enormous vault as if the three jewels in the

Magian's breast had mingled and been transformed into a living heart of light.

He bowed his head. He covered his brow with his hands.

"It is the sign," he said. "The King is coming, and I will go to meet him."

BY THE WATERS OF BABYLON

All night long Vasda, the swiftest of Artaban's horses, had been waiting, saddled and bridled, in her stall, pawing the ground impatiently, and shaking her bit as if she shared the eagerness of her master's purpose, though she knew not its meaning.

Before the birds had fully roused to their strong, high, joyful chant of morning song, before the white mist had begun to lift lazily from the plain, the other wise man was in the saddle, riding swiftly along the high-road, which skirted the base of Mount Orontes, westward.

How close, how intimate is the comradeship between a man and his favorite horse on a long journey. It is a silent, comprehensive friendship, an intercourse beyond the need of words.

They drink at the same wayside springs, and sleep under the same guardian stars. They are conscious together of the subduing spell of nightfall and the quickening joy of daybreak. The master shares his evening meal with his hungry companion, and feels the soft, moist lips caressing the palm of his hand as they close over the morsel of bread. In the gray dawn he is roused from his bivouac by the gentle stir of a warm, sweet breath over his sleeping face, and looks up into the eyes of his faithful fellow-traveler, ready and waiting for the toil of the day. Surely, unless he is pagan and an unbeliever, by whatever name he calls upon his God, he will thank Him for this voiceless sympathy, this dumb affection, and his morning prayer will embrace a double blessing—God bless us both, and keep our feet from falling and our souls from death!

And then, through the keen morning air, the swift hoofs beat their spirited music along the road, keeping time to the pulsing of two hearts that are moved with the same eager desire—to conquer space, to devour the distance, to attain the goal of the journey.

Artaban must indeed ride wisely and well if he would keep the appointed hour with the other Magi; for the route was a hundred and fifty parasangs, and fifteen was the utmost that he could travel in a day. But he knew Vasda's strength, and pushed forward without anxiety, making the fixed distance every day, though he must travel late into the night, and in the morning long before sunrise.

He passed along the brown slopes of Mount Orontes, furrowed by the rocky courses of a hundred torrents.

He crossed the level plains of the Nisaeans, where the famous herds of horses, feeding in the wide pastures, tossed their heads at Vasda's approach, and galloped away with a thunder of many hoofs, and flocks of wild birds rose suddenly from the swampy meadows, wheeling in great circles with a shining flutter of innumerable wings and shrill cries of surprise.

He traversed the fertile fields of Concabar, where the dust from the threshing-floors filled the air with a golden mist, half hiding the huge temple of Astarte with its four-hundred pillars.

At Baghistan, among the rich gardens watered by fountains from the rock, he looked up at the mountain thrusting its immense rugged brow out over the road, and saw the figure of King Darius trampling upon his fallen foes, and the proud list of his wars and conquests graven high upon the face of the eternal cliff.

Over many a cold and desolate pass, crawling painfully across the windswept shoulders of the hills; down many a black mountain-gorge, where the river roared and raced before him like a savage guide; across many a smiling vale, with terraces of yellow limestone full of vines and fruit trees; through the oak groves of Carine and the dark Gates of Zagros, walled in by precipices; into the ancient city of Chala, where the people of Samaria had been kept in captivity long ago; and out again by the mighty portal, riven through the encircling hills, where he saw the image of the High Priest of the Magi sculptured on the wall of rock, with hand uplifted as if to bless the centuries of pilgrims; past the entrance of the narrow defile, filled from end to end with orchards of peaches and figs, through which the river Gyndes foamed down to meet him; over the broad rice-fields, where the autumnal vapors spread their deathly mists; following along the course of the river, under tremulous shadows of poplar and tamarind, among the lower hills; and out upon the flat plain, where the road ran straight as an arrow through the stubble-fields and parched meadows; past the city of Ctesiphon, where the Parthian emperors reigned and the vast metropolis of Seleucia which Alexander built; across the swirling floods of Tigris and the many channels of Euphrates, flowing yellow through the corn-lands— Artaban pressed onward until he arrived at nightfall of the tenth day, beneath the shattered walls of populous Babylon.

Vasda was almost spent, and he would gladly have turned into the city to find rest and refreshment for himself and for her. But he knew that it was three hours' journey yet to the Temple of the Seven Spheres, and he must reach the place by midnight if he would find his comrades waiting. So he did not halt, but rode steadily across the stubble-fields.

A grove of date-plums made an island of gloom in the pale yellow sea. As she passed into the shadow Vasda slackened her pace, and began to pick her way more carefully.

Near the farther end of the darkness an access of caution seemed to fall upon her. She scented some danger or difficulty; it was not in her heart to fly from it—only to be prepared for it, and to meet it wisely, as a good horse should do. The grove was close and silent as the tomb; not a leaf rustled, not a bird sang.

She felt her steps before her delicately, carrying her head low, and sighing now and then with apprehension. At last she gave a quick breath of anxiety and dismay, and stood stock-still quivering in every muscle, before a dark object in the shadow of the last palm-tree.

Artaban dismounted. The dim star-light revealed the form of a man lying across the road. His humble dress and the outline of his haggard face showed that he was probably one of the poor Hebrew exiles who still dwelt in great numbers in the vicinity. His pallid skin, dry and yellow as parchment, bore the mark of the deadly fever which ravaged the marshlands in autumn. The chill of death was in his lean hand, and as Artaban released it the arm fell back inertly upon the motionless breast.

He turned away with a thought of pity, consigning the body to that strange burial which the Magians deemed most fitting—the funeral of the desert, from which the kites and vultures rise on dark wings, and the beasts of prey slink furtively away, leaving only a heap of white bones in the sand.

But, as he turned, a long, faint, ghostly sigh came from the man's lips. The brown, bony fingers closed convulsively on the hem of the Magian's robe and held him fast.

Artaban's heart leaped to his throat, not with fear, but with a dumb resentment at the importunity of this blind delay.

How could he stay here in the darkness to minister to a dying stranger? What claim had this unknown fragment of human life upon his compassion or his service? If he lingered but for an hour he could hardly reach Borsippa at the appointed time. His companions would think he had given up the journey. They would go without him. He would lose his quest.

But if he went on now, the man would surely die. If he stayed, life might be restored. His spirit throbbed and fluttered with the urgency of the crisis. Should he risk the great reward of his divine faith for the sake of a single deed of human love? Should he turn aside, if only for a moment, from the following of the star, to give a cup of cold water to a poor, perishing Hebrew?

"God of truth and purity," he prayed, "direct me in the holy path, the way of wisdom which Thou only knowest."

Then he turned back to the sick man. Loosening the grasp of his hand, he carried him to a little mound at the foot of the palm-tree.

He unbound the thick folds of the turban and opened the garment above the sunken breast. He brought water from one of the small canals near by, and moistened the sufferer's brow and mouth. He mingled a draught of one of those simple but potent remedies which he carried always in his girdle—for the Magians were physicians as well as astrologers—and poured it slowly between the colorless lips. Hour after hour he labored as only a skillful healer of disease can do; and at last the man's strength returned; he sat up and looked about him.

"Who art thou?" he said in the rude dialect of the country, "and why hast thou sought me here to bring back my life?"

"I am Artaban the Magian, of the city of Ecbatana, and I am going to Jerusalem in search of one who is to be born King of the Jews, a great Prince and Deliverer of all men. I dare not delay any longer upon my journey, for the caravan that has waited for me may depart without me. But see, here is all that I have left of bread and wine, and here is a potion of healing herbs. When thy strength is restored thou canst find the dwellings of the Hebrews among the houses of Babylon."

The Jew raised his trembling hand solemnly to heaven.

"Now may the God of Abraham and Isaac and Jacob bless and prosper the journey of the merciful, and bring him in peace to his desired haven. But stay; I have nothing to give thee in return—only this: that I can tell thee where the Messiah must be sought. For our prophets have said that he should be born not in Jerusalem, but in Bethlehem of Judah. May the Lord bring thee in safety to that place, because thou has had pity upon the sick."

It was already long past midnight. Artaban rode in haste, and Vasda, restored by the brief rest, ran eagerly through the silent plain and swam the channels of the river. She put forth the remnant of her strength, and fled over the ground like a gazelle.

But the first beam of the sun sent her shadow before her as she entered upon the final stadium of the journey, and the eyes of Artaban, anxiously scanning the great mound of Nimrod and the Temple of the Seven Spheres, could discern no trace of his friends.

The many-colored terraces of black and orange and red and yellow and green and blue and white, shattered by the convulsions of nature, and crumbling under the repeated blows of human violence, still glittered like a ruined rainbow in the morning light.

Artaban rode swiftly around the hill. He dismounted and climbed to the highest terrace, looking out toward the west.

The huge desolation of the marshes stretched away to the horizon and the border of the desert. Bitterns stood by the stagnant pools and jackals skulked through the low bushes; but there was no sign of the caravan of the wise men, far or near.

At the edge of the terrace he saw a little cairn of broken bricks, and under them a piece of parchment. He caught it up and read: "We have waited past the midnight, and can delay no longer. We go to find the King. Follow us across the desert."

Artaban sat down upon the ground and covered his head in despair.

"How can I cross the desert," said he, "with no food and with a spent horse? I must return to Babylon, sell my sapphire, and buy a train of camels, and provision for the journey. I may never overtake my friends. Only God the merciful knows whether I shall not lose the sight of the King because I tarried to show mercy."

FOR THE SAKE OF A LITTLE CHILD

There was silence in the Hall of Dreams, where I was listening to the story of the Other Wise Man. And through this silence I saw, but very dimly, his figure passing over the dreary undulations of the desert, high upon the back of his camel, rocking steadily onward like a ship over the waves.

The land of death spread its cruel net around him. The stony wastes bore no fruit but briers and thorns. The dark ledges of rock thrust themselves above the surface here and there, like the bones of perished monsters. Arid and inhospitable mountain ranges rose before him, furrowed with dry channels of ancient torrents, white and ghastly as scars on the face of nature. Shifting hills of treacherous sand were heaped like tombs along the horizon. By day, the fierce heat pressed its intolerable burden on the quivering air; and no living creature moved on dumb, swooning earth, but tiny jerboas scuttling through the parched bushes, or lizards vanishing in the clefts of the rock. By night the jackals prowled and barked in the distance, and the lion made the black ravines echo with his hollow roaring, while a bitter blighting chill followed the fever of the day. Through heat and cold, the Magian moved steadily onward.

Then I saw the gardens and orchards of Damascus, watered by the streams of Abana and Pharpar with their sloping swards inlaid with bloom, and their thickets of myrrh and roses. I saw also the long, snowy ridge of Hermon, and the dark groves of cedars, and the valley of the Jordan, and the blue waters of the Lake of Galilee, and fertile plain of Esdraelon, and the hills of Ephraim, and the highlands of Judah. Through all these I followed the figure of Artaban moving steadily onward, until he arrived at Bethlehem. And it was the third day after the three wise men had come to that place and had found Mary and Joseph, with the young child, Jesus, and had laid their gifts of gold and frankincense and myrrh at his feet.

Then the other wise man drew near, weary, but full of hope, bearing his ruby and pearl to offer to the King. "For now at last," he said, "I shall surely find him, though it be alone, and later than my brethren. This is the place of which the Hebrew exile told me that the prophets had spoken, and here I shall behold the rising of the great light. But I must inquire about the visit of my brethren, and to what house the star directed them, and to whom they presented their tribute."

The streets of the village seemed to be deserted, and Artaban wondered whether the men had all gone up to the hill-pastures to bring down their sheep. From the open door of a low stone cottage he heard the sound of a woman's voice singing softly. He entered and found a young mother hushing her baby to rest. She told him of the strangers from the far East who had appeared in the village three days ago, and how they said that a star had guided them to the place where Joseph of Nazareth was lodging with his wife and her newborn child, and how they had paid reverence to the child and given him many rich gifts.

"But the travelers disappeared again," she continued, "as suddenly as they had come. We were afraid at the strangeness of their visit. We could not understand it. The man of Nazareth took the babe and his mother and fled away that same night secretly, and it was whispered that they were going far away to Egypt. Ever since, there has been a spell upon the village; something evil hangs over it. They say that the Roman soldiers are coming from Jerusalem to force a new tax from us, and the men have driven the flocks and herds far back among the hills, and hidden themselves to escape it."

Artaban listened to her gentle, timid speech, and the child in her arms looked up in his face and smiled, stretching out its rosy hands to grasp at the winged circle of gold on his breast. His heart warmed to the touch. It seemed like a greeting of love and trust to one who had journeyed in loneliness and perplexity, fighting with his own doubts and fears, and following a light that was veiled in clouds.

"Might not this child have been the promised Prince?" he asked within himself, as he touched its soft cheek. "Kings have been born ere now in lowlier houses than this, and the favorite of the stars may rise even from a cottage. But it has not seemed good to the God of Wisdom to reward my search so soon and so easily. The one whom I seek has gone before me and I must follow the King to Egypt."

The young mother laid the babe in its cradle, and rose to minister to the wants of the strange guest that fate had brought into her house. She set food before him, the plain fare of peasants, but willingly offered, and therefore full of refreshment for the soul as well as for the body. Artaban accepted it gratefully; and, as he ate, the child fell into a happy slumber, and murmured sweetly in its dreams, and a great peace filled the quiet room.

But suddenly there came the noise of a wild confusion and uproar in the streets of the village, a shrieking and wailing of women's voices, a clangor of brazen trumpets and a clashing of swords, and a desperate cry: "The soldiers! the soldiers of Herod! They are killing our children."

The young mother's face grew white with terror. She clasped her child to her bosom, and crouched motionless in the darkest corner of the room, covering him with the folds of her robe, lest he should wake and cry.

But Artaban went quickly and stood in the doorway of the house. His broad shoulders filled the portal from side to side, and the peak of his white cap all but touched the lintel.

The soldiers came hurrying down the street with bloody hands and dripping swords. At the sight of the stranger in his imposing dress they hesitated with surprise. The captain of the band approached the threshold to thrust him aside. But Artaban did not stir. His face was as calm as though he were watching the stars, and in his eyes there burned that steady radiance before which even the half-tamed hunting leopard shrinks and the fierce bloodhound pauses in his leap. He held the soldier silently for an instant, and then said in a low voice:

"I am all alone in this place, and I am waiting to give this jewel to the prudent captain who will leave me in peace."

He showed the ruby, glistening in the hollow of his hand like a great drop of blood.

The captain was amazed at the splendor of the gem. The pupils of his eyes expanded with desire, and the hard lines of greed wrinkled around his lips. He stretched out his hand and took the ruby.

"March on!" he cried to his men, "there is no child here. The house is still."

The clamor and the clang of arms passed down the street as the headlong fury of the chase sweeps by the secret covert where the trembling deer is hidden. Artaban re-entered the cottage. He turned his face to the east and prayed:

"God of truth, forgive my sin! I have said the thing that is not, to save the life of a child. And two of my gifts are gone. I have spent for man that which was meant for God. Shall I ever be worthy to see the face of the King?"

But the voice of the woman, weeping for joy in the shadow behind him, said very gently:

"Because thou has saved the life of my little one, may the Lord bless thee and keep thee; the Lord make His face to shine upon thee and be gracious unto thee; the Lord lift up His countenance upon thee and give thee peace."

IN THE HIDDEN WAY OF SORROW

Then again there was a silence in the Hall of Dreams, deeper and more mysterious than the first interval, and I understand that the years of Artaban were flowing very swiftly under the stillness of that clinging fog, and I caught only a glimpse, here and there, of the river of his life shining through the shadows that concealed its course.

I saw him moving among the throngs of men in populous Egypt, seeking everywhere for traces of the household that had come down from Bethlehem, and finding them under the spreading sycamore-trees of Heliopolis, and beneath the walls of the Roman fortress of New Babylon beside the Nile—traces so faint and dim that they vanished before him continually, as footprints on the hard river-stand glisten for a moment with moisture and then disappear.

I saw him again at the foot of the pyramids, which lifted their sharp points into the intense saffron glow of the sunset sky, changeless monuments of the perishable glory and the imperishable hope of man. He looked up into the vast countenance of the crouching Sphinx, and vainly tried to read the meaning of the calm eyes and smiling mouth. Was it, indeed, the mockery of all effort and all aspiration, as Tigranes had said—the cruel jest of a riddle that has no answer, a search that never can succeed? Or was there a touch a pity and encouragement in that inscrutable smile—a promise that even the defeated should attain a victory, and the disappointed should discover a prize, and the ignorant should be made wise, and the blind should see, and the wandering should come into the haven at last?

I saw him again in an obscure house of Alexandria, taking counsel with a Hebrew rabbi. The venerable man, bending over the rolls of parchment on which the prophecies of Israel were written, read aloud the pathetic words which foretold the sufferings of the promised Messiah—and the despised and rejected of men, the man of sorrows and the acquaintance of grief.

"And remember, my son," said he, fixing his deep-set eyes upon the face of Artaban, "the King whom you are seeking is not to be found in a palace, nor among the rich and powerful. If the light of the world and the glory of Israel had been appointed to come with the greatness of earthly splendor, it must have appeared long ago. For no son of Abraham will ever again rival the power which Joseph had in the palaces of Egypt, or the magnificence of Solomon throned between the lions in Jerusalem. But the light for which the world is waiting is a new light, the glory that shall rise out of patient and triumphant suffering. And the kingdom which is to be established forever is a new kingdom, the royalty of perfect and unconquerable love.

"I do not know how this shall come to pass, nor how the turbulent kings and peoples of earth shall be brought to acknowledge the Messiah and pay homage to Him. But this I know. Those who seek Him will do well to look among the poor and the lowly, the sorrowful and the oppressed."

So I saw the Other Wise Man again and again, traveling from place to place, and searching among the people of the dispersion, with whom the little family from Bethlehem might, perhaps, have found a refuge. He passed through countries where famine lay heavy upon the land and the poor were crying for bread. He made his dwelling in plague-stricken cities where the sick were languishing in the bitter companionship of helpless misery. He visited the oppressed and the afflicted in the gloom of subterranean prisons, and the crowded wretchedness of slave-markets, and the weary toil of galley-ships. In all this populous and intricate world of anguish, though he found none to worship, he found many to help. He fed the hungry, and clothed the naked, and healed the sick, and comforted the captive; and his years went by more swiftly than the weaver's shuttle that flashes back and forth through the loom while the web grows and the invisible pattern is completed.

It seemed almost as if he had forgotten his quest. But once I saw him for a moment as he stood alone at sunrise, waiting at the gate of a Roman prison. He had taken from a secret resting-place in his bosom the pearl, the last of his jewels. As he looked at it, a mellower lustre, a soft and iridescent light, full of shifting gleams of azure and rose, trembled upon its surface. It seemed to have absorbed some reflection of the colors of the lost sapphire and ruby. So the profound, secret purpose of a noble life draws into itself the memories of past joy and past sorrow. All that has helped it, all that has hindered it, is transfused by a subtle magic into its very essence. It becomes more luminous and precious the longer it is carried close to the warmth of the beating heart.

Then, at last, while I was thinking of this pearl, and of its meaning, I heard the end of the story of the Other Wise Man.

A PEARL OF GREAT PRICE

Three-and-thirty years of the life of Artaban had passed away, and he was still a pilgrim, and a seeker after light. His hair, once darker than the cliffs of Zagros, was now white as the wintry snow that covered them. His eyes, that once flashed like flames of fire, were dull as embers smouldering among the ashes.

Worn and weary and ready to die, but still looking for the King, he had come for the last time to Jerusalem. He had often visited the old city before, and had searched through all its lanes and crowded hovels and black prisons without finding any trace of the family of Nazarenes who had fled from Bethlehem long ago. But now it seemed as if he must make one more effort, and something whispered in this heart that at last, he might succeed.

It was the season of the Passover. The city was thronged with strangers. The children of Israel, scattered in far lands all over the world, had returned to the Temple for the great feast, and there had been a confusion of tongues in the narrow streets for many days.

But on this day there was a singular agitation visible in the multitude. The sky was veiled with a portentous gloom, and currents of excitement seemed to flash through a crowd like the thrill which shakes the forest on the eve of a storm. A secret tide was sweeping them all one way. The clutter of sandals, and the soft, thick sound of thousands of bare feet shuffling over the stones, flowed unceasingly along the street that leads to the Damascus gate.

Artaban joined company with a group of people from his own country, Parthian Jews who had come up to keep the Passover, and inquired of them the cause of the tumult, and where they were going.

"We are going," they answered, "to the place called Golgotha, outside the city walls, where there is to be an execution. Have you not heard what has happened? Two famous robbers are to be crucified, and with them another, called Jesus of Nazareth, a man who had done many wonderful works among the people, so that they love him greatly. But the priests and elders have said that he must die, because he gave himself out to be the Son of God. And Pilate has sent him to the cross because he said that he was the 'King of the Jews.'"

How strangely these familiar words fell upon the tired heart of Artaban! They had led him for a lifetime over land and sea. And now they came to him darkly and mysteriously like a message of despair. The King had arisen, but He had been denied and cast out. He was about to perish. Perhaps He was already dying. Could it be the same who had been born in Bethlehem thirty-three years ago, at whose birth the star had appeared in heaven, and of whose coming the prophets had spoken?

Artaban's heart beat unsteadily with that troubled, doubtful apprehension which is the excitement of old age. But he said within himself: "The ways of God are stranger than the thoughts of men, and it may be that I shall find the King, at last, in the hands of His enemies, and shall come in time to offer my pearl for his ransom before He dies."

So the old man followed the multitude with slow and painful steps toward the Damascus gate of the city. Just beyond the entrance of the guardhouse a troop of Macedonian soldiers came down the street, dragging a young girl with torn dress and dishevelled hair. As the Magian paused to look at her with compassion, she broke suddenly from the hands of her tormentors and threw herself at his feet, clasping him around the knees. She had seen his white cap and the winged circle on his breast.

"Have pity on me," she cried, "and save me, for the sake of the God of purity! I also am a daughter of the true religion which is taught by the Magi. My father was a merchant of Parthia, but he is dead, and I am seized for his debts to be sold as a slave. Save me from worse than death."

Artaban trembled.

It was the old conflict in his soul, which had come to him in the palm-grove of Babylon and in the cottage at Bethlehem—the conflict between the expectation of faith and the impulse of love. Twice the gift which he had consecrated to the worship of religion had been drawn from his hand to the service of humanity. This was the third trial, the ultimate probation, the final and irrevocable choice.

Was it his great opportunity or his last temptation? He could not tell. One thing only was clear in the darkness of his mind—it was inevitable. And does not the inevitable come from God?

One thing only was sure to his divided heart—to rescue this helpless girl would be a true deed of love. And is not love the light of the soul?

He took the pearl from his bosom. Never had it seemed so luminous, so radiant, so full of tender, living lustre. He laid it in the hand of the slave.

"This is thy ransom, daughter! It is the last of my treasure which I kept for the King."

While he spoke the darkness of the sky thickened, and shuddering tremors ran through the earth, heaving convulsively like the breast of one who struggles with mighty grief.

The walls of the houses rocked to and fro. Stones were loosened and crashed into the street. Dust clouds filled the air. The soldiers fled in terror, reeling like drunken men. But Artaban and the girl whom he had ransomed crouched helpless beneath the wall of the Praetorium.

What had he to fear? What had he to live for? He had given away the last remnant of his tribute for the King. He had parted with the last hope of finding Him. The quest was over, and it had failed. But even in that thought, accepted and embraced, there was peace. It was not resignation. It was not submission. It was something more profound and searching. He knew that all was well, because he had done the best that he could, from day to day. He had been true to the light that had been given to him. He had looked for more. And if he had not found it, if a failure was all that came out of his life, doubtless that was the best that was possible. He had not seen the revelation of "life everlasting, incorruptible and immortal." But he knew that even if he could live his earthly life over again, it could not be otherwise than it had been.

One more lingering pulsation of the earthquake quivered through the ground. A heavy tile, shaken from the roof, fell and struck the old man on the temple. He lay breathless and pale, with his gray head resting on the young girl's shoulder, and the blood trickling from the wound. As she bent over him, fearing that he was dead, there came a voice through the twilight, very small and still, like music sounding from a distance, in which the notes are clear but the words are lost. The girl turned to see if some one had spoken from the window above them, but she saw no one.

Then the old man's lips began to move, as if in answer, and she heard him say in the Parthian tongue:

"Not so, my Lord: For when saw I thee hungered and fed thee? Or thirsty, and gave thee drink? When saw I thee a stranger, and took thee in? Or naked, and clothed thee? When saw I thee sick or in prison, and came unto thee? Three-and-thirty years have I looked for thee; but I have never seen thy face, nor ministered to thee, my King."

He ceased, and the sweet voice came again. And again the maid heard it, very faintly and far away. But now it seemed as though she understood the words:

"Verily I say unto thee, Inasmuch as thou has done it unto one of the least of these my brethren, thou has done it unto me."

A calm radiance of wonder and joy lighted the pale face of Artaban like the first ray of dawn on a snowy mountain-peak. One long, last breath of relief exhaled gently from his lips.

His journey was ended. His treasures were accepted. The Other Wise Man had found the King.

Henry Van Dyke, 1896

The Gift of the Magi

One dollar and eighty-seven cents. That was all. And sixty cents of it was in pennies. Pennies saved one and two at a time by bulldozing the grocer and vegetable man and the butcher until one's cheeks burned with the silent imputation of parsimony that such close dealing implied. Three times Della counted it. One dollar and eighty-seven cents. And the next day would be Christmas.

There was clearly nothing to do but flop down on the shabby little couch and howl. So Della did it. Which instigates the moral reflection that life is made up of sobs, sniffles, and smiles, with sniffles predominating.

While the mistress of the home is gradually subsiding from the first stage to the second, take a look at the home. A furnished flat at $8 per week. It did not exactly beggar description, but it certainly had that word on the lookout for the mendicancy squad.

In the vestibule below was a letter-box into which no letter would go, and an electric button from which no mortal finger could coax a ring. Also appertaining thereunto was a card bearing the name "Mr. James Dillingham Young."

The "Dillingham" had been flung to the breeze during a former period of prosperity when its possessor was being paid $30 per week. Now, when the income was shrunk to $20, the letters of "Dillingham" looked blurred, as though they were thinking seriously of contracting to a modest and unassuming D. But whenever Mr. James Dillingham Young came home and reached his flat above he was called "Jim" and greatly hugged by Mrs. James Dillingham Young, already introduced to you as Della. Which is all very good.

Della finished her cry and attended to her cheeks with the powder rag. She stood by the window and looked out dully at the gray cat walking a gray fence in a gray backyard. Tomorrow would be Christmas Day, and she had only $1.87 with which to buy Jim a present. She had been saving every penny she could for months, with this result. Twenty dollars a week doesn't go far. Expenses had been greater than she had calculated. They always are. Only $1.87 to buy a present for Jim. Her Jim. Many a happy hour she had spent planning for something nice for him. Something fine and rare and sterling—something just a little bit near to being worthy of the honor of being owned by Jim.

There was a pier-glass between the windows of the room. Perhaps you have seen a pier-glass in an $8 flat. A very thin and very agile person may, by observing his reflection in a rapid sequence of longitudinal strips, obtain a fairly accurate conception of his looks. Della, being slender, had mastered the art.

Suddenly she whirled from the window and stood before the glass. Her eyes were shining brilliantly, but her face had lost its color within twenty seconds. Rapidly she pulled down her hair and let it fall to its full length.

Now, there were two possessions of the James Dillingham Youngs in which they both took a mighty pride. One was Jim's gold watch that had been his father's and his grandfather's. The other was Della's hair. Had the Queen of Sheba lived in the flat across the airshaft, Della would have let her hair hang out the window some day to dry just to depreciate Her Majesty's jewels and gifts. Had King Solomon been the janitor, with all his treasures piled up in the basement, Jim would have pulled out his watch every time he passed, just to see him pluck at his beard from envy.

So now Della's beautiful hair fell about her rippling and shining like a cascade of brown waters. It reached below her knee and made itself almost a garment for her. And then she did it up again nervously and quickly. Once she faltered for a minute and stood still while a tear or two splashed on the worn red carpet.

On went her old brown jacket; on went her old brown hat. With a whirl of skirts and with the brilliant sparkle still in her eyes, she fluttered out the door and down the stairs to the street.

Where she stopped the sign read: "Mme. Sofronie. Hair Goods of All Kinds." One flight up Della ran, and collected herself, panting. Madame, large, too white, chilly, hardly looked the "Sofronie."

"Will you buy my hair?" asked Della.

"I buy hair," said Madame. "Take ye hat off and let's have a sight at the looks of it."

Down rippled the brown cascade.

"Twenty dollars," said Madame, lifting the mass with a practiced hand.

"Give it to me quick," said Della.

Oh, and the next two hours tripped by on rosy wings. Forget the hashed metaphor. She was ransacking the stores for Jim's present.

She found it at last. It surely had been made for Jim and no one else. There was no other like it in any of the stores, and she had turned all of them inside out. It was a platinum fob chain simple and chaste in design, properly proclaiming its value by substance alone and not by meretricious ornamentation—as all good things should do. It was even worthy of The Watch. As soon as she saw it she knew that it must be Jim's. It was like him. Quietness and value—the description applied to both. Twenty-one dollars they took from her for it, and she hurried home with the 87 cents. With that chain on his watch Jim might be properly anxious about the time in any company. Grand as the watch was, he sometimes looked at it on the sly on account of the old leather strap that he used in place of a chain.

When Della reached home her intoxication gave way a little to prudence and reason. She got out her curling irons and lighted the gas and went to work repairing the ravages made by generosity added to love. Which is always a tremendous task, dear friends—a mammoth task.

Within forty minutes her head was covered with tiny, close-lying curls that made her look wonderfully like a truant schoolboy. She looked at her reflection in the mirror long, carefully, and critically.

"If Jim doesn't kill me," she said to herself, "before he takes a second look at me, he'll say I look like a Coney Island chorus girl. But what could I do—oh! what could I do with a dollar and eighty-seven cents?"

At 7 o'clock the coffee was made and the frying-pan was on the back of the stove hot and ready to cook the chops.

Jim was never late. Della doubled the fob chain in her hand and sat on the corner of the table near the door that he always entered. Then she heard his step on the stair away down on the first flight, and she turned white for just a moment. She had a habit of saying little silent prayers about the simplest everyday things, and now she whispered: "Please God, make him think I am still pretty."

The door opened and Jim stepped in and closed it. He looked thin and very serious. Poor fellow, he was only twenty-two—and to be burdened with a family! He needed a new overcoat and he was without gloves.

Jim stopped inside the door, as immovable as a setter at the scent of quail. His eyes were fixed upon Della, and there was an expression in them that she could not read, and it terrified her. It was not anger, nor surprise, nor disapproval, nor horror, nor any of the sentiments

271

that she had been prepared for. He simply stared at her fixedly with that peculiar expression on his face.

Della wriggled off the table and went for him.

"Jim, darling," she cried, "don't look at me that way. I had my hair cut off and sold it because I couldn't have lived through Christmas without giving you a present. It'll grow out again—you won't mind, will you? I just had to do it. My hair grows awfully fast. Say 'Merry Christmas!' Jim, and let's be happy. You don't know what a nice—what a beautiful, nice gift I've got for you."

"You've cut off your hair?" asked Jim, laboriously, as if he had not arrived at that patent fact yet even after the hardest mental labor.

"Cut it off and sold it," said Della. "Don't you like me just as well, anyhow? I'm me without my hair, ain't I?"

Jim looked about the room curiously.

"You say your hair is gone?" he said, with an air almost of idiocy.

"You needn't look for it," said Della. "It's sold, I tell you—sold and gone, too. It's Christmas Eve, boy. Be good to me, for it went for you. Maybe the hairs of my head were numbered," she went on with a sudden serious sweetness, "but nobody could ever count my love for you. Shall I put the chops on, Jim?"

Out of his trance Jim seemed quickly to wake. He enfolded his Della. For ten seconds let us regard with discreet scrutiny some inconsequential object in the other direction. Eight dollars a week or a million a year—what is the difference? A mathematician or a wit would give you the wrong answer. The magi brought valuable gifts, but that was not among them. This dark assertion will be illuminated later on.

Jim drew a package from his overcoat pocket and threw it upon the table.

"Don't make any mistake, Dell," he said, "about me. I don't think there's anything in the way of a haircut or a shave or a shampoo that could make me like my girl any less. But if you'll unwrap that package you may see why you had me going a while at first."

White fingers and nimble tore at the string and paper. And then an ecstatic scream of joy; and then, alas! a quick feminine change to hysterical tears and wails, necessitating the immediate employment of all the comforting powers of the lord of the flat.

For there lay The Combs—the set of combs, side and back, that Della had worshipped for long in a Broadway window. Beautiful combs, pure tortoise shell, with jewelled rims—just the shade to wear in the beautiful vanished hair. They were expensive combs, she knew, and her heart had simply craved and yearned over them without the least hope of possession. And now, they were hers, but the tresses that should have adorned the coveted adornments were gone.

But she hugged them to her bosom, and at length she was able to look up with dim eyes and a smile and say: "My hair grows so fast, Jim!"

And then Della leaped up like a little singed cat and cried, "Oh, oh!"

Jim had not yet seen his beautiful present. She held it out to him eagerly upon her open palm. The dull precious metal seemed to flash with a reflection of her bright and ardent spirit.

"Isn't it a dandy, Jim? I hunted all over town to find it. You'll have to look at the time a hundred times a day now. Give me your watch. I want to see how it looks on it."

Instead of obeying, Jim tumbled down on the couch and put his hands under the back of his head and smiled.

"Dell," said he, "let's put our Christmas presents away and keep 'em a while. They're too nice to use just at present. I sold the watch to get the money to buy your combs. And now suppose you put the chops on."

The magi, as you know, were wise men—wonderfully wise men—who brought gifts to the Babe in the manger. They invented the art of giving Christmas presents. Being wise, their gifts were no doubt wise ones, possibly bearing the privilege of exchange in case of duplication. And here I have lamely related to you the uneventful chronicle of two foolish children in a flat who most unwisely sacrificed for each other the greatest treasures of their house. But in a last word to the wise of these days let it be said that of all who give gifts these two were the wisest. Of all who give and receive gifts, such as they are wisest. Everywhere they are wisest. They are the magi.

O. Henry (William Sydney Porter), 1908

Incident on Fourth Street

One Christmas Eve, when I was a small boy, I was out with my father doing some last-minute errands on Fourth Street in Cincinnati. The packages I was carrying grew heavier with every step, and I could hardly wait to get home so that Christmas could begin.

For this was the night when we three boys trimmed the tree and hung our stockings in front of the fireplace; then the neighbors gathered around our piano for carols so lovely they made a lump in my throat.

It was while I was thinking these things that a hand touched mine. Beside me on the sidewalk stood a bleary-eyed, unshaven, dirty old man, his other hand clutching a ragged cap in which lay a few pennies.

I recoiled from the grimy fingers, turned my shoulder to him, and the old man crept away.

My father had seen. "You shouldn't treat a man that way, Norman," he said.

"Aw, Dad, he's nothing but a bum."

"A bum?" my father said. "There is no such thing as a bum. He is a child of God. Maybe he hasn't made the most of himself, but he is God's beloved child just the same. Now I want you to go and give him this."

My father pulled out his pocketbook and handed me a dollar. This was a large sum for our family; most of our gifts to each other hadn't cost that much. "Now do exactly as I tell you. Go up to him, hand him this dollar, speak to him respectfully, and tell him you are giving him this dollar in the name of Christ."

"Oh, Dad!" I objected, "I couldn't say that!"

My father insisted, "Go and do as I tell you."

Reluctantly, I ran after the old man, caught up with him and said, "Excuse me, Sir, I give you this dollar in the name of Christ."

The old man looked at me in absolute surprise. Then a curious change came over his whole bearing, a new dignity into his manner. Graciously, with a sort of joy, he said, "And I thank you, young Sir, in the name of Christ."

Suddenly the packages in my arms were lighter, the air was warmer, the very sidewalk was beautiful. No Christmas tree stood there, no carols filled the air, but all at once, on Fourth Street, Christmas had begun.

Norman Vincent Peale, 1965

An American, Bill Lederer, wrote the following story/letter, which reflects the power of Christmas. It was published in the Saturday Evening Post *and later in a* Guideposts *magazine Christmas card. Sal Lazzaroti, for many years art director of* Guideposts, *sent the story to me one Christmas.*

A Sailor's Christmas Gift

Chief of Naval Operations
Washington, D.C.

Dear Admiral:
Last year at Christmas time my wife, our three boys and I were in France, on our way from Paris to Nice in a rented car. For five wretched

days everything had gone wrong. On Christmas Eve, when we checked into our hotel in Nice, there was no Christmas spirit in our hearts.

It was raining and cold when we went out to eat. We found a drab little restaurant shoddily decorated for the holiday. Only five tables were occupied. There were two German couples, two French families, and an American sailor. While eating, he was writing a letter.

My wife ordered our meal in French. The waiter brought us the wrong thing. I scolded my wife for being stupid.

Then, at the table with the French family on our left, the father slapped one of his children for some minor infraction, and the boy began to cry.

On our right, the German wife began berating her husband.

All of us were interrupted by an unpleasant blast of cold air. Through the front door came an old flower woman. She wore a dripping, tattered overcoat, and shuffled in on wet, rundown shoes. She went from one table to the other.

"Flowers, *Monsieur?* Only one *franc.*" No one bought any.

Wearily she sat down at a table between the sailor and us. To the waiter she said, "A bowl of soup. I haven't sold a flower all afternoon." To the piano player she said hoarsely, "Can you imagine, Joseph, soup on Christmas Eve?"

He pointed to his empty "tipping plate."

278

The young sailor finished his meal and got up. Putting on his coat, he walked over to the flower woman's table.

"Happy Christmas," he said, smiling and picking out two corsages. "How much are they?"

"Two *francs, Monsieur.*"

Pressing one of the small corsages flat, he put it into the letter he had written, then handed the woman a 20-*franc* note.

"I don't have change, *Monsieur,*" she said. "I'll get some from the waiter."

"No, Ma'am," said the sailor, leaning over and kissing the ancient cheek. "This is my Christmas present to you."

Then he came to our table, holding the other corsage in front of him. "Sir," he said to me, "may I have permission to present these flowers to your beautiful daughter?"

In one quick motion he gave my wife the corsage, wished us a Merry Christmas and departed. Everyone had stopped eating. Everyone had been watching the sailor.

A few seconds later Christmas exploded throughout the restaurant like a bomb.

The old flower woman jumped up, waving the 20-*franc* note, shouted to the piano player, "Joseph, my Christmas present! And you shall have half so you can have a feast too."

The piano player began to belt out *Good King Wenceslaus*.

My wife waved her corsage in time to the music. She appeared 20 years younger. She began to sing, and our three sons joined her, bellowing with enthusiasm.

"Gut! Gut!" shouted the Germans. They began singing in German.

The waiter embraced the flower woman. Waving their arms, they sang in French.

The Frenchman who had slapped the boy beat rhythm with his fork against a glass. The lad, now on his lap, sang in a youthful soprano.

A few hours earlier 18 persons had been spending a miserable evening. It ended up being the happiest, the very best Christmas Eve they ever had experienced.

This, Admiral, is what I am writing you about. As the top man in the Navy, you should know about the very special gift that the U.S. Navy gave to my family, to me and to the other people in that French restaurant. Because your young sailor had Christmas spirit in his soul, he released the love and joy that had been smothered within us by anger and disappointment. He gave us Christmas.

Thank you, Sir, and Merry Christmas!

Bill Lederer, 1963

One Christmas was so meaningful for me that I take the liberty of including its story here. I like to call it "Faraway Christmas."

Faraway Christmas

Golden stars and angels. Festive lights and carols. Shoppers with gaily wrapped packages. Windows glowing with Yuletide pageantry. "Oh," a friend said to me, "aren't they wonderful, all these warm, familiar symbols? Christmas wouldn't be Christmas without them!"

I had to smile a little. Let me tell you why.

Not too long ago, my wife Ruth and the other members of our family—our three children and their spouses and assorted grandchildren—persuaded me that it would be a great adventure to spend Christmas in a completely different setting, one with a totally new atmosphere. "What if we went to Africa," they said with great excitement, "and lived in tents in one of those game parks surrounded by all those wonderful animals? Wouldn't a faraway Christmas be exciting? Wouldn't it be terrific? Wouldn't family ties be strengthened by such a unique experience?"

I protested feebly that perhaps someone who had passed his eighty-seventh birthday, as I had, might find living in a tent surrounded by wild animals a bit strenuous. But no one seemed to be listening. "You'll love every minute of it," Ruth assured me. And so, on this high note of excitement and enthusiasm, we made our preparations to go to East Africa.

The Samburu Game Park in Kenya was indeed far away. And indeed it was different. Ruth and I shared a tent pitched near a fast-flowing brown river. In tents on either side were our children and grandchildren. There was heat and dust and burning sun. At night the forest resounded with barks, screeches, splashes, and once, just behind our tents, a grunting sound that they told me next day had probably been made by a leopard.

So I did not sleep very well, but these unfamiliar things were not what troubled me. What troubled me was that nothing seemed like Christmas. I tried to shrug off the feeling, but it persisted, a kind of emptiness, a sadness almost, a small voice that whispered, "Christmas means coming home, doesn't it? Why have all of you chosen to turn your backs on home like this?"

I did my best to conceal such thoughts from the others, but I couldn't conceal them from myself. And they kept coming back, often at unexpected moments.

On the afternoon of Christmas Eve, for example, we had come back from a splendid day of viewing the animals. We had seen a beautiful herd of zebras, seventy-six elephants, a cheetah chasing an impala, and a nursing lioness, all magnificent in their natural surroundings. Then it was time for a shower before dinner, which was a bit of an adventure, too. The camp helpers heated water, put it in a bucket, then hoisted the bucket to the top of a pole behind the tent. From there the water ran down a pipe into the rear of the tent where, standing on slats, the bather could soap and rinse himself, after a fashion.

I was drying myself off when suddenly—I don't know what triggered it—I found myself remembering long-ago Christmases spent in Cincinnati during my impressionable boyhood years. The city was full of people of German descent, and the Germans are very sentimental about Christmas. I found myself recalling Fountain Square as it looked on Christmas Eve; I thought it the biggest, brightest, most beautiful place I had ever seen. The Christmas tree was enormous, and the streets were alive with carols, many sung in German: *"Stille Nacht"* and *"O Tannenbaum."* I could see myself walking with my father, my small hand in his big one, the snow crunching under our feet. Up on East Liberty Street, where we lived, my mother always had a tree with real candles on it. The smell of those tallow candles mingled with the scent of fir, an aroma unlike any other. Now, standing in our little tent with the vastness of Africa all around me, I remembered that wonderful smell, and I missed it terribly.

We had been told that there would be a special dinner for us that evening. Even this did not cheer me; I thought it might be an artificial occasion with everyone trying too hard to be merry. When I came out near dinnertime, I saw that, in the eating tent, a straggly brown bush had been set up, decorated with small colored lights and some tinsel and red ribbon. I thought of the great tree in Fountain Square and the even greater one in Rockefeller Center in New York City and the magnificent one on the great lawn of the White House in Washington.

We were called to the edge of the river, where chairs had been set up for all of us so that we could see, on the other side, two herders guarding their cattle, their spear tips gleaming like points of light in the gathering dusk. And at the peaceful, almost timeless sight, I felt something stir within me, for I knew that these herders and their charges had not changed in thousands of years. They belonged to their landscape just as the shepherds on the hills outside Bethlehem belonged to theirs. And, at that moment, one of the grandchildren began to sing, hesitantly, tentatively, "O Little Town of Bethlehem." Gradually others joined in with "Hark! the Herald Angels Sing" and then "Joy to the World." Soon we were all singing and, as we sang, everything seemed to change; the sense of strangeness was gone. I looked around the group—our children, their children, singing songs, sharing feelings that in a very real way went back almost 2,000 years to that simple manger in a simple town, with the herders standing by in a parched and primitive land.

Then someone began to read the immortal story from Luke: "And there were in the same country shepherds abiding in the field, keeping watch over their flock by night. . . ." As the story went on, I thought, *How wonderful and simple it is—so wonderful and simple that only God could have thought of it.*

I found myself remembering a radio talk given many years ago by Sam Shoemaker, a much-loved pastor and a good friend of mine. In it, Sam was speculating on what God the Father might have said to Jesus his Son on the night before Jesus left him to go down to earth. He imagined Father and Son conversing much as a human boy and his father might do before the son leaves home to go out into the world. Only Sam, with his great simplicity, could picture it this way. According to this conception, God might have said, "Son, I hate to see you go. I sure am going to miss you. I love you with all my heart. But I do want you to go down to earth and tell those poor souls down there how to live and point them to the way that will lead them back home."

Sam said he thought the last thing God said to Jesus was, "Give them all my love." Now that's simple—but it's human and it's divine.

So when the carols and the Bible reading ended and we walked back to the eating tent for our dinner, I knew with a complete sense of peace that where Christmas is concerned, surroundings do not matter, because the spirit of Jesus is everywhere, knocking on the door of our hearts, asking to be taken in.

The festive lights and the gifts and the ornaments are fine, but they are only a setting for the real jewel: the birth of a Baby that marked the descent of God himself to mankind. That's where the true meaning of Christmas lies. And it can be found in that simple sentence: "Give them all my love."

Norman Vincent Peale, 1990

V.
Christmas Thoughts

*I*N THE PRECEDING pages, we have read the words of Christmas from the Bible, in hymns and carols, in songs and poems, and in stories. But they are also expressed in words we remember from editorials, sermons, letters, plays, and short quotations. And now, to bring this collection of my own favorite words about Christmas to a close, here are some of these other words to bring you joy at Christmas.

Frank Church, editor of the New York Sun, *in 1897 wrote one of the most enduring editorials to appear in an American newspaper. It was captioned*

Is There a Santa Claus?

September 21, 1897

We take pleasure in answering at once and thus prominently the communication below, expressing at the same time our great gratification that its faithful author is numbered among the friends of The Sun:

Dear Editor:

I am 8 years old. Some of my little friends say there is no Santa Claus. Papa says 'If you see it in The Sun it's so.' Please tell me the truth, is there a Santa Claus?

Virginia O'Hanlon
115 West 95th Street

Virginia, your little friends are wrong. They have been affected by the skepticism of a skeptical age. They do not believe except they see. They think that nothing can be which is not comprehensible by their little minds. All minds, Virginia, whether they be men's or children's, are little. In this great universe of ours man is a mere insect, an ant, in his intellect, as compared with the boundless world about him, as measured by the intelligence capable of grasping the whole of truth and knowledge.

Yes, Virginia, there is a Santa Claus. He exists as certainly as love and generosity and devotion exist, and you know that they abound and give to your life its highest beauty and joy. Alas! how dreary would be the world if there were no Santa Claus! It would be as dreary as if there were no Virginias. There would be no childlike faith then, no poetry, no romance to make tolerable this existence. We should have no enjoyment, except in sense and sight. The eternal light with which childhood fills the world would be extinguished.

Not believe in Santa Claus! You might as well not believe in fairies! You might get your papa to hire men to watch in all the chimneys on Christmas Eve to catch Santa Claus; but even if they did not see Santa Claus coming down, what would that prove? Nobody sees Santa Claus, but that is no sign that there is no Santa Claus. The most real things in the world are those that neither children nor men can see. Did you ever see fairies dancing on the lawn? Of course not, but that's no proof that they are not there. Nobody can conceive or imagine all the wonders there are unseen and unseeable in the world.

You tear apart the baby's rattle and see what makes the noise inside, but there is a veil covering the unseen world which not the strongest men that ever lived could tear apart. Only faith, fancy, poetry, love, romance, can push aside that curtain and view and picture the supernal beauty and glory beyond. Is it all real? Ah, Virginia, in all this world there is nothing else real and abiding.

No Santa Claus! Thank God he lives, and he lives forever. A thousand years from now, Virginia, nay, ten times ten thousand years from now, he will continue to make glad the heart of childhood.

Francis Pharcellus Church, 1897

From "A Christmas Sermon"

To be honest, to be kind—to earn a little and to spend a little less, to make upon the whole a family happier for his presence, to renounce when that shall be necessary and not be embittered, to keep a few friends but these without capitulation—above all, on the same grim condition, to keep friends with himself—here is a task for all that a man has of fortitude and delicacy. He has an ambitious soul who would ask more: he has a hopeful spirit who should look in such an enterprise to be successful.

Robert Louis Stevenson, 1888

Cradle Hymn

Away in a manger, no crib for a bed,
The little Lord Jesus laid down His sweet head.
The stars in the bright sky looked down where He lay—
The little Lord Jesus, asleep on the hay.

Martin Luther, 1535

From Hamlet

Some say that ever 'gainst that season comes
Wherein our Saviour's birth is celebrated,
The bird of dawning singeth all night long:
And then, they say, no spirit can walk abroad;
The nights are wholesome; then no plants strike,
No fairy takes, nor witch hath power to charm,
So hallow'd and so gracious is the time.

William Shakespeare, 1602

From "A Christmas Tree"

And I *do* come home at Christmas. We all do, or we all should. We all come home, or ought to come home, for a short holiday—the longer, the better—from the great boardingschool, where we are forever working at our arithmetical slates, to take, and give a rest.

Charles Dickens, 1846

From "Vagabond"

Forget, forgive, for who may say that Christmas day may ever come to host or guest again.

William H. H. Murray, 1872

From "A Thought"

I love the Christmas-tide, and yet,
    I notice this each year I live;
I always like the gifts I get,
    But how I love the gifts I give!

Booth Tarkington, 1921

Long Walk

One of my favorite stories is about a missionary teaching in Africa. Before Christmas, he had been telling his native students how

Christians, as an expression of their joy, gave one another presents on Christ's birthday.

On Christmas morning, one of the natives brought the missionary a seashell of lustrous beauty. When asked where he had discovered such an extraordinary shell, the native said he had walked many miles to a certain bay, the only spot where such shells could be found.

"I think it was wonderful of you to travel so far to get this lovely gift for me," the teacher exclaimed.

His eyes brightening, the native answered, "Long walk, part of gift."

Gerald Horton Bath, 1960

Preface for Christmas Day

Because thou didst give Jesus Christ, thine only Son, to be born at this time for us; who, by the operation of the Holy Ghost, was made very man, of the substance of the Virgin Mary his mother; and that without spot of sin, to make us clean from all sin. Therefore with Angels and Archangels, and with all the company of heaven, we laud and glorify thy glorious Name; evermore praising thee, and saying, Holy,

holy, holy, Lord God of hosts, Heaven and earth are full of thy glory;
Glory be to thee, O Lord Most High. Amen.

Book of Common Prayer, 1549

*One of the most beloved Roman Catholic popes of our time was Pope
John XXIII (1958–63). It is said that when he was elected pope he went
back to see his family in the small village where he was born. The people
were speechless when they saw him. However, in his kind way, he said,
"Don't be afraid. It's only me." In the book* Prayers and Devotions
from Pope John XXIII, *he wrote about Christmas:*

Christmas Is for the Whole World

How eagerly and lovingly we read the pages of the Sacred Book
which describe the birth of Jesus!

A stable, out in the open country, in the darkness of night. Perhaps
the gleam of a small lantern. Here is St. Joseph, the just man, chosen by
God, here is the Mother of the new-born child, radiant with joy at this
surpassing miracle, and here is the divine Babe in the arms of the purest
of creatures. He has been so long awaited, through untold ages. But he

has come in the hour appointed by God himself. He is tiny, and already subject to the harshest privations, and to suffering: but he is the Word of the Father, the Saviour of the World. The greater the poverty and simplicity, the greater the fascination and appeal of this Child.

Around him the world is stirring: the just have become aware that the great promise is about to be fulfilled. So the day of our redemption dawns, the day of reparation for what is past, of happiness for the eternal future. . . .

The shepherds draw near: they see and feel that peace, joy and love flow out from that tiny Child. The history of twenty centuries begins in this stable, for the Child is in very truth the source of all things. Through him, in fact, everything is renewed, death is overcome, sin is forgiven and Paradise restored.

We feel new fervour of love when we pause in prayer before the Crib.

Mankind also is a great, an immense family. . . . This is proved by what we feel in our hearts at Christmas. The divine Child smiles at everyone; his beloved eyes shine in grace and splendour. Hard hearts are softened, anxieties soothed, suffering relieved.

Calm follows the storm, and sadness ends in joy.

Pope John XXIII, 1966

Book III

My Inspirational Favorites

Acknowledgments

THE EDITOR AND PUBLISHERS gratefully acknowledge permission to use copyrighted material in this volume. While every effort has been made to secure permissions, if we have failed to acknowledge copyrighted material, we apologize and will make suitable acknowledgment in any future edition.

American Youth Foundation and Ralston-Purina Company for "You Can Be Bigger Than You Are" from *I Dare You*, by William H. Danforth.

McGraw-Hill, Inc., for "Lee and Grant at Appomattox" from *A Dual Biography: Lee and Grant*, by Gene Smith, copyright 1984.

The Helen Steiner Rice Foundation for "Look on the Sunny Side," by Helen Steiner Rice, used with permission of the Helen Steiner Rice Foundation, Cincinnati, Ohio.

Contents

CONTENTS

A Word to the Reader

IN THIS BOOK, I am privileged to share some of the essays, poems, stories, and portions of books that have been inspirations to me in my lifetime of reading.

I have made my selections not as a literary critic but because I like them. They have inspired and helped me, and I hope they do the same for you. Many people have told me that these particular pieces have appealed to them also.

If I had collected all my favorites from my reading over the years, they would make up an enormous volume. Instead, I have chosen to assemble a little book that can be easily carried or read in bed. I have tried sincerely to make it a book that will be a joy to have in a personal library. May you find it a rewarding and pleasant companion for many a happy hour.

Norman Vincent Peale

NOT MANY PEOPLE TODAY have heard of Henry Drummond, but toward the end of the last century he was widely known throughout Great Britain and the United States. A Scottish geologist who taught natural science and later theology in a Glasgow college, Drummond had a burning passion to speak and write profound truths about Christianity in simple terms that could be easily understood.

In 1883 he wrote "The Greatest Thing in the World," a speech he gave in Africa and, in 1887, all over the United States. Reports on this speech attested to the thrill audiences felt when they heard Drummond talk about "the supreme good," Love. And when his speech was printed into a little book, it sold more than 350,000 copies—an astounding number for the day.

His passionate belief made him one of the most popular figures of his time. I hope you will enjoy and profit from reading this great scientific thinker of the preceding century.

It was Henry Drummond's custom, at the beginning of each lecture, to read from the Bible, I Corinthians, chapter 13, which follows:

THOUGH I SPEAK with the tongues of men and of angels, and have not Love, I am become as sounding brass, or a tinkling cymbal. And though I have the gift of prophecy, and understand all mysteries, and all knowledge; and though I have all faith, so that I could remove mountains, and have not Love, I am nothing. And though I bestow all my goods to feed the poor, and though I give my body to be burned, and have not Love, it profiteth me nothing.

Love suffereth long, and is kind;
Love envieth not;
Love vaunteth not itself, is not puffed up,
Doth not behave itself unseemly,
Seeketh not her own,
Is not easily provoked,
Thinketh no evil;
Rejoiceth not in iniquity, but rejoiceth in the truth;
Beareth all things, believeth all things, hopeth all
things, endureth all things.

Love never faileth: but whether there be prophecies, they shall fail;
whether there be tongues, they shall cease; whether there be knowledge,
it shall vanish away. For we know in part, and we prophesy in part. But
when that which is perfect is come, then that which is in part shall be
done away. When I was a child, I spake as a child, I understood as a
child, I thought as a child: but when I became a man, I put away childish
things. For now we see through a glass, darkly; but then face to face: now
I know in part; but then shall I know even as also I am known. And now
abideth faith, hope, Love, these three; but the greatest of these is Love.

The Greatest Thing in the World

Henry Drummond (1851–1897)

EVERY ONE has asked himself the great question of antiquity as of the modern world: What is the *summum bonum*—the supreme good? You have life before you. Once only you can live it. What is the noblest object of desire, the supreme gift to covet?

We have been accustomed to be told that the greatest thing in the religious world is Faith. That great word has been the keynote for centuries of the popular religion; and we have easily learned to look upon it as the greatest thing in the world. Well, we are wrong. If we have been told that, we may miss the mark. I have taken you in the chapter which I have just read, to Christianity at its source; and there we have seen, "The greatest of these is love." It is not an oversight. Paul was speaking of faith just a moment before. He says, "If I have all faith, so that I can remove mountains, and have not love; I am nothing." So far from forgetting he deliberately contrasts them, "Now abideth Faith, Hope, Love," and without a moment's hesitation the decision falls, "The greatest of these is Love."

And it is not prejudice. A man is apt to recommend to others his own strong point.

Love was not Paul's strong point. The observing student can detect a beautiful tenderness growing and ripening all through his character as Paul gets old; but the hand that wrote "The greatest of these is love," when we meet it first, is stained with blood.

Nor is this letter to the Corinthians peculiar in singling out love as the than *summum bonum*. The masterpieces of Christianity are agreed about it. Peter says, "Above all things have fervent love among yourselves." *Above all things.* And John goes farther, "God is love." And you remember the profound remark which Paul makes elsewhere, "Love is the fulfilling of the law." Did you ever think what he meant by that? In those days men were working their passage to Heaven by keeping the Ten Commandments, and the hundred and ten other commandments which they had manufactured out of them. Christ said, I will show you a more simple way. If you do one thing, you will do these hundred and ten things, without ever thinking about them. If you love, you will unconsciously fulfil the whole law. And you can readily see for yourselves how that must be so. Take any of the commandments. "Thou shalt have no other gods before Me." If a man love God, you will not require to tell him that. Love is the fulfilling of that law. "Take not His name in vain." Would he ever dream of taking His name in vain if he loved Him? "Remember the Sabbath day to keep it holy." Would he not be too glad to have one day in seven to dedicate more exclusively to the object of his affection? Love would fulfil all these laws regarding God. And so, if he loved Man you would never think of telling him to honor his father and mother. He could not do anything else. It would be preposterous to tell him not to kill. You could only insult him if you suggested that he should not steal—how could he steal from those he loved. It would be superfluous to beg him not to bear false witness against his neighbor. If he loved him it would be the last thing he would do.

And you would never dream of urging him not to covet what his neighbors had. He would rather they possessed it than himself. In this way "Love is the fulfilling of the law." It is the rule for fulfilling all rules, the new commandment for keeping all the old commandments, Christ's one secret of the Christian life.

Now Paul had learned that; and in this noble eulogy he has given us the most wonderful and original account extant of the *summum bonum*. We may divide it into three parts. In the beginning of the short chapter, we have Love *contrasted;* in the heart of it, we have Love *analyzed;* toward the end, we have Love *defended* as the supreme gift.

THE CONTRAST

Paul begins by contrasting Love with other things that men in those days thought much of. I shall not attempt to go over those things in detail. Their inferiority is already obvious.

He contrasts it with eloquence. And what a noble gift it is, the power of playing upon the souls and wills of men, and rousing them to lofty purposes and holy deeds. Paul says, "If I speak with the tongues of men and of angels, and have not love, I am become as sounding brass, or a tinkling cymbal." And we all know why. We have all felt the brazenness of words without emotion, the hollowness, the unaccountable unpersuasiveness, of eloquence behind which lies no Love.

He contrasts it with prophecy. He contrasts it with mysteries. He contrasts it with faith. He contrasts it with charity. Why is Love greater than faith? Because the end is greater than the means. And why is it greater than charity? Because the whole is greater than the part. Love is greater faith, because the end is greater than the means. What is the use of having faith? It is to connect the soul with God. And what is the object of connecting man with God? That he may become like God. But God is Love. Hence Faith, the means, is in order to Love, the end. Love, therefore, obviously is greater than faith. It is greater than charity, again, because the whole is greater than a part. Charity is only a little bit of Love, one of the innumerable avenues of Love, and there may even be, and there is, a great deal of charity without Love. It is a very easy thing to toss a copper to a beggar on the street; it is generally an easier thing than not to do it. Yet Love is just as often in the withholding. We purchase relief from the sympathetic feelings roused by the spectacle of misery, at the copper's cost. It is too cheap—too cheap for us, and often too dear for the beggar. If we really loved him we would either do more for him, or less.

Then Paul contrasts it with sacrifice and martyrdom. And I beg the little band of would-be missionaries—and I have the honor to call some of you by this name for the first time—to remember that though you give your bodies to be burned, and have not Love, it profits nothing—nothing! You can take nothing greater to the heathen world than the impress and the reflection of the Love of God upon your own character. That is the universal language. It will take you years to speak in Chinese, or in the dialects of India. From the day you land, that language of Love, understood by all, will be pouring forth its unconscious eloquence. It is the man who is the missionary, it is not his words. His character is his message. In the heart of Africa, among the great Lakes, I have come across black men and women who remembered the only white man they ever saw before—David Livingstone; and as you cross his footsteps in that dark continent, men's faces light up as they speak of the kind Doctor who passed there years ago. They could not understand him; but they felt the Love that beat in his heart. Take into your new sphere of labor, where you also mean to lay down your life, that simple charm, and your lifework must succeed. You can take nothing greater, you need take nothing less. It is not worth while going if you take anything less. You may take every accomplishment; you may be braced for every sacrifice; but if you give your body to be burned, and have not Love, it will profit you and the cause of Christ *nothing*.

THE ANALYSIS

After contrasting Love with these things, Paul, in three verses, very short, gives us an amazing analysis of what this supreme thing is. I ask you to look at it. It is a compound thing, he tells us. It is like light. As you have seen a man of science take a beam of light and pass it through a crystal prism, as you have seen it come out on the other side of the prism broken up into its component colors—red, and blue, and yellow, and violet, and orange, and all the colors of the rainbow—so Paul passes this thing, Love, through the magnificent prism of his inspired intellect, and it comes out on the other side broken up into its elements. And in these few words we have what one might call the Spectrum of Love, the analysis of Love. Will you observe what its elements are? Will you notice that they have common names; that they are virtues which we hear about every day; that they are things which can be practiced by every man in every place in life; and how, by a multitude of small things and ordinary virtues, the supreme thing, the *summum bonum,* is made up.

The Spectrum of Love has nine ingredients:

Patience—"Love suffereth long."
Kindness—"And is kind."
Generosity—"Love envieth not."
Humility—"Love vaunteth not itself, is not puffed up."
Courtesy—"Doth not behave itself unseemly."
Unselfishness—"Seeketh not her own."
Good Temper—"Is not easily provoked."
Guilelessness—"Thinketh no evil."
Sincerity—"Rejoiceth not in iniquity, but rejoiceth in the truth."

Patience; kindness; generosity; humility; courtesy; unselfishness; good temper; guilelessness; sincerity—these make up the supreme gift, the stature of the perfect man. You will observe that all are in relation to men, in relation to life, in relation to the known to-day and the near to-morrow, and not to the unknown eternity. We hear much of love to God; Christ spoke much of love to man. We make a great deal of peace with heaven; Christ made much of peace on earth. Religion is not a strange or added thing, but the inspiration of the secular life, the breathing of an eternal spirit through this temporal world. The supreme thing, in short, is not a thing at all, but the giving of a further finish to the multitudinous words and acts which make up the sum of every common day.

314

There is no time to do more than make a passing note upon each of these ingredients. Love is *Patience*. This is the normal attitude of Love; Love passive, Love waiting to begin; not in a hurry; calm; ready to do its work when the summons comes, but meantime wearing the ornament of a meek and quiet spirit. Love suffers long; beareth all things; believeth all things; hopeth all things. For love understands, and therefore waits.

Kindness. Love active. Have you ever noticed how much of Christ's life was spent in doing kind things—in *merely* doing kind things? Run over it with that in view, and you will find that He spent a great proportion of His time simply in making people happy, in doing good turns to people. There is only one thing greater than happiness in the world, and that is holiness; and it is not in our keeping; but what God *has* put in our power is the happiness of those about us, and that is largely to be secured by our being kind to them.

"The greatest thing," says some one, "a man can do for his Heavenly Father is to be kind to some of His other children." I wonder why it is that we are not all kinder than we are? How much the world needs it. How easily it is done. How instantaneously it acts. How infallibly it is remembered. How superabundantly it pays itself back—for there is no debtor in the world so honorable, so superbly honorable, as Love. "Love never faileth." Love is success, Love is happiness, Love is life. "Love I say," with Browning, "is energy of Life."

For life, with all it yields of joy or woe
And hope and fear,

Is just our chance o' the prize of learning love,—
How love might be, hath been indeed, and is.

Where Love is, God is. He that dwelleth in Love dwelleth in God.
God is Love. Therefore *love*. Without distinction, without calculation,
without procrastination, love. Lavish it upon the poor, where it is very easy;
especially upon the rich, who often need it most; most of all upon our
equals, where it is very difficult, and for whom perhaps we each do least of
all. There is a difference between *trying to please* and *giving pleasure*. Give
pleasure. Lose no chance of giving pleasure. For that is the ceaseless and
anonymous triumph of a truly loving spirit. "I shall pass through this world
but once. Any good thing therefore that I can do, or any kindness that I can
show to any human being, let me do it now. Let me not defer it or neglect
it, for I shall not pass this way again."

Generosity. "Love envieth not." This is love in competition with others. Whenever you attempt a good work you will find other men doing the
same kind of work, and probably doing it better. Envy them not. Envy is a
feeling of ill-will to those who are in the same line as ourselves, a spirit of
covetousness and detraction. How little Christian work even is a protection
against un-Christian feeling. That most despicable of all the unworthy
moods which cloud a Christian's soul assuredly waits for us on the threshold
of every work, unless we are fortified with this grace of magnanimity. Only
one thing truly need the Christian envy, the large, rich, generous soul
which "envieth not."

And then, after having learned all that, you have to learn this further thing, *Humility*—to put a seal upon your lips and forget what you have done. After you have been kind, after Love has stolen forth into the world and done its beautiful work, go back into the shade again and say nothing about it. Love hides even from itself. Love waives even self-satisfaction. "Love vaunteth not itself, is not puffed up."

The fifth ingredient is a somewhat strange one to find in this *summum bonum: Courtesy*. This is Love in society, Love in relation to etiquette. "Love doth not behave itself unseemly." Politeness has been defined as love in trifles. Courtesy is said to be love in little things. And the one secret of politeness is to love. Love *cannot* behave itself unseemly. You can put the most untutored persons into the highest society, and if they have a reservoir of Love in their heart, they will not behave themselves unseemly. They simply cannot do it. Carlyle said of Robert Burns that there was no truer gentleman in Europe than the ploughman-poet. It was because he loved everything—the mouse, and the daisy, and all the things, great and small, that God had made. So with this simple passport he could mingle with any society, and enter courts and palaces from his little cottage on the banks of the Ayr. You know the meaning of the word "gentleman." It means a gentle man—a man who does things gently with love. And that is the whole art and mystery of it. The gentleman cannot in the nature of things do an ungentle, and ungentlemanly thing. The ungentle soul, the inconsiderate, unsympathetic nature cannot do anything else. "Love doth not behave itself unseemly."

Unselfishness. "Love seeketh not her own." Observe: Seeketh not even that which is her own. In Britain the Englishman is devoted, and rightly, to his rights. But there come times when a man may exercise even the higher right of giving up his rights. Yet Paul does not summon us to give up our rights. Love strikes much deeper. It would have us not seek them at all, ignore them, eliminate the personal element altogether from our calculations. It is not hard to give up our rights. They are often external. The difficult thing is to give up ourselves. The more difficult thing still is not to seek things for ourselves at all. After we have sought them, bought them, won them, deserved them, we have taken the cream off them for ourselves already. Little cross then to give them up. But not to seek them, to look every man not on his own things, but on the things of others—*id opus est.* "Seekest thou great things for thyself?" said the prophet; "*seek them not.*" Why? Because there is no greatness in *things.* Things cannot be great. The only greatness is unselfish love. Even self-denial in itself is nothing, is almost a mistake. Only a great purpose or a mightier love can justify the waste. It is more difficult, I have said, not to seek our own at all, than, having sought it, to give it up. I must take that back. It is only true of a partly selfish heart. Nothing is a hardship to Love, and nothing is hard. I believe that Christ's "yoke" is easy. Christ's "yoke" is just His way of taking life. And I believe it is an easier way than any other. I believe it is a happier way than any other. The most obvious lesson in Christ's teaching is that there is no happiness in having and getting anything, but only in giving. I repeat, *there is no happiness in having or in getting, but only in giving.* And half the world is on the wrong scent in pursuit of happiness. They think it consists in having and getting, and in being served by others. It consists in giving, and in serving others. He that would be great among you, said Christ, let him serve.

He that would be happy, let him remember that there is but one way—it is more blessed, it is more happy, to give than to receive.

The next ingredient is a very remarkable one: *Good Temper*. "Love is not easily provoked." Nothing could be more striking than to find this here. We are inclined to look upon bad temper as a very harmless weakness. We speak of it as a mere infirmity of nature, a family failing, a matter of temperament, not a thing to take into very serious account in estimating a man's character. And yet here, right in the heart of this analysis of love, it finds a place; and the Bible again and again returns to condemn it as one of the most destructive elements in human nature.

The peculiarity of ill temper is that it is the vice of the virtuous. It is often the one blot on an otherwise noble character. You know men who are all but perfect, and women who would be entirely perfect, but for an easily ruffled, quick-tempered, or "touchy" disposition. This compatibility of ill temper with high moral character is one of the strangest and saddest problems of ethics. The truth is there are two great classes of sins—sins of the *Body,* and sins of the *Disposition*. The Prodigal Son may be taken as a type of the first, the Elder Brother of the second. Now, society has no doubt whatever as to which of these is the worse. Its brand falls, without a challenge, upon the Prodigal. But are we right? We have no balance to weigh one another's sins, and coarser and finer are but human words; but faults in the higher nature may be less venial than those in the lower, and to the eye of Him who is Love, a sin against Love may seem a hundred times more base. No form of vice, not worldliness, not greed of gold, not drunkenness itself, does more to un-Christianize society than evil temper. For embittering life, for breaking up communities, for destroying the most sacred relationships, for devastating homes, for withering up men and women, for taking the bloom of childhood, in short, for sheer gratuitous misery-producing power, this influence stands alone. Look at the Elder Brother, moral, hard-working, patient, dutiful—let him get all credit for his virtues—look at this man, this baby, sulking outside his own father's door. "He was angry," we read, "and would not go in." Look at the effect upon the father, upon the servants, upon the happiness of the guests. Judge of the effect upon the Prodigal—and how many prodigals are kept out of the Kingdom of God by the unlovely character of those who profess to be inside? Analyze, as a study in Temper, the thunder-cloud as it gathers upon the Elder-Brother's brow. What is it made of? Jealousy, anger, pride, un-charity, cruelty, self-righteousness, touchiness, doggedness, sullenness,— these are the ingredients of this dark and loveless soul. In varying proportions, also, these are the ingredients of all ill temper. Judge if such sins of the disposition are not worse to live in, and for others to live with, than sins of the body. Did Christ indeed not answer the question Himself when He said, "I say unto you, that the publicans and the harlots go into the Kingdom of Heaven before you"? There is really no place in Heaven for a disposition like this. A man with such a mood could only make Heaven miserable for all the people in it. Except, therefore, such a man be born again, he cannot, he simply *cannot,* enter the Kingdom of Heaven. For it is perfectly certain—and you will not misunderstand me—that to enter Heaven a man must take it with him.

You will see then why Temper is significant. It is not in what it is alone, but in what it reveals. This is why I take the liberty now of speaking of it with such unusual plainness. It is a test for love, a symptom, a revelation of an unloving nature at bottom. It is the intermittent fever which bespeaks unintermittent disease within; the occasional bubble escaping to the surface which betrays some rottenness underneath; a sample of the most hidden products of the soul dropped involuntarily when off one's guard; in a word, the lightning form of a hundred hideous and un-Christian sins. For a want of patience, a want of kindness, a want of generosity, a want of courtesy, a want of unselfishness, all are instantaneously symbolized in one flash of Temper.

Hence it is not enough to deal with the Temper. We must go to the source, and change the inmost nature, and the angry humors will die away of themselves. Souls are made sweet not by taking the acid fluids out, but by putting something in—a great Love, a new Spirit, the Spirit of Christ. Christ, the Spirit of Christ, interpenetrating ours, sweetens, purifies, transforms all. This only can eradicate what is wrong, work a chemical change, renovate and regenerate, and rehabilitate the inner man. Will-power does not change men. Time does not change men. Christ does. Therefore "Let that mind be in you which was also in Christ Jesus." Some of us have not much time to lose. Remember, once more, that this is a matter of life or death. I cannot help speaking urgently, for myself, for yourselves. "Whoso shall offend one of these little ones, which believe in me, it were better for him that a millstone were hanged about his neck, and that he were drowned in the depth of the sea." That is to say, it is the deliberate verdict of the Lord Jesus that it is better not to live than not to love. *It is better not to live than not to love.*

Guilelessness and *Sincerity* may be dismissed almost with a word. Guilelessness is the grace for suspicious people. And the possession of it is the great secret of personal influence. You will find, if you think for a moment, that the people who influence you are people who believe in you. In an atmosphere of suspicion men shrivel up; but in that atmosphere they expand, and find encouragement and educative fellowship. It is a wonderful thing that here and there in this hard, uncharitable world there should still be left a few rare souls who think no evil. This is the great unworldliness. Love "Thinketh no evil," imputes no motive, sees the bright side, puts the best construction on every action. What a delightful state of mind to live in! What a stimulus and benediction even to meet with it for a day! To be trusted is to be saved. And if we try to influence or elevate others, we shall soon see that success is in proportion to their belief of our belief in them. For the respect of another is the first restoration of the self-respect a man has lost; our ideal of what he is becomes to him the hope and pattern of what he may become.

"Love rejoiceth not in iniquity, but rejoiceth in the truth." I have called this *Sincerity* from the words rendered in the Authorized Version by "rejoiceth in the truth." And certainly, were this the real translation, nothing could be more just. For he who loves will love Truth not less than men. He will rejoice in the Truth—rejoice not in what he has been taught to believe; not in this Church's doctrine or in that; not in this ism or in that ism; but "in *the Truth.*" He will accept only what is real; he will strive to get at facts; he will search for *Truth* with a humble and unbiassed mind, and cherish whatever he finds at any sacrifice. But the more literal translation of the Revised Version calls for just such a sacrifice for truth's sake here. For what Paul really meant is, as we there read, "Rejoiceth not in unrighteousness, but rejoiceth with the truth," a quality which probably no one English word—and certainly not *Sincerity*—adequately defines. It includes, perhaps more strictly, the self-restraint which refuses to make capital out of others' faults; the charity which delights not in exposing the weakness of others, but "covereth all things"; the sincerity of purpose which endeavors to see things as they are, and rejoices to find them better than suspicion feared or calumny denounced.

So much for the analysis of Love. Now the business of our lives is to have these things fitted into our characters. That is the supreme work to which we need to address ourselves in this world, to learn Love. Is life not full of opportunities for learning Love? Every man and woman every day has a thousand of them. The world is not a playground; it is a schoolroom. Life is not a holiday, but an education. And the one eternal lesson for us all is *how better we can love*. What makes a man a good cricketer? Practice. What makes a man a good artist, a good sculptor, a good musician? Practice. What makes a man a good linguist, a good stenographer? Practice. What makes a man a good man? Practice. Nothing else. There is nothing capricious about religion. We do not get the soul in different ways, under different laws, from those in which we get the body and the mind. If a man does not exercise his arm he develops no biceps muscle; and if a man does not exercise his soul, he acquires no muscle in his soul, no strength of character, no vigor of moral fibre, nor beauty of spiritual growth. Love is not a thing of enthusiastic emotion. It is a rich, strong, manly, vigorous expression of the whole round Christian character—the Christlike nature in its fullest development. And the constituents of this great character are only to be built up by ceaseless practice.

What was Christ doing in the carpenter's shop? Practicing. Though perfect, we read that He *learned* obedience, and grew in wisdom and in favor with God. Do not quarrel therefore with your lot in life. Do not complain of its never ceasing cares, its petty environment, the vexations you have to stand, the small and sordid souls you have to live and work with. Above all, do not resent temptation; do not be perplexed because it seems to thicken round you more and more, and ceases neither for effort nor for agony nor prayer. That is your practice. That is the practice which God appoints you; and it is having its work in making you patient, and humble, and generous, and unselfish, and kind, and courteous. Do not grudge the hand that is moulding the still too shapeless image within you. It is growing more beautiful, though you see it not, and every touch of temptation may add to its perfection. Therefore keep in the midst of life. Do not isolate yourself. Be among men, and among things, and among troubles, and difficulties, and obstacles. You remember Goethe's words: *Es bildet ein Talent sich in der Stille, Doch ein Charakter in dem Strom der Welt.* "Talent develops itself in solitude; character in the stream of life." Talent develops itself in solitude—the talent of prayer, of faith, of meditation, of seeing the unseen; Character grows in the stream of the world's life. That chiefly is where men are to learn love.

How? Now, how? To make it easier, I have named a few of the elements of love. But these are only elements. Love itself can never be defined. Light is a something more than the sum of its ingredients—a glowing, dazzling, tremulous ether. And love is something more than all its elements—a palpitating, quivering, sensitive, living thing. By synthesis of all the colors, men can make whiteness, they cannot make light. By synthesis of all the virtues, men can make virtue, they cannot make love. How then are we to have this transcendent living whole conveyed into our souls? We brace our wills to secure it. We try to copy those who have it. We lay down rules about it. We watch. We pray. But these things alone will not bring Love into our nature. Love is an *effect*. And only as we fulfil the right condition can we have the effect produced. Shall I tell you what the *cause* is?

If you turn to the Revised Version of the First Epistle of John you will find these words: "We love because He first loved us." "We love," not "We love *Him*." That is the way the old version has it, and it is quite wrong. "*We love*—because He first loved us." Look at that word "because." It is the *cause* of which I have spoken. "*Because* He first loved us," the effect follows that we love, we love Him, we love all men. We cannot help it. Because He loved us, we love, we love everybody. Our heart is slowly changed. Contemplate the love of Christ, and you will love. Stand before that mirror, reflect Christ's character and you will be changed into the same image from tenderness to tenderness. There is no other way. You cannot love to order. You can only look at the lovely object, and fall in love with it, and grow into likeness to it. And so look at this Perfect Character, this Perfect Life. Look at the great Sacrifice as He laid down Himself, all through life, and upon the Cross of Calvary, and you must love Him. And loving Him, you must become like Him. Love begets love. It is a process of induction. Put a piece of iron in the presence of an electrified body, and that piece of iron for a time becomes electrified. It is changed into a temporary magnet in the mere presence of a permanent magnet, and as long as you leave the two side by side, they are both magnets alike. Remain side by side with Him who loved us, and gave Himself for us, and you too will become a permanent magnet, a permanently attractive force; and like Him you will draw all men unto you, like Him you will be drawn unto all men. That is the inevitable effect of Love. Any man who fulfils that cause must have that effect produced in him. Try to give up the idea that religion comes to us by chance, or by mystery, or by caprice. It comes to us by natural law, or by supernatural law, for all law is Divine. Edward Irving went to see a dying boy once, and when he entered the room he just put his hand on the sufferer's head, and said, "My boy, God loves you," and went away. And the boy started from his bed, and called out to the people in the house, "God loves me! God loves me!" It changed that boy. The sense that God loved him overpowered him, melted him down, and began the creating of a new heart in him. And that is how the love of God melts down the unlovely heart in man, and begets in him the new creature, who is patient and humble and gentle and unselfish. And there is no other way to get it. There is no mystery about it. We love others, we love everybody, we love our enemies, because He first loved us.

THE DEFENCE

Now I have a closing sentence or two to add about Paul's reason for singling out love as the supreme possession. It is a very remarkable reason. In a single word it is this: *it lasts*. "Love," urges Paul, "never faileth." Then he begins again one of his marvellous lists of the great things of the day, and exposes them one by one. He runs over the things that men thought were going to last, and shows that they are all fleeting, temporary, passing away.

"Whether there be prophecies, they shall fail." It was the mother's ambition for her boy in those days that he should become a prophet. For hundreds of years God had never spoken by means of any prophet, and at that time the prophet was greater than the King. Men waited wistfully for another messenger to come and hung upon his lips when he appeared as upon the very voice of God. Paul says, "Whether there be prophecies, they shall fail." This book is full of prophecies. One by one they have "failed"; that is, having been fulfilled, their work is finished; they have nothing more to do now in the world except to feed a devout man's faith.

Then Paul talks about tongues. That was another thing that was greatly coveted. "Whether there be tongues, they shall cease." As we all know, many, many centuries have passed since tongues have been known in this world. They have ceased. Take it in any sense you like. Take it, for illustration merely, as languages in general—a sense which was not in Paul's mind at all, and which though it cannot give us the specific lesson will point the general truth. Consider the words in which these chapters were written—Greek. It has gone. Take the Latin—the other great tongue of those days. It ceased long ago. Look at the Indian language. It is ceasing. The language of Wales, of Ireland, of the Scottish Highlands, is dying before our eyes. The most popular book in the English tongue at the present time, except the Bible, is one of Dickens's works, his *Pickwick Papers*. It is largely written in the language of London street-life; and experts assure us that in fifty years it will be unintelligible to the average English reader.

Then Paul goes farther, and with even greater boldness adds, "Whether there be knowledge, it shall vanish away." The wisdom of the ancients, where is it? It is wholly gone. A schoolboy to-day knows more than Sir Isaac Newton knew. His knowledge has vanished away. You put yesterday's newspaper in the fire. Its knowledge has vanished away. You buy the old editions of the great encyclopaedias for a few pence. Their knowledge has vanished away. Look how the coach has been superseded by the use of steam. Look how electricity has superseded that, and swept a hundred almost new inventions into oblivion. One of the greatest living authorities, Sir William Thomson, said the other day, "The steam-engine is passing away." "Whether there be knowledge, it shall vanish away." At every workshop you will see, in a back yard, a heap of old iron, a few wheels, a few levers, a few cranks, broken and eaten with rust. Twenty years ago that was the pride of the city. Men flocked in from the country to see the great invention; now it is superseded, its day is done. And all the boasted science and philosophy of this day will soon be old. But yesterday, in the University of Edinburgh, the greatest figure in the faculty was Sir James Simpson, the discoverer of chloroform. The other day his successor and nephew, Professor Simpson, was asked by the librarian of the University to go to the library and pick out the books on his subject that were no longer needed. And his reply to the librarian was this: "Take every text-book that is more than ten years old, and put it down in the cellar." Sir James Simpson was a great authority only a few years ago: men came from all parts of the earth to consult him; and almost the whole teaching of that time is consigned by the science of to-day to oblivion. And in every branch of science it is the same. "Now we know in part. We see through a glass darkly."

Can you tell me anything that is going to last? Many things Paul did not condescend to name. He did not mention money, fortune, fame; but he picked out the great things of his time, the things the best men thought had something in them, and brushed them peremptorily aside. Paul had no charge against these things in themselves. All he said about them was that they would not last. They were great things, but not supreme things. There were things beyond them. What we are stretches past what we do, beyond what we possess. Many things that men denounce as sins are not sins; but they are temporary. And that is a favorite argument of the New Testament. John says of the world, not that it is wrong, but simply that it "passeth away." There is a great deal in the world that is delightful and beautiful; there is a great deal in it that is great and engrossing; but it will not last. All that is in the world, the lust of the eye, the lust of the flesh, and the pride of life, are but for a little while. Love not the world therefore. Nothing that it contains is worth the life and consecration of an immortal soul. The immortal soul must give itself to something that is immortal. And the only immortal things are these: "Now abideth faith, hope, love, but the greatest of these is love."

329

Some think the time may come when two of these three things will also pass away—faith into sight, hope into fruition. Paul does not say so. We know but little now about the conditions of the life that is to come. But what is certain is that Love must last. God, the Eternal God, is Love. Covet therefore that everlasting gift, that one thing which it is certain is going to stand, that one coinage which will be current in the Universe when all the other coinages of all the nations of the world shall be useless and un-honored. You will give yourselves to many things, give yourself first to Love. Hold things in their proportion. *Hold things in their proportion.* Let at least the first great object of our lives be to achieve the character defended in these words, the character—and it is the character of Christ—which is built round Love.

I have said this thing is eternal. Did you ever notice how continually John associates love and faith with eternal life? I was not told when I was a boy that "God so loved the world that He gave His only-begotten Son, that whosoever believeth in Him should have everlasting life." What I was told, I remember, was, that God so loved the world that, if I trusted in Him, I was to have a thing called peace, or I was to have rest, or I was to have joy, or I was to have safety. But I had to find out for myself that whosoever trusteth in Him—that is, whosoever loveth Him, for trust is only the avenue to Love—hath everlasting *life*. The Gospel offers a man life. Never offer men a thimbleful of Gospel. Do not offer them merely joy, or merely peace, or merely rest, or merely safety; tell them how Christ came to give men a more abundant life than they have, a life abundant in love, and therefore abun-dant in salvation for themselves, and large in enterprise for the alleviation and redemption of the world. Then only can the Gospel take hold of the whole of a man, body, soul, and spirit, and give to each part of his nature its exercise and reward. Many of the current Gospels are addressed only to a part of man's nature. They offer peace, not life; faith, not Love; justification, not regeneration. And men slip back again from such religion because it has never really held them. Their nature was not all in it. It offered no deeper and gladder life-current than the life that was lived before. Surely it stands to reason that only a fuller love can compete with the love of the world.

To love abundantly is to live abundantly, and to love forever is to live forever. Hence, eternal life is inextricably bound up with love. We want to live forever for the same reason that we want to live to-morrow. Why do you want to live to-morrow? It is because there is some one who loves you, and whom you want to see to-morrow, and be with, and love back. There is no other reason why we should live on than that we love and are beloved. It is when a man has no one to love him that he commits suicide. So long as he has friends, those who love him and whom he loves, he will live, because to live is to love. Be it but the love of a dog, it will keep him in life; but let that go and he has no contact with life, no reason to live. He dies by his own hand. Eternal life also is to know God, and God is love. This is Christ's own definition. Ponder it. "This is life eternal, that they might know Thee the only true God, and Jesus Christ whom Thou hast sent." Love must be eternal. It is what God is. On the last analysis, then, love is life. Love never faileth, and life never faileth, so long as there is love. That is the philosophy of what Paul is showing us; the reason why in the nature of things Love should be the supreme thing—because it is going to last;

331

because in the nature of things it is an Eternal Life. It is a thing that we are living now, not that we get when we die; that we shall have a poor chance of getting when we die unless we are living now. No worse fate can befall a man in this world than to live and grow old alone, unloving and unloved. To be lost is to live in an unregenerate condition, loveless and unloved; and to be saved is to love; and he that dwelleth in love dwelleth already in God. For God is Love.

Now I have all but finished. How many of you will join me in reading this chapter once a week for the next three months? A man did that once and it changed his whole life. Will you do it? It is for the greatest thing in the world. You might begin by reading it every day, especially the verses which describe the perfect character. "Love suffereth long, and is kind; love envieth not; love vaunteth not itself." Get these ingredients into your life. Then everything that you do is eternal. It is worth doing. It is worth giving time to. No man can become a saint in his sleep; and to fulfil the condition required demands a certain amount of prayer and meditation and time, just as improvement in any direction, bodily or mental, requires preparation and care. Address yourselves to that one thing; at any cost have this transcendent character exchanged for yours. You will find as you look back upon your life that the moments that stand out, the moments when you have really lived, are the moments when you have done things in a spirit of love. As memory scans the past, above and beyond all the transitory pleasures of life, there leap forward those supreme hours when you have been enabled to do unnoticed kindnesses to those round about you, things too trifling to speak about, but which you feel have entered into your eternal life. I have seen almost all the beautiful things God has made; I have enjoyed almost every pleasure that He has planned for man; and yet as I look back I see standing out above all the life that has gone four or five short experiences when the love of God reflected itself in some poor imitation, some small act of love of mine, and these seem to be the things which alone of all one's life abide. Everything else in all our lives is transitory. Every other good is visionary. But the acts of love which no man knows about, or can ever know about—they never fail.

In the book of Matthew, where the Judgment Day is depicted for us in the imagery of One seated upon a throne and dividing the sheep from the goats, the test of a man then is not, "How have I believed?" but "How have I loved?" The test of religion, the final test of religion, is not religiousness but Love. I say the final test of religion at that great Day is not religiousness, but Love; not what I have done, not what I have believed, not what I have achieved, but how I have discharged the common charities of life. Sins of commission in that awful indictment are not even referred to. By what we have not done, *by sins of omission*, we are judged. It could not be otherwise. For the withholding of love is the negation of the spirit of Christ, the proof that we never knew Him, that for us He lived in vain. It means that He suggested nothing in all our thoughts, that He inspired nothing in all our lives, that we were not once near enough to Him to be seized with the spell of His compassion for the world. It means that—

333

I lived for myself, I thought for myself,
For myself, and none beside—
Just as if Jesus had never lived,
As if He had never died.

It is the Son of *Man* before whom the nations of the world shall be gathered. It is in the presence of *Humanity* that we shall be charged. And the spectacle itself, the mere sight of it, will silently judge each one. Those will be there whom we have met and helped; or there, the unpitied multitude whom we neglected or despised. No other Witness need be summoned. No other charge than lovelessness shall be preferred. Be not deceived. The words which all of us shall one Day hear sound not of theology but of life, not of churches and saints but of the hungry and the poor, not of creeds and doctrines but of shelter and clothing, not of Bibles and prayer-books but of cups of cold water in the name of Christ. Thank God the Christianity of to-day is coming nearer the world's need. Live to help that on. Thank God men know better, by a hair's-breadth, what religion is, what God is, who Christ is, where Christ is. Who is Christ? He who fed the hungry, clothed the naked, visited the sick. And where is Christ? Where?— whoso shall receive a little child in My name receiveth Me. And who are Christ's? Every one that loveth is born of God.

The Autobiography of Benjamin Franklin is one of my favorite books. My mother recommended it to me when I was young. And I have reread it regularly ever since.

In its sixth chapter Franklin undertakes to improve his character and rid himself of his faults. He goes about doing so with a scientific method that could be a model for anyone.

I have tried it myself and it works. Of course, I have not attained perfect results, but I assure you it is worth diligent persistence. In reading this chapter of Franklin's life story, we get a clue to his success and enduring wisdom. It provides an insight into the mind of one of our greatest Americans. I have condensed the chapter, but Franklin's method of self-improvement is there, and trying it will enhance your life.

From "The Autobiography of Benjamin Franklin"

(1706–1790)

AT THE TIME I established myself in Pennsylvania, there was not a good bookseller's shop in any of the colonies to the southward of Boston. In New York and Philadelphia the printers were indeed stationers, but they sold only paper, almanacs, ballads, and a few common school-books. Those who loved reading were obliged to send for their books from England. Some did this and a club was formed, a room hired where we could all bring our books, be ready to consult in our conferences, but of a more common benefit, each of us were at liberty to borrow any book he wished to read at home. This was accordingly done, and for some time contented us.

335

Finding the advantage of this little collection, I proposed to render the benefit from the books more common, by commencing a public subscription library. I drew a sketch of the plan and rules that would be necessary, and got a skillful conveyancer, Mr. Charles Brockden, to put the whole in form of articles of agreement to be subscribed, by which each subscriber engaged to pay a certain sum down for the first purchase of the books, and an annual contribution for increasing them.

So few were the readers at that time in Philadelphia, and the majority of us so poor, that I was not able, with great industry, to find more than fifty persons, mostly young tradesmen, willing to pay down for this purpose forty shillings each, and ten shillings per annum. With this little fund we began.

The books were imported; the library was opened one day in the week for lending them to the subscribers, on their promissory notes to pay double the value, if not duly returned. The institution soon manifested its utility, was imitated by other towns, and in other provinces. The libraries were augmented by donations; reading became fashionable; and our people, having no public amusements to divert their attention from study, became better acquainted with books, and in a few years were observed by strangers to be better instructed and more intelligent than people of the same rank generally are in other countries.

When we were about to sign the above-mentioned articles, which were to be binding on us, our heirs, &c., for fifty years, Mr. Brockden, the scrivener, said to us, "You are young men, but it is scarcely probable that any of you will live to see the expiration of the term fixed in the instrument." A number of us, however, are yet living; but the instrument was after a few years rendered null by a charter that incorporated and gave perpetuity to the company.

The objections and reluctances I met with in soliciting the subscriptions, made me soon feel the impropriety of presenting one's self as the proposer of any useful project, that might be supposed to raise one's reputation in the smallest degree above that of one's neighbors, when one has need of their assistance to accomplish that project. I therefore put myself as much as I could out of sight, and stated it as a scheme of a *number of friends*, who had requested me to go about and propose it to such as they thought lovers of reading. In this way my affair went on more smoothly, and I ever after practiced it on such occasions; and, from my frequent successes, can heartily recommend it. The present little sacrifice of your vanity will afterward be amply repaid. If it remains a while uncertain to whom the merit belongs, some one more vain than yourself may be encouraged to claim it.

This library afforded me the means of improvement by constant study, for which I set apart an hour or two each day, and thus repaired in some degree the loss of the learned education my father once intended for me. Reading was the only amusement I allowed myself. I spent no time in taverns, games, or frolics of any kind; and my industry in my business continued as indefatigable as it was necessary. I was indebted for my printing-house; I had a young family coming on to be educated, and I had two competitors to contend with for business, who were established in the place before me.

My circumstances, however, grew daily easier. My original habits of frugality continuing, and my father having, among his instructions to me when a boy, frequently repeated a proverb of Solomon, "*Seest thou a man diligent in his calling, he shall stand before kings, he shall not stand before mean men,*" I thence considered industry as a means of obtaining wealth and distinction, which encouraged me, though I did not think that I should ever literally *stand before kings*, which, however, has since happened; for I have stood before *five*, and even had the honor of sitting down with one, the King of Denmark, to dinner.

We have an English proverb that says, "*He that would thrive, must ask his wife.*" It was lucky for me that I had one as much disposed to industry and frugality as myself. She assisted me cheerfully in my business, folding and stitching pamphlets, tending shop, purchasing old linen rags for the paper makers, &c. We kept no idle servants, our table was plain and simple, our furniture of the cheapest. For instance, my breakfast was for a long time bread and milk (no tea), and I ate it out of a two penny earthen porringer, with a pewter spoon.

But mark how luxury will enter families, and make a progress, in spite of principle: being called one morning to breakfast, I found it in a China bowl, with a spoon of silver! They had been bought for me without my knowledge by my wife, and had cost her the enormous sum of three-and-twenty shillings, for which she had no other excuse or apology to make, but that she thought *her* husband deserved a silver spoon and China bowl as well as any of his neighbors. This was the first appearance of plate and China in our house, which afterward, in a course of years, as our wealth increased, augmented gradually to several hundred pounds in value.

I had been religiously educated as a Presbyterian; but, though some of the dogmas of that persuasion, such as *the eternal decrees of God, election, reprobation, &c.*, appearing to me unintelligible, others doubtful, and I early absented myself from the public assemblies of the sect, Sunday being my studying day, I never was without some religious principles. I never doubted, for instance, the existence of a Deity; that he made the world, and governed it by his providence; that the most acceptable service of God was the doing good to man; that our souls are immortal; and that all crimes will be punished, and virtue rewarded, either here or hereafter.

Though I seldom attended any public worship, I had still an opinion of its propriety, and of its utility when rightly conducted, and I regularly paid my annual subscription for the support of the only Presbyterian minister or meeting we had in Philadelphia. He used to visit me sometimes as a friend, and admonish me to attend his administrations, and I was now and then prevailed on to do so, once for five Sundays successively.

Had he been in my opinion a good preacher, perhaps I might have continued, notwithstanding the occasion I had for the Sunday's leisure in my course of study; but his discourses were chiefly either polemic arguments, or explications of the peculiar doctrines of our sect, and were all to me very dry, uninteresting, and unedifying, since not a single moral principle was inculcated or enforced, their aim seeming to be rather to make *us Presbyterians* than *good citizens*.

At length he took for his text that verse of the fourth chapter to the Philippians, "*Finally, brethren, whatsoever things are true, honest, just, pure, lovely, or of good report, if there be any virtue, or any praise, think on these things.*" And I imagined, in a sermon on such a text, we could not miss of having some morality. But he confined himself to five points only, as meant by the apostle: 1. Keeping holy the Sabbath day. 2. Being diligent in reading the holy Scriptures. 3. Attending duly the public worship. 4. Partaking of the Sacrament. 5. Paying a due respect to God's ministers. These might be all good things; but, as they were not the kind of good things that I expected from the text, I despaired of ever meeting with them from any other, was disgusted, and attended his preaching no more. I had some years before composed a little Liturgy, or form of prayer, for my own private use (in 1728), entitled, *Articles of Belief and Acts of Religion*. I returned to the use of this, and went no more to the public assemblies. My conduct might be blamable, but I leave it, without attempting further to excuse it; my present purpose being to relate facts, and not to make apologies for them.

It was about this time I conceived the bold and arduous project of arriving at *moral perfection*. I wished to live without committing any fault at any time, and to conquer all that either natural inclination, custom, or company might lead me into. As I knew, or thought I knew, what was right and wrong, I did not see why I might not *always* do the one and avoid the other. But I soon found I had undertaken a task of more difficulty than I had imagined. While my attention was taken up, and employed in guarding against one fault, I was often surprised by another; habit took the advantage of inattention; inclination was sometimes too strong for reason. I concluded, at length, that the mere speculative conviction that it was our interest to be completely virtuous, was not sufficient to prevent our slipping; and that the contrary habits must be broken, and good ones acquired and established, before we can have any dependence on a steady, uniform rectitude of conduct. For this purpose I therefore tried the following method.

In the various enumerations of the *moral virtues* I had met with in my reading, I found the catalogue more or less numerous, as different writers included more or fewer ideas under the same name. *Temperance*, for example, was by some confined to eating and drinking, while by others it was extended to mean the moderating every other pleasure, appetite, inclination, or passion, bodily or mental, even to our avarice and ambition. I proposed to myself, for the sake of clearness, to use rather more names, with fewer ideas annexed to each, than a few names with more ideas; and I included under thirteen names of virtues all that at that time occurred to me as necessary or desirable, and annexed to each a short precept, which fully expressed the extent I gave to its meaning.

These names of *virtues*, with their precepts, were,

1. *Temperance*. Eat not to dullness; drink not to elevation.
2. *Silence*. Speak not but what may benefit others or yourself; avoid trifling conversation.
3. *Order*. Let all your things have their places; let each part of your business have its time.
4. *Resolution*. Resolve to perform what you ought; perform without fail what you resolve.
5. *Frugality*. Make no expense but to do good to others or yourself; that is, waste nothing.

6. *Industry*. Lose no time; be always employed in something useful; cut off all unnecessary actions.
7. *Sincerity*. Use no hurtful deceit; think innocently and justly; and, if you speak, speak accordingly.
8. *Justice*. Wrong none by doing injuries, or omitting the benefits that are your duty.
9. *Moderation*. Avoid extremes; forbear resenting injuries so much as you think they deserve.
10. *Cleanliness*. Tolerate no uncleanliness in body, clothes, or habitation.
11. *Tranquility*. Be not disturbed at trifles, or at accidents common or unavoidable.
12. *Chastity*. . . .
13. *Humility*. Imitate Jesus and Socrates.

My intention being to acquire and *habitude* of all these virtues, I judged it would be well not to distract my attention by attempting the whole at once, but to fit it on *one* of them at a time; and, when I should be master of that, then to proceed to another, and so on, till I should have gone through the thirteen; and, as the previous acquisition of some might facilitate the acquisition of certain others, I arranged them with that view, as they stand above. *Temperance* first, as it tends to procure that coolness and clearness of head, which is so necessary where constant vigilance was to be kept up, and a guard maintained against the unremitting attraction of ancient habits, and the force of perpetual temptations.

This being acquired and established, *Silence* would be more easy; and my desire being to gain knowledge at the same time that I improved in virtue, and considering that in conversation it was obtained rather by the use of the ear than of the tongue, and therefore wishing to break a habit I was getting into of prattling, punning, and jesting, which only made me acceptable to trifling company, I gave *Silence* the second place.

This and the next, *Order*, I expected would allow me more time for attending to my project and my studies. *Resolution*, once become habitual, would keep me firm in my endeavors to obtain all the subsequent virtues; *Frugality* and *Industry* relieving me from my remaining debt, and producing affluence and independence, would make more easy the practice of *Sincerity* and *Justice*, &c., &c. Conceiving then, that, agreeably to the advice of Pythagoras in his *Golden Verses,* daily examination would be necessary, I contrived the following method for conducting that examination.

I made a little book, in which I allotted a page for each of the virtues. I ruled each page with red ink, so as to have seven columns, one for each day of the week, marking each column with a letter for the day. I crossed these columns with thirteen red lines, marking the beginning of each line with the first letter of one of the virtues, on which line, and in its proper column, I might mark, by a little black spot, every fault I found upon examination to have been committed respecting that virtue upon that day.[1]

I determined to give a week's strict attention to each of the virtues successively. Thus, in the first week, my great guard was to avoid every least of-

---

1. This "title book" is dated 1st July, 1733.

Form of the pages.

TEMPERANCE

Eat not to dullness; drink not to elevation.

	Sun.	M.	T.	W.	Th.	F.	S.
Tem.							
Sil.	*	*		*		*	
Ord.	*	*			*	*	*
Res.		*				*	
Fru.		*				*	
Ind.			*				
Sinc.							
Jus.							
Mod.							
Clea.							
Tran.							
Chas.							
Hum.							

fense against *Temperance,* leaving the other virtues to their ordinary chance, only marking every evening the faults of the day. Thus, if in the first week I could keep my first line, marked T, clear of spots, I supposed the habit of that virtue so much strengthened, and its opposite weakened, that I might venture extending my attention to include the next, and for the following week keep both lines clear of spots.

Proceeding thus to the last, I could get through a course complete in thirteen weeks, and four courses in a year. And like him who, having a gar-

344

den to weed, does not attempt to eradicate all the bad herbs at once, which would exceed his reach and his strength, but works on one of the beds at a time, and, having accomplished the first, proceeds to a second, so I should have, I hoped, the encouraging pleasure of seeing on my pages the progress made in virtue, by clearing successively my lines of their spots, till in the end, by a number of courses, I should be happy in viewing a clean look, after a thirteen weeks' daily examination.

And conceiving God to be the fountain of wisdom, I thought it right and necessary to solicit his assistance for obtaining it; to this end I formed the following little prayer, which was prefixed to my tables of examination, for daily use.

> O powerful Goodness! bountiful Father! merciful Guide! Increase in me
> that wisdom which discovers my truest interest. Strengthen my resolution
> to perform what that wisdom dictates. Accept my kind offices to thy other
> children as the only return in my power for thy continual favors to me.

I used also sometimes a little prayer which I took from Thomson's *Poems*, viz.:

> Father of light and life, thou Good Supreme!
> O teach me what is good; teach me Thyself!
> Save me from folly, vanity, and vice,
> From every low pursuit; and feed my soul
> With knowledge, conscious peace, and virtue pure;
> Sacred, substantial, never-fading bliss!

345

The precept of *Order* requiring that *every part of my business should have its allotted time*, one page in my little book contained a scheme of employment for the twenty-four hours of a natural day.

I entered upon the execution of this plan for self-examination, and continued it with occasional intermissions for some time. I was surprised to find myself so much fuller of faults than I had imagined; but I had the satisfaction of seeing them diminish.

Because of my many faults, my scheme of *Order* gave me the most trouble; and I found that, though it might be practicable where a man's business was such as to leave him the disposition of his time, that of a journeyman printer, for instance, it was not possible to be exactly observed by a master, who must mix with the world, and often receive people of business at their own hours.

Order, too, with regard to places for things, papers, &c., I found extremely difficult to acquire. I had not been early accustomed to *method*, and, having an exceedingly good memory, I was not so sensible of the inconvenience attending want of method. This article, therefore, cost me much painful attention, and my faults in it vexed me so much, and I made so little progress in amendment, and had such frequent relapses, that I was almost ready to give up the attempt, and content myself with a faulty character in that respect, like the man who, in buying an ax of a smith, my neighbor, desired to have the whole of its surface as bright as the edge.

The smith consented to grind it bright for him if he would turn the wheel; he turned, while the smith pressed the broad face of the ax hard and heavily on the stone, which made the turning of it very fatiguing. The man came every now and then from the wheel to see how the work went on, and at length would take his ax as it was, without further grinding. "No," said the smith, "turn on, turn on; we shall have it bright by-and-by; as yet, it is only speckled." "Yes," said the man, "but *I think I like a speckled ax best.*"

And I believe this may have been the case with many, who, having, for want of some such means as I employed, found the difficulty of obtaining good and breaking bad habits in other points of vice and virtue, have given up the struggle, and concluded that *"a speckled ax is best"*; for something, that pretended to be reason, was every now and then suggesting to me that such extreme nicety as I exacted of myself might be a kind of foppery in morals, which, if it were known, would make me ridiculous; that a perfect character might be attended with the inconvenience of being envied and hated; and that a benevolent man should allow a few faults in himself, to keep his friends in countenance.

In truth, I found myself incorrigible with respect to *Order;* and now I am grown old, and my memory bad, I feel very sensibly the want of it. But, on the whole, though I never arrived at the perfection I had been so ambitious of obtaining, but fell far short of it, yet I was, by the endeavor, a better and a happier man than I otherwise should have been if I had not attempted it; as those who aim at perfect writing by imitating the engraved copies, though they never reach the wished-for excellence of those copies, their hand is mended by the endeavor, and is tolerable while it continues fair and legible.

It may be well my posterity should be informed that to this little artifice, with the blessing of God, their ancestor owed the constant felicity of his life, down to his seventy-ninth year, in which this is written. What reverses may attend the remainder is in the hand of Providence; but, if they arrive, the reflection on past happiness enjoyed ought to help his bearing them with more resignation.

To *Temperance* he ascribes his long-continued health, and what is still left to him of a good constitution; to *Industry and Frugality*, the early easiness of his circumstances and acquisition of his fortune, with all that knowledge that enabled him to be a useful citizen, and obtained for him some degree of reputation among the learned; to *Sincerity* and *Justice*, the confidence of his country, and the honorable employs it conferred upon him; and to the joint influence of the whole mass of the virtues, even in the imperfect state he was able to acquire them, all that evenness of temper, and that cheerfulness in conversation, which makes his company still sought for, and agreeable even to his young acquaintance. I hope, therefore, that some of my descendants may follow the example and reap the benefit.

It will be remarked that, though my scheme was not wholly without religion, there was in it no mark of any of the distinguishing tenets of any particular sect. I had purposely avoided them; for, being fully persuaded of the utility and excellency of my method, and that it might be serviceable to people in all religions, and intending some time or other to publish it, I would-not have any thing in it that should prejudice any one, of any sect, against it. I proposed writing a little comment on each virtue, in which I would have shown the advantages of possessing it, and the mischiefs attending its opposite vice; I should have called my book THE ART OF VIRTUE, because it would have shown the means and manner of obtaining virtue, which would have distinguished it from the mere exhortation to be good, that does not instruct and indicate the means, but is like the apostle's man of verbal charity, who, without showing to the naked and hungry how or where they might get clothes or victuals, only exhorted them to be fed and clothed. —*James, ii., 15, 16.*

But it so happened that my intention of writing and publishing this comment was never fulfilled. I had, indeed, from time to time, put down short hints of the sentiments and reasoning to be made use of in it, some of which I have still by me; but the necessary close attention to private business in the earlier part of life, and public business since, have occasioned my postponing it; for, it being connected in my mind with *a great and extensive project,* that required the whole man to execute, and which an unforeseen succession of employs prevented my attending to, it has hitherto remained unfinished.

In this piece it was my design to explain and enforce this doctrine, *that vicious actions are not hurtful because they are forbidden, but forbidden because they are hurtful,* the nature of man alone considered; that it was, therefore, every one's interest to be virtuous who wished to be happy even in this world; and I should, from this circumstance (there being always in the world a number of rich merchants, nobility, states, and princes, who have need of honest instruments for the management of their affairs, and such being so rare), have endeavored to convince young persons that no qualities are so likely to make a poor man's fortune as those of *probity* and *integrity.*

My list of virtues contained at first but twelve; but a Quaker friend having kindly informed me that I was generally thought proud; that my pride showed itself frequently in conversation; that I was not content with being in the right when discussing any point, but was overbearing, and rather insolent, of which he convinced me by mentioning several instances; I determined to endeavor to cure myself, if I could, of this vice or folly among the rest, and I added *Humility* to my list, giving an extensive meaning to the word.

I can not boast of much success in acquiring the *reality* of this virtue, but I had a good deal with regard to the appearance of it. I made it a rule to forbear all direct contradiction to the sentiments of others, and all positive assertion of my own. I even forbid myself the use of every word or expression in the language that imported a fixed opinion, such as *certainly, undoubtedly, &c.*, and I adopted, instead of them, *I conceive, I apprehend,* or *I imagine* a thing to be so or so; or *it so appears to me at present.* When another asserted something that I thought an error, I denied myself the pleasure of contradicting him abruptly, and of showing immediately some absurdity in his proposition; and in answering I began by observing that in certain cases or circumstances his opinion would be right, but in the present case there *appeared* or *seemed to me* some difference, &c. I soon found the advantage of this change in my manners; the conversations I engaged in went on more pleasantly. The modest way in which I proposed my opinions procured them a readier reception and less contradiction; I had less mortification when I was found to be in the wrong, and I more easily prevailed with others to give up their mistakes and join with me when I happened to be in the right.

And this mode, which I at first put on with some violence to natural inclination, became at length easy, and so habitual to me, that perhaps for

350

the last fifty years no one has ever heard a dogmatical expression escape me. And to this habit (after my character of integrity) I think it principally owing that I had early so much weight with my fellow-citizens when I proposed new institutions, or alterations in the old, and so much influence in public councils when I became a member; for I was but a bad speaker, never eloquent, subject to much hesitation in my choice of words, hardly correct in language, and yet I generally carried my point.

In reality, there is, perhaps, no one of our natural passions so hard to subdue as *pride*. Disguise it, struggle with it, stifle it, mortify it as much as one pleases, it is still alive, and will every now and then peep out and show itself; you will see it, perhaps, often in this history; for, even if I could conceive that I had completely overcome it, I should probably be *proud* of my *humility*.

❧

I Can

Ralph Waldo Emerson
(1803–1882)

So NIGH is grandeur to our dust,
So near is God to man,
When Duty whispers low, Thou must,
The youth replies, I can.

❧

Look on the Sunny Side

Helen Steiner Rice
(1901–1981)

THERE ARE always two sides,
    the GOOD and the BAD,
The DARK and the LIGHT,
    the SAD and the GLAD—
But in looking back over
    the GOOD and the BAD
We're aware of the number
    of GOOD THINGS we've had—
And in counting our blessings
    we find when we're through
We've no reason at all
    to complain or be blue—
So thank God for GOOD things
    He has already done;
And be grateful to Him
    for the battles you've won,
And know that the same God
    who helped you before

Is ready and willing
    to help you once more—
Then with faith in your heart
    reach out for God's Hand
And accept what He sends,
    though you can't understand—
For OUR FATHER in heaven
    always knows what is best,
And if you trust in His wisdom
    your life will be blest,
For always remember
    that whatever betides you,
You are never alone
    for God is beside you.

EDITOR WILLIAM ALLEN WHITE wrote a moving editorial for the *Emporia Gazette* about Mary White, his daughter, who had died. I find the grief, love, and pride of the famous editor most affecting.

353

Mary White

William Allen White
(1868–1944)

THE ASSOCIATED PRESS reports carrying the news of Mary White's death declared that it came as a result of a fall from a horse. How she would have hooted at that! She never fell from a horse in her life. Horses have fallen on her and with her—"I'm always trying to hold 'em in my lap," she used to say. But she was proud of few things, and one was that she could ride anything that had four legs and hair. Her death resulted not from a fall, but from a blow on the head which fractured her skull, and the blow came from the limb of an overhanging tree on the parking.

The last hour of her life was typical of its happiness. She came home from a day's work at school, topped off by a hard grind with the copy on the High School Annual, and felt that a ride would refresh her. She climbed into her khakis, chattering to her mother about the work she was doing, and hurried to get her horse and be put out on the dirt roads for the country air and the radiant green fields of the spring. As she rode through the town on an easy gallop, she kept waving at passers-by. She knew everyone in town. For a decade the little figure with the long pig-tail and the red hair-ribbon has been familiar on the streets of Emporia, and she got in the way of speaking to those who nodded at her. She passed the Kerrs—walking the horse—in front of the Normal Library, and waved at them; passed another friend a few hundred feet further on, and waved at her. The horse was walking and, as she turned into North Merchant Street, she took

354

off her cowboy hat, and the horse swung into a lope. She passed the Tripletts and waved her cowboy hat at them, still moving gayly north on Merchant Street. A *Gazette* carrier passed—a High School boy friend—and she waved at him, but with her bridle hand; the horse veered quickly, plunged into the parking where the low-hanging limb faced her, and, while she still looked back waving, the blow came. But she did not fall from the horse; she slipped off, dazed a bit, staggered, and fell in a faint. She never quite recovered consciousness.

But she did not fall from the horse, neither was she riding fast. A year or so ago she used to go like the wind. But that habit was broken, and she used the horse to get into the open to get fresh, hard exercise and to work off a certain surplus energy that welled up in her and needed a physical out-let. That need has been in her heart for years. It was back of the impulse that kept the dauntless little brown-clad figure on the streets and country roads of this community and built into a strong, muscular body what had been a frail and sickly frame during the first years of her life. But the riding gave her more than a body. It released a gay and hardy soul. She was the happiest thing in the world. And she was happy because she was enlarging her horizon. She came to know all sorts and conditions of men; Charley O'Brien, the traffic cop, was one of her best friends. W. L. Holtz, the Latin teacher, was another. Tom O'Connor, farmer-politician, and Rev. J. H. J. Rice, preacher and police judge, and Frank Beach, music master, were her special friends, and all the girls, black and white, above the track and below the track, in Pepville and Stringtown, were among her acquaintances. And she brought home riotous stories of her adventures. She loved to rollick;

persiflage was her natural expression at home. Her humor was a continual bubble of joy. She seemed to think in hyperbole and metaphor. She was mischievous without malice, as full of faults as an old shoe. No angel was Mary White, but an easy girl to live with, for she never nursed a grouch five minutes in her life.

With all her eagerness for the out-of-doors, she loved books. On her table when she left her room were a book by Conrad, one by Galsworthy, *Creative Chemistry*, by E. E. Slosson, and a Kipling book. She read Mark Twain, Dickens, and Kipling before she was ten—all of their writings. Wells and Arnold Bennett particularly amused and diverted her. She was entered as a student in Wellesley in 1922; was assistant editor of the High School Annual this year, and in line for election to the editorship of the Annual next year. She was a member of the executive committee of the High School Y.W.C.A.

Within the last two years she had begun to be moved by an ambition to draw. She began as most children do by scribbling in her school books, funny pictures. She bought cartoon magazines and took a course—rather casually, naturally, for she was, after all, a child with no strong purposes— and this year she tasted the first fruits of success by having her pictures accepted by the High School Annual. But the thrill of delight she got when Mr. Ecord, of the Normal Annual, asked her to do the cartooning for that book this spring was too beautiful for words. She fell to her work with all her enthusiastic heart. Her drawings were accepted, and her pride—always repressed by a lively sense of the ridiculousness of the figure she was cutting—was a really gorgeous thing to see. No successful artist ever drank a deeper draft of satisfaction than she took from the little fame her work was getting among her schoolfellows. In her glory she almost forgot her horse—but never her car.

For she used the car as a jitney bus. It was her social life. She never had a "party" in all her nearly seventeen years—wouldn't have one; but she never drove a block in the car in her life that she didn't begin to fill the car with pick-ups! Everyone rode with Mary White—white and black, old and young, rich and poor, men and women. She liked nothing better than to fill the car full of long-legged High School boys and an occasional girl, and parade the town. She never had a "date," nor went to a dance, except once with her brother Bill, and the "boy proposition" didn't interest her—yet. But young people—great spring-breaking, vanish-cracking, fender-bending, door-sagging carloads of "kids"—gave her great pleasure. Her zests were keen. But the most fun she ever had in her life was acting as chairman of the committee that got up the big turkey dinner for the poor folks at the county home; scores of pies, gallons of slaw, jam, cakes, preserves, oranges, and a wilderness of turkey were loaded in the car and taken to the county home. And, being of a practical turn of mind, she risked her own Christmas dinner by staying to see that the poor folks actually got it all. Not that she was a cynic; she just disliked to tempt folks. While there she found a blind colored uncle, very old, who could do nothing but make rag rugs, and she rustled up from her school friends rags enough to keep him busy for a season. The last engagement she tried to make was to take the guests at the county home out for a car ride. And the last endeavor of her life was to try to get a rest room for colored girls in the High School. She found one girl reading in the toilet, because there was no better place for a colored girl to loaf, and it inflamed her sense of injustice and she became a nagging harpie to those who, she thought, could remedy the evil. The poor she had always with her, and was glad of it. She hungered and thirsted for righteousness; and was the most impious creature in the world. She joined the Congregational Church without consulting her parents; not particularly for her soul's good. She never had a thrill of piety in her life, and would have hooted at "testimony." But even as a little child she felt the church was an agency for helping people to more of life's abundance, and she wanted to help. She never wanted help for herself. Clothes meant little to her. It was a fight to get a new rig on her; but eventually a harder fight to get it off. She never wore a jewel and had no ring but her High School class ring, and never asked for anything but a wrist watch. She refused to have her hair up, though she was nearly seventeen. "Mother," she protested, "you don't know how much I get by with, in my braided pig-tails, that I could not with my hair up." Above every other passion of her life was her passion not to grow up, to be a child. The tomboy in her, which was big, seemed to loathe to be put away forever in skirts. She was a Peter Pan, who refused to grow up.

Her funeral yesterday at the Congregational Church was as she would have wished it; no singing, no flowers save the big bunch of red roses from her Brother Bill's Harvard classmen—Heavens, how proud that would have made her!—and the red roses from the *Gazette* force—in vases at her head and feet. A short prayer, Paul's beautiful essay on "Love" from the Thirteenth Chapter of First Corinthians, some remarks about her democratic spirit by her friend, John H. J. Rice, pastor and police judge, which she would have deprecated if she could, a prayer sent down for her by her friend, Carl Nau, and opening the service the slow, poignant movement from Beethoven's *Moonlight Sonata*, which she loved, and closing the service a cutting from the joyously melancholy first movement of Tschaikowski's *Pathetic Symphony*, which she liked to hear in certain moods on the phonograph, then the Lord's Prayer by her friends in the High School.

That was all.

For her pall-bearers only her friends were chosen: her Latin teacher, W. L. Holtz, her High School principal, Rice Brown, her doctor, Frank Foncannon; her friend, W. W. Finney; her pal at the *Gazette* office, Walter Hughes; and her brother Bill. It would have made her smile to know that her friend Charley O'Brien, the traffic cop, had been transferred from Sixth and Commercial to the corner near the church to direct her friends who came to bid her good-by.

A rift in the clouds in a gray day threw a shaft of sunlight upon her coffin as her nervous energetic little body sank to its last sleep. But the soul of her, the glowing, gorgeous, fervent soul of her, surely was flaming in eager joy upon some other dawn.

⚜

Little Boy Blue

Eugene Field
(1850–1895)

THE LITTLE TOY DOG is covered with dust,
　　But sturdy and stanch he stands;
And the little toy soldier is red with rust,
　　And his musket moulds in his hands.
Time was when the little toy dog was new,
　　And the soldier was passing fair,
And that was the time when our Little Boy Blue
　　Kissed them and put them there.

"Now, don't you go till I come," he said,
　　"And don't you make any noise!"
So toddling off to his trundle-bed
　　He dreamt of the pretty toys.
And as he was dreaming, an angel song
　　Awakened our Little Boy Blue,—
Oh, the years are many, the years are long,
　　But the little toy friends are true!

Ay, faithful to Little Boy Blue they stand,
    Each in the same old place,
Awaiting the touch of a little hand,
    The smile of a little face.
And they wonder, as waiting these long years through,
    In the dust of that little chair,
What has become of our Little Boy Blue
    Since he kissed them and put them there.

꧁꧂

The Eternal Goodness

John Greenleaf Whittier
(1807–1892)

I SEE the wrong that round me lies,
    I feel the guilt within;
I hear, with groan and travail-cries,
    The world confess its sin.

Yet, in the maddening maze of things,
    And tossed by storm and flood,
To one fixed trust my spirit clings:
    I know that God is good!

꧁꧂

361

ELBERT HUBBARD WAS an American lecturer and essayist. He was also a successful magazine publisher. "A Message to Garcia" (1899) was a thrilling account of an army officer's ability to get things done, however difficult. This is a lesson on: "It must be done and I can do it."

A Message to Garcia
Elbert Hubbard
(1865–1915)

IN ALL THIS Cuban business there is one man stands out on the horizon of my memory.

When war broke out between Spain and the United States, it was very necessary to communicate quickly with the leader of the Insurgents. Garcia was somewhere in the mountain fastnesses of Cuba—no one knew where. No mail or telegraph message could reach him. The President must secure his cooperation, and quickly.

What to do!

Someone said to the President, "There is a fellow by the name of Rowan will find Garcia for you, if anybody can."

Rowan was sent for and given a letter to be delivered to Garcia. How the "fellow by the name of Rowan" took the letter, sealed it up in an oilskin pouch, strapped it over his heart, in four days landed by night off the coast of Cuba from an open boat, disappeared into the jungle, and in three weeks came out on the other side of the Island, having traversed a hostile country on foot, and delivered his letter to Garcia—are things I have no special desire to tell in detail. The point that I wish to make is this: McKinley gave Rowan a letter to be delivered to Garcia; Rowan took the letter and did not ask, "Where is he at?"

By the Eternal! there is a man whose form should be cast in deathless bronze and the statue placed in every college of the land. It is not book-learning young men need, nor instruction about this and that, but a stiff-ening of the vertebrae which will cause them to be loyal to a trust, to act promptly, concentrate their energies: do the thing—"Carry a message to Garcia."

General Garcia is dead now, but there are other Garcias. No man who has endeavored to carry out an enterprise where many hands were needed, but has been well-nigh appalled at times by the imbecility of the average man—the inability or unwillingness to concentrate on a thing and do it.

Slipshod assistance, foolish inattention, dowdy indifference, and half-hearted work seem the rule; and no man succeeds, unless by hook or crook or threat he forces or bribes other men to assist him; or mayhap, God in His goodness performs a miracle, and sends him an Angel of Light for an assistant.

You, reader, put this matter to a test: You are sitting now in your of-fice—six clerks are within call. Summon any one and make this request: "Please look in the encyclopedia and make a brief memorandum for me concerning the life of Correggio."

Will the clerk quietly say, "Yes, sir," and go do the task?

On your life he will not. He will look at you out of a fishy eye and ask one or more of the following questions:

Who was he?

Which encyclopedia?

Where is the encyclopedia?

Was I hired for that?

Don't you mean Bismarck?

What's the matter with Charlie doing it?

Is he dead?

Is there any hurry?

Sha'n't I bring you the book and let you look it up yourself?

What do you want to know for?

And I will lay you ten to one that after you have answered the questions, and explained how to find the information, and why you want it, the clerk will go off and get one of the other clerks to help him try to find Garcia—and then come back and tell you there is no such man. Of course I may lose my bet, but according to the Law of Average I will not.

Now, if you are wise, you will not bother to explain to your "assistant" that Correggio is indexed under the C's, not in the K's, but you will smile very sweetly and say, "Never mind," and go look it up yourself. And this incapacity for independent action, this moral stupidity, this infirmity of the will, this unwillingness to cheerfully catch hold and lift . . . If men will not act for themselves, what will they do when the benefit of their effort is for all?

A first mate with knotted club seems necessary; and the dread of getting "the bounce" Saturday night holds many a worker to his place.

Advertise for a stenographer, and nine out of ten who apply can neither spell nor punctuate—and do not think it necessary to.

Can such a one write a letter to Garcia?

"You see that bookkeeper," said the foreman to me in a large factory.

"Yes; what about him?"

"Well, he's a fine accountant, but if I'd send him up town on an errand, he might accomplish the errand all right, and on the other hand, might stop at four saloons on the way, and when he got to Main Street would forget what he had been sent for."

Can such a man be entrusted to carry a message to Garcia?

We have recently been hearing much maudlin sympathy expressed for the "downtrodden denizens of the sweatshop" and the "homeless wanderer searching for honest employment," and with it all often go many hard words for the men in power.

Nothing is said about the employer who grows old before his time in a vain attempt to get frowsy ne'er-do-wells to do intelligent work; and his long, patient striving after "help" that does nothing but loaf when his back is turned. In every store and factory there is a constant weeding out process going on. The employer is constantly sending away "help" that have shown their incapacity to further the interests of the business, and others are being taken on. No matter how good times are, this sorting continues: only, if times are hard and work is scarce, the sorting is done finer—but out and forever out the incompetent and unworthy go. It is the survival of the fittest. Self-interest prompts every employer to keep the best—those who can carry a message to Garcia.

I know one man of really brilliant parts who has not the ability to manage a business of his own, and yet who is absolutely worthless to anyone else, because he carries with him constantly the insane suspicion that his employer is oppressing, or intending to oppress, him. He cannot give orders, and he will not receive them. Should a message be given him to take to Garcia, his answer would probably be, "Take it yourself!"

Tonight this man walks the streets looking for work, the wind whistling through his threadbare coat. No one who knows him dare employ him, for he is a regular firebrand of discontent. He is impervious to reason, and the only thing that can impress him is the toe of a thick-soled Number Nine boot.

Of course, I know that one so morally deformed is no less to be pitied than a physical cripple; but in our pitying let us drop a tear, too, for the men who are striving to carry on a great enterprise, whose working hours are not limited by the whistle, and whose hair is fast turning white through the struggle to hold in line dowdy indifference, slipshod imbecility, and the heartless ingratitude which, for their enterprise, would be both hungry and homeless.

Have I put the matter too strongly? Possibly I have; but when all the world has gone aslumming I wish to speak a word of sympathy for the man who succeeds—the man who, against great odds, has directed the efforts of others, and having succeeded, finds there's nothing in it: nothing but bare board and clothes. I have carried a dinner-pail and worked for day's wages, and I have also been an employer of labor, and I know there is something to be said on both sides. There is no excellence, per se, in poverty; rags are no recommendation; and all employers are not rapacious and high-handed, any more than all poor men are virtuous. My heart goes out to the man who does his work when the "boss" is away, as well as when he is at home. And the man who, when given a letter for Garcia, quietly takes the missive, without asking any idiotic questions, and with no lurking intention of chucking it into the nearest sewer, or of doing aught else but deliver it, never gets "laid off," nor has to go on a strike for higher wages. Civilization is one long, anxious search for just such individuals. Anything such a man asks shall be granted. He is wanted in every city, town and village—in every office, shop, store and factory. The world cries out for such; he is needed and needed badly—the man who can "Carry a Message to Garcia."

⚜

Not in Vain

Emily Dickinson
(1830–1886)

IF I CAN STOP one heart from breaking,
I shall not live in vain:
If I can ease one life the aching,
Or cool one pain,
Or help one fainting robin
Unto his nest again,
I shall not live in vain.

Be Strong

Maltbie Davenport Babcock
(1858–1901)

BE STRONG!
We are not here to play, to dream, to drift;
We have hard work to do, and loads to lift;
Shun not the struggle—face it; 'tis God's gift.

Be strong!
Say not, "The days are evil. Who's to blame?"
And fold the hands and acquiesce—oh shame!
Stand up, speak out, and bravely, in God's name.

Be strong!
It matters not how deep intrenched the wrong,
How hard the battle goes, the day how long;
Faint not—fight on! To-morrow comes the song.

※

WHEN I WAS a young man I went one Sunday morning to give a talk in the chapel of an old and famous New England university. The chapel was filled with students and faculty.

I was startled at the close of my address because the students began a great snapping of fingers. Afterward, an elderly professor took me to his home for lunch, and I asked, "Why the general snapping of fingers at the close of my talk?"

"Oh, that is their form of applause in chapel in lieu of handclapping," he explained.

As I prepared to leave, my host presented me with a little book, *Courage* by J. M. Barrie. "You are young and have a long life ahead and you will need courage all along the way," he said. "This will help you." It has helped. I have it still. It was Barrie's 1922 rectorial address at St. Andrews University in Scotland.

The speech is so wise and expressed in such gracious words that I include it here almost whole. It is one of the world's greatest masterpieces of spoken English.

Courage

J. M. Barrie (1860–1957)

YOU HAVE HAD many rectors here in St. Andrews who will continue in bloom long after the lowly ones such as I am are dead and rotten and forgotten. They are the roses in December; you remember some one said that God gave us memory so that we might have roses in December. But I do not envy the great ones. In my experience—and you may find in the end it is yours also—the people I have cared for—my December roses—have been very simple folk. Yet I wish that for this hour I could swell into someone of importance, so as I do you credit. I suppose you had a melting for me because I was hewn out of one of your own quarries, walked similar academic groves, and have trudged the road on which you will soon set forth. I would that I could put into your hands a staff for that somewhat bloody march, for though there is much about myself that I conceal from other people, to help you I would expose every cranny of my mind.

But, alas, when the hour strikes for the Rector to answer to his call he is unable to become the undergraduate he used to be, and so the only door into you is closed. We, your elders, are much more interested in you than you are in us. We are not really important to you. I have utterly forgotten the address of the Rector of my time, and even who he was, but I recall vividly climbing up a statue to tie his colours around its neck and being hurled therefrom the contumely. We remember the important things. I cannot provide you with that staff for your journey; but perhaps I can tell you a little about it, how to use it and lose it and find it again, and cling to it more than ever. You shall cut it—so it is ordained—every one of you for himself, and its name is Courage. You must excuse me if I talk a good deal about courage to you to-day. There is nothing else much worth speaking about to undergraduates or graduates or white-haired men and women. It is the lovely virtue—the rib of Himself that God sent down to His children.

My special difficulty is that though you have had literary rectors here before, they were the big guns, the historians, the philosophers; you have had none, I think, who followed my more humble branch, which may be described as playing hide and seek with angels. My puppets seem more real to me than myself, and I could get on much more swingingly if I made one of them deliver this address. It is M'Connachie who has brought me to this pass. M'Connachie, I should explain, as I have undertaken to open the innermost doors, is the name I give to the unruly half of myself: the writing half. We are complement and supplement. I am the half that is dour and practical and canny, he is the fanciful half; my desire is to be the family solicitor, standing firm on my hearthrug among the harsh realities of the office furniture; while he prefers to fly around on one wing. I should not mind him doing that, but he drags me with him. I have sworn that M'Connachie shall not interfere with the address today; but there is no telling. I might have done things worthwhile if it had not been for M'Connachie, and my first piece of advice to you at any rate shall be sound: don't copy me. A good subject for a rectorial address would be the mess the Rector himself has made of life. I merely cast this forth as a suggestion, and leave the working of it out to my successor. I do not think it has been used yet.

My theme is Courage, as you should use it in the great fight that seems to be coming between youth and their betters; by youth, meaning, of course, you, and by your betters, us. I want you to take up this position: That youth have for too long left exclusively in our hands the decisions in national matters that are more vital to them than to us. Things about the next war, for instance, and why the last one ever had a beginning. I use the word fight because it must, I think, begin with a challenge; but the aim is the reverse of antagonism, it is partnership. I want you to hold that the time has arrived for youth to demand that partnership, and to demand it courageously. That to gain courage is what you come to St. Andrews for, with some alarums and excursions into college life. That is what I propose, but, of course, the issue lies with M'Connachie.

Your betters had no share in the immediate cause of the war; we know what nation has that blot to wipe out; but for fifty years or so we heeded not the rumblings of the distant drum—I do not mean by lack of military preparations; and when war did come we told youth, who had to get us out of it, tall tales of what it really is and of the clover beds to which it leads. We were not meaning to deceive, most of us were as honourable and as ignorant as the youth themselves; but that does not acquit us of failings such as stupidity and jealousy, the two black spots in human nature which, more than love of money, are at the root of all evil. If you prefer to leave things as they are we shall probably fail you again. Do not be too sure that we have learned our lesson, and are not at this very moment doddering down some brimstone path.

I am far from implying that even worse things than war may not come to a State. There are circumstances in which nothing can so well become a land, as I think this land proved which the late war did break out and there was but one thing to do. There is a form of anaemia that is more rotting than even an unjust war. The end will indeed have come to our courage and to us when we are afraid in dire mischance to refer the final appeal to the arbitrament of arms. I suppose all the lusty of our race alive and dead, join hands on that.

And he is dead who will not fight;
And who dies fighting has increase.

But if you must be in the struggle, the more reason you should know why, before it begins and have a say in the decision whether, it is to begin. The youth who went to the war had no such knowledge, no such say; I am sure the survivors, of whom there must be a number here today, want you to be wiser that they were, and are certainly determined to be wiser next time themselves. If you are to get that partnership which, once gained, is to be for, mutual benefit it will be, I should say, by banding yourselves, with these men, not defiantly but firmly, not for selfish ends but for your country's good. In the meantime they have one bulwark; they have a General who is befriending them as I think never, after the fighting was over, has a General befriended his men before. Perhaps the seemly thing would be for us, their betters, to elect one of these young survivors of the carnage to be our Rector. He ought now to know a few things about war that are worth our hearing. If his theme were the Rector's favourite, diligence, I should be afraid of his advising a great many of us to be diligent in sitting still and doing no more harm.

Of course he would put it more suavely than that, though it is not, I think, by gentleness that you will get your rights; we are dogged ones at sticking to what we have got, and so will you be at our age. But avoid calling us ugly names; we may be stubborn and we may be blunderers, but we love you more than aught else in the world, and once you have won your partnership we shall all be welcoming you. I urge you not to use ugly names about any one. In the war it was not the fighting men who were distinguished for abuse; as has been well said, "Hell hath no fury like a non-combatant." Never ascribe to an opponent motives meaner than your own. There may be students here to-day who have decided this session to go in for immortality, and would like to know of an easy way of accomplishing it. That is a way, but not so easy as you think. Go through life without ever ascribing to your opponents motives meaner than your own. Nothing so lowers the moral currency; give it up, and be great.

Another sure way to fame is to know what you mean. It is a solemn thought that almost no one—if he is truly eminent—knows what he means. Look at the great ones of the earth, the politicians. We do not discuss what they say but what they may, have meant when they said it. In 1922 we are all wondering, and so are they, what they meant in 1914 and afterwards. They are publishing books trying to find out; the men of action as well as the men of words. There are exceptions. It is not that our statesmen are "sugared mouths with minds therefrae"; many of them are the best men we have got, upright and anxious, nothing cheaper than to miscall them. The explanation seems just to be that it is so difficult to know what you mean, especially when you have become a swell. No longer, apparently, can you deal in "russet yeas and honest kersey noes"; gone for ever is simplicity, which is as beautiful as the divine plain face of Lamb's Miss Kelly. Doubts breed suspicions, a dangerous air. Without suspicion there might have been no war. When you are called to Downing Street to discuss what you want of your betters with the Prime Minister, he won't be suspicious, not as far as you can see; but remember the atmosphere or generations you are in, and when he passes you the toast-rack say to yourselves, if you would be in the mode, "Now, I wonder what he meant by that."

Even without striking out in the way I suggest, you are already disturbing your betters considerably. I sometimes talk this over with M'Connachie, with whom, as you may guess, circumstances compel me to pass a good deal of my time. In our talks we agree that we, your betters, constantly find you forgetting that we are your betters. Your answer is that the war and other happenings have shown you that age is not necessarily another name for sapience; that our avoidance of frankness in life and in the arts is often, but not so often as you think, a cowardly way of shirking unpalatable truths, and that you have taken us off our pedestals because we look more natural on the ground. You who are at the rash age even accuse your elders, sometimes not without justification, of being more rash than yourselves. "If Youth but only knew," we used to teach you to sing; but now, just because Youth has been to the war, it wants to change the next line into "If Age had only to do."

In so far as this attitude of yours is merely passive, sullen, negative, as it mainly is, despairing of our capacity and anticipating a future of gloom, it is no game for man or woman. It is certainly the opposite of that for which I plead. Do not stand aloof, despising, disbelieving, but come in and help insist on coming in and helping. After all, we have shown a good deal of courage; and your part is to add a greater courage to it. There are glorious years lying ahead of you if you choose to make them glorious. God's in His heaven still. So forward, brave hearts. To what adventures I cannot tell, but I know that your God is watching to see whether you are adventurous. I

375

know that the great partnership is only a first step, but I do not know what are to be the next and the next. The partnership is but a tool; what are you to do with it? Very little, I warn you, if you are merely thinking of yourselves; much, if what is at the marrow of your thoughts is a future that even you can scarcely hope to see.

Learn as a beginning how world-shaking situations arise and how they may be countered. Doubt all your betters who would deny you that right of partnership. Begin by doubting all such in high places except, of course, your professors. But doubt all other professors—yet not conceitedly, as some do, with their noses in the air; avoid all such physical risks. If it necessitates your pushing some of us out of our places, still push; you will find it needs some shoving. But the things courage can do! The things that even incompetence can do if it works with singleness of purpose. The war has done at least one big thing: it has taken spring out of the year. And, this accomplished, our leading people are amazed to find that the other seasons are not conducting themselves as usual. The spring of the year lies buried in the fields of France and elsewhere. By the time the next eruption comes it may be you who are responsible for it and your sons who are in the lava. All, perhaps, because this year you let things slide.

We are a nice and kindly people, but it is already evident that we are stealing back into the old grooves, seeking cushions for our old bones, rather than attempting to build up a fairer future. That is what we mean when we say that the country is settling down. Make haste, or you will become like us, with only the thing we proudly call experience to add to your stock, a poor exchange for the generous feelings that time will take away.

We have no intention of giving you your share. Look around and see how much share Youth has now that the war is over. You got a handsome share while it lasted.

I expect we shall beat you; unless your fortitude be doubly girded by a desire to send a message of cheer to your brothers who fell, the only message, I believe, for which they crave; they are not worrying about their Aunt Jane. They want to know if you have learned wisely from what befell them; if you have, they will be braced in the feeling that they did not die in vain. Some of them think they did. They will not take our word for it that they did not. You are their living image; they know you could not lie to them, but they distrust our flattery and our cunning faces. To us they have passed away; but are you who stepped into their heritage only yesterday, whose books are scarcely cold to their hands, you who still hear their cries being blown across the links are you already relegating them to the shades? The gaps they have left in this University are among the most honourable of her wounds. But we are not here to acclaim them. Where they are now, hero is, I think, a very little word. They call to you to find out in time the truth about this great game, which your elders play for stakes and Youth plays for its life.

I do not know whether you are grown a little tired of that word hero, but I am sure the heroes are. That is the subject of one of our unfinished plays, M'Connachie is the one who writes the plays. If any one of you here proposes to be playwright you can take this for your own and finish it. The scene is a school, schoolmasters present, but if you like you could make it a university, professors present. They are discussing an illuminated scroll

377

about a student fallen in the war, which they have kindly presented to his parents; and unexpectedly the parents enter. They are an old pair, back-bent, they have been stalwarts in their day but have now gone small; they are poor, but not so poor that they could not send their boy to college. They are in black, not such a rusty black either, and you may be sure she is the one who knows what to do with his hat. Their faces are gnarled, I suppose—but I do not need to describe that pair to Scottish students. They have come to thank the Senatus for their lovely scroll and to ask them to tear it up. At first they had been enamoured to read of what a scholar their son was, how noble and adored by all. But soon a fog settled over them, for this grand person was not the boy they knew. He had many a fault well known to them; he was not always so noble; as a scholar he did no more than scrape through; and he sometimes made his father rage and his mother grieve. They had liked to talk such memories as these together, and smile over them, as if they were bits of him he had left lying about the house. So thank you kindly, and would you please give them back their boy by tearing up the scroll? I see nothing else for our dramatist to do. I think he should ask an alumna of St. Andrews to play the old lady (indicating Miss Ellen Terry). The loveliest of all young actresses, the dearest of all old ones; it seems only yesterday that all the men of imagination proposed to their beloved in some such frenzied words as these, "As I can't get Miss Terry, may I have you?"

This play might become historical as the opening of your propaganda in the proposed campaign. How to make a practical advance? The League of Nations is a very fine thing, but it cannot save you, because it will be run by us. Beware your betters bringing presents. What is wanted is something run by yourselves. You have more in common with the youth of other lands than Youth and Age can ever have with each other; even the hostile countries sent out many a son very like ours, from the same sort of homes, the same sort of universities, who had as little to do as our youth had with the origin of the great adventure. Can we doubt that many of these on both sides who have gone over and were once opponents are now friends? You ought to have a League of Youth of all countries as your beginning, ready to say to all Governments, "We will fight each other, but only when we are sure of the necessity." Are you equal to your job, you young men? If not, I call upon the red-gowned women to lead the way. I sound to myself as if I were advocating a rebellion, though I am really asking for a larger friendship. Perhaps I may be arrested on leaving the hall. In such a cause I should think that I had at last proved myself worthy to be your Rector.

You will have to work harder than ever, but possibly not so much at the same things; more at modern languages certainly if you are to discuss that League of Youth with the students of other nations when they come over to St. Andrews for the Conference. I am far from taking a side against the classics. I should as soon argue against your having tops to your heads; that way lie the best tops. Science, too, has at last come to its own in St. Andrews. It is the surest means of teaching you how to know what you mean when you say. So you will have to work harder. Izaak Walton quotes the saying that doubtless the Almighty could have created a finer fruit than the strawberry, but that doubtless also He never did. Doubtless also He could have provided us with better fun than hard work, but I don't know what it is. To be born poor is probably the next best thing. The greatest glory that has ever come to me was to be swallowed up in London, not knowing a soul, with no means of subsistence, and the fun of working till the stars went out. To have known any one would have spoilt it. I did not even quite know the language. I rang for my boots, and they thought I said a glass of water, so I drank the water and worked on. There was no food in the cupboard, so I did not need to waste time in eating. The pangs and agonies when no proof came. How courteously tolerant was I of the postman without a proof for us; how M'Connachie, on the other hand, wanted to punch his head. The magic days when our article appeared in an evening paper. The promptitude with which I counted the lines to see how much we should get for it. Then M'Connachie's superb air of dropping it into the gutter. Oh, to be a free lance of journalism again—that darling jade! Those were days. Too good to last. Let us be grave. Here comes a Rector.

But now, on reflection, a dreadful sinking assails me, that this was not really work. The artistic callings—you remember how Stevenson thumped them—are merely doing what you are clamorous to be at; it is not real work unless you would rather be doing something else. My so-called labours were just M'Connachie running away with me. Still, I have sometimes worked; for instance, I feel that I am working at this moment. And the big guns are in the same plight as the little ones. Carlyle, the king of all rectors, has always been accepted as the arch-apostle of toil, and has registered his many woes. But it will not do. Despite sickness, poortith, want and all, he was grinding all his life at the one job he revelled in. An extraordinarily happy man, though there is no direct proof that he thought so.

There must be many men in other callings besides the arts lauded as hard workers who are merely out for enjoyment. Our Chancellor? (indicating Lord Haig). If our Chancellor had always a passion to be a soldier, we must reconsider him as a worker. Even our Principal? How about the light that burns in our Principal's room after decent people have gone to bed? If we could climb up and look in—I should like to do something of that kind for the last time—should we find him engaged in honest toil, or guiltily engrossed in chemistry?

You will all fall into one of those two callings, the joyous or the uncongenial; and one wishes you into the first, though our sympathy, our esteem, must go rather to the less fortunate, the braver ones who "turn their necessity to glorious gain" after they have put away their dreams. To the others will go the easy prizes of life—success, which has become a somewhat odious onion nowadays, chiefly because we so often give the name to the wrong thing. When you reach the evening of your days you will, I think, see—with, I hope, becoming cheerfulness—that we are all failures, at least all the best of us. The greatest Scotsman that ever lived wrote himself down a failure:

The poor inhabitant below
Was quick to learn and wise to know,
And keenly felt the friendly glow
And softer flame.
But thoughtless follies laid him low,
And stained his name.

381

Perhaps the saddest lines in poetry, written by a man who could make things new for the gods themselves.

If you want to avoid being like Burns there are several possible ways. Thus you might copy us, as we shine forth in our published memoirs, practically without a flaw. No one so obscure nowadays but that he can have a book about him. Happy the land that can produce such subjects for the pen.

But do not put your photograph at all ages into your autobiography. That may bring you to the ground. "My Life; and what I have done with it"; that is the sort of title, but it is the photographs that give what you have done with it. Grim things, those portraits; if you could read the language of them you would often find it unnecessary to read the book. The face itself, of course, is still more tell-tale, for it is the record of all one's past life. There the man stands in the dock, page by page; we ought to be able to see each chapter of him melting into the next like the figures in the cinematograph. Even the youngest of you has got through some chapters already. When you go home for the next vacation some one is sure to say "John has changed a little; I don't quite see in what way, but he has changed." You remember they said that last vacation. Perhaps it means that you look less like your father. Think that out. I could say some nice things of your betters if I chose.

In youth you tend to look rather frequently into a mirror, not at all necessarily from vanity. You say to yourself, "What an interesting face; I wonder what he is to be up to?" Your elders do not look into the mirror so often. We know what he has been up to. As yet there is unfortunately no science of reading other people's faces; I think a chair for this should be founded in St. Andrews.

The new professor will need to be a sublime philosopher, and for obvious reasons he ought to wear spectacles before his senior class. It will be a gloriously optimistic chair, for he can tell his students the glowing truth, that what their faces are to be like presently depends mainly on themselves. Mainly, not altogether—

I am the master of my fate,
I am the captain of my soul.

I found the other day an old letter from Henley that told me of the circumstances in which he wrote that poem. "I was a patient," he writes, "in the old infirmary of Edinburgh. I had heard vaguely of Lister, and went there as a sort of forlorn hope on the chance of saving my foot. The great surgeon received me, as he did and does everybody, with the greatest kindness, and for twenty months I lay in one or other ward of the old place under his care. It was a desperate business, but he saved my foot, and here I am." There he was, ladies and gentlemen, and what he was doing during that "desperate business" was singing that he was master of his fate.

If you want an example of courage try Henley. Or Stevenson. I could tell you some stories about these two, but they would not be dull enough for a rectorial address. For courage, again, take Meredith, whose laugh was "as broad as a thousand beeves at pasture." Take, as I think, the greatest figure literature has still left to us, to be added to-day to the roll of St. Andrews' alumni, though it must be in absence. The pomp and circumstance of war will pass, and all others now alive may fade from the scene, but I think the quiet figure of Hardy will live on.

I seem to be taking all my examples from the calling I was lately pretending to despise. I should like to read you some passages of a letter from a man of another calling, which I think will hearten you. I have the little filmy sheets here. I thought you might like to see the actual letter; it has been a long journey; it has been to the South Pole. It is a letter to me from Captain Scott of the Antarctic, and was written in the tent you know of, where it was found long afterwards with his body and those of some other very gallant gentlemen, his comrades. The writing is in pencil, still quite clear, though toward the end some of the words trail away as into the great silence that was waiting for them. It begins:

> We are pegging out in a very comfortless spot. Hoping this letter may be found and sent to you, I write you a word of farewell. I want you to think well of me and my end." (After some private instructions too intimate to read, he goes on): "Goodbye—I am not at all afraid of the end, but sad to miss many a simple pleasure which I had planned for the future in our long marches . . . We are in a desperate state—feet frozen, etc., no fuel, and a long way from food, but it would do your heart good to be in our tent, to hear our songs and our cheery conversation . . ." (Later it is here that the words become difficult)—"We are very near the end . . . We did intend to finish ourselves when things proved like this, but we have decided to die naturally without."

I think it may uplift you all to stand for a moment by that tent and listen, as he says, to their songs and cheery conversation. When I think of Scott I remember the strange Alpine story of the youth who fell down a glacier and was lost, and of how a scientific companion, one of several who accompanied him, all young, computed that the body would again appear at a certain date and place many years afterwards. When that time came round some of the survivors returned to the glacier to see if the prediction would be fulfilled; all old men now; and the body reappeared as young as on the day he left them. So Scott and his comrades emerge out of the white immensities always young.

How comely a thing is affliction borne cheerfully, which is not beyond the reach of the humblest of us. What is beauty? It is these hardbitten men singing courage to you from their tent; it is the waves of their island home crooning of their deeds to you who are to follow them. Sometimes beauty boils over and then spirits are abroad. Ages may pass as we look or listen, for time is annihilated. There is a very old legend told to me by Nansen the explorer—I like well to be in the company of explorers—the legend of a monk who had wandered into the fields and a lark began to sing. He had never heard a lark before, and he stood there entranced until the bird and its song had become part of the heavens. Then he went back to the monastery and found there a doorkeeper whom he did not know and who did not know him. Other monks came, and they were all strangers to him. He told them he was Father Anselm, but that was no help. Finally they looked through the books of the monastery, and these revealed that there had been a Father Anselm there a hundred or more years before. Time had been blotted out while he listened to the lark.

That, I suppose, was a case of beauty boiling over, or a soul boiling over; perhaps the same thing. Then spirits walk.

They must sometimes walk St. Andrews. I do not mean the ghosts of queens or prelate; but one that keeps step, as soft as snow, with some poor student. He sometimes catches sight of it. That is why his fellows can never quite touch him, their best beloved; he half knows something of which they know nothing—the secret that is hidden in the face of the Mona Lisa. As I see him, life is so beautiful to him that its proportions are monstrous. Perhaps his childhood may have been overfull of gladness; they don't like that. If the seekers were kind he is the one for whom the flags of his college would fly one day. But the seeker I am thinking of is unfriendly, and so our student is "the lad that will never be old." He often gaily forgets, and thinks he has slain his foe by daring him, like him who, dreading water, was always the first to leap into it. One can see him serene, astride a Scotch cliff, singing to the sun the farewell thanks of a boy:

> Throned on a cliff serene Man saw the sun
> hold a red torch above the farthest seas,
> and the fierce island pinnacles put on
> in his defence their sombre panoplies;
> Foremost the white mists eddied, trailed and
> spun like seekers, emulous to clasp his knees,
> till all the beauty of the scene seemed one,
> led by the secret whispers of the breeze.
> "The sun's torch suddenly flashed upon his face
> and died; and he sat content in subject night
> and dreamed of an old dead foe that had

sought and found him;
a beast stirred boldly in his resting-place;
And the cold came; Man rose to his masterheight,
shivered, and turned away; but the mists
were round him."

If there is any of you here so rare that the seekers have taken an ill-will to him, as to the boy who wrote those lines, I ask you to be careful. Henley says in that poem we were speaking of:

Under the bludgeonings of chance
My head is bloody but unbowed.

A fine mouthful, but perhaps "My head is bloody and bowed" is better. Let us get back to that tent with its songs and cheery conversations. Courage. I do not think it is to be got by your becoming solemn-sides before your time. You must have been warned against letting the golden hours slip by. Yes, but some of them are golden only because we let them slip. Diligence—ambition; noble words, but only if "touched to fine issues." Prizes may be dross, learning lumber, unless they bring you into the arena with increased understanding. Hanker not too much after worldly prosperity that corpulent cigar; if you became a millionaire you would probably go swimming around for more like a diseased goldfish. Look to it that what you are doing is not merely toddling to a competency. Perhaps that must be your fate, but fight it and then, though you fail, you may still be among the elect of whom we have spoken. Many a brave man has had to come to it at last. But there are the complacent toddlers from the start. Favour them not, ladies, especially now that every one of you carries a possible maréchal's baton under her gown. "Happy," it has been said by a distinguished man, "is he who can leave college with an unreproaching conscience and an unsullied heart." I don't know; he sounds to me like a sloppy, watery sort of fellow; happy, perhaps, but if there be red blood in him, impossible. Be not disheartened by ideals of perfection which can be achieved only by those who run away. Nature, that "thrifty goddess," never gave you "the smallest scruple of her excellence" for that. Whatever bludgeonings may be gathering for you, I think one feels more poignantly at your age than ever again in life. You have not our December roses to help you; but you have June coming, whose roses do not wonder, as do ours even while they give us their fragrance—wondering most when they give us most—that we should linger on an empty scene. It may indeed be monstrous but possibly courageous.

Courage is the thing. All goes if courage goes. What says our glorious Johnson of courage: "Unless a man has that virtue he has no security for preserving any other." We should thank our Creator three times daily for courage instead of for our bread, which, if we work, is surely the one thing we have a right to claim of Him. This courage is a proof of our immortality, greater even than gardens "when the eve is cool." Pray for it. "Who rises from prayer a better man, his prayer is answered." Be not merely courageous, but light-hearted and gay. There is an officer who was the first of our Army to land at Gallipoli. He was dropped overboard to light decoys on the shore,

388

so as to deceive the Turks as to where the landing was to be. He pushed a raft containing these in front of him. It was a frosty night, and he was naked and painted black. Firing from the ships was going on all around. It was a two-hours' swim in pitch darkness. He did it, crawled through the scrub to listen to the talk of the enemy, who were so near that he could have shaken hands with them, lit his decoys and swam back. He seems to look on this as a gay affair. He is a V.C. now, and you would not think to look at him that he could ever have presented such a disreputable appearance. Would you? (indicating Colonel Freyberg).

Those men of whom I have been speaking as the kind to fill the fife could all be light-hearted on occasion. I remember Scott by Highland streams trying to rouse me by maintaining that haggis is boiled bagpipes; Henley in dispute as to whether, say, Turgenieff or Tolstoi could hang the other on his watch-chain; he sometimes clenched the argument by casting his crutch at you; Stevenson responded in the same gay spirit by giving that crutch to John Silver; you remember with what adequate results. You must cultivate this lightheartedness if you are to hang your betters on your watch-chains. Dr. Johnson—let us have him again—does not seem to have discovered in his travels that the Scotts are a light-hearted nation. Boswell took him to task for saying that the death of Garrick had eclipsed the gaiety of nations. "Well, sir," Johnson said, "there may be occasions when it is permissible to," etc. But Boswell would not let go. "I cannot see, sir, how it could in any case have eclipsed the gaiety of nations, as England was the only nation before whom he had ever played." Johnson was really stymied, but you would never have known it. "Well, sir," he said, holding out, "I understand that Garrick once played in Scotland, and if Scotland has any gaiety to eclipse, which, sir, I deny——."

Prove Johnson wrong for once at the Students' Union and in your other societies. I much regret that there was no Students' Union at Edinburgh in my time. I hope you are fairly noisy and that members are sometimes led out. Do you keep to the old topics? King Charles's head; and Bacon wrote Shakespeare, or if he did not he missed the opportunity of his life. Don't forget to speak scornfully of the Victorian age; there will be time for meekness when you try to better it. Very soon you will be Victorian or that sort of thing yourselves; next session probably, when the freshmen come up. Afterwards, if you go in for my sort of calling, don't begin by thinking you are the last word in art; quite possibly you are not; steady yourselves by remembering that there were great men before William K. Smith. Make merry while you may. Yet lightheartedness is not for ever and a day. At its best it is the gay companion of innocence; and when innocence goes as go it must—they soon trip off together, looking for something younger. But courage comes all the way:

Fight on, my men, says Sir Andrew Barton,
I am hurt, but I am not slaine;
I'll lie me down and bleed a-while,
And then I'll rise and fight againe.

Another piece of advice; almost my last. For reasons you may guess I must give this in a low voice. Beware of M'Connachie. When I look in a mirror now it is his face I see. I speak with his voice. I once had a voice of my own, but nowadays I hear it from far away only, a melancholy, lonely, lost little pipe. I wanted to be an explorer, but he willed otherwise. You will all have your M'Connachies luring you off the high road. Unless you are constantly on the watch, you will find that he has slowly pushed you out of yourself and taken your place. He has rather done for me. I think in his youth he must somehow have guessed the future and been fleggit by it, flichtered from the nest like a bird, and so our eggs were left, cold. He has clung to me, less from mischief than for companionship; I half like him and his penny whistle; with all his faults he is as Scotch as peat; he whispered to me just now that you elected him, not me, as your Rector.

A final passing thought. Were an old student given an hour in which to revisit the St. Andrews of his day, would he spend more than half of it at lectures? He is more likely to be heard clattering up bare stairs in search of old companions. But if you could choose your hour from all the five hundred years of this seat of learning, wandering at your will from one age to another, how would you spend it? A fascinating theme; so many notable shades at once astir that St. Leonard's and St. Mary's grow murky with them. Hamilton, Melville, Sharpe, Chalmers, down to Herkless, that distinguished Principal, ripe scholar and warm friend, the loss of whom I deeply deplore with you. I think if that hour were mine, and though at St. Andrews he was but a passerby, I would give a handsome part of it to a walk with Dr. Johnson. I should like to have the time of day passed to me in twelve languages by the Admirable Crichton. A wave of the hand to Andrew Lang; and then for the archery butts with the gay Montrose, all a-

391

ruffled and ringed, and in the gallant St. Andrews studentmanner, continued as I understand to this present day, scattering largess as he rides along,

> But where is now the courtly troupe
> That once went riding by?
> I miss the curls of Canteloupe,
> The laugh of Lady Di.

We have still left time for a visit to a house in South Street, hard by St. Leonard's. I do not mean the house you mean. I am a Knox man. But little will that avail, for M'Connachie is a Queen Mary man. So, after all, it is at her door we chap, a last futile effort to bring that woman to heel. One more house of call, a student's room, also in South Street. I have chosen my student, you see, and I have chosen well; him that sang—

> Life has not since been wholly vain,
> And now I bear
> Of wisdom plucked from joy and pain
> Some slender share.

> But howsoever rich the store,
> I'd lay it down
> To feel upon my back once more
> The old red gown.

Well, we have at last come to an end. Some of you may remember when I began this address; we are all older now. I thank you for your patience. This is my first and last public appearance, and I never could or would have made it except to a gathering of Scottish students. If I have concealed my emotions in addressing you it is only the thrawn national way that deceives everybody except Scotsmen. I have not been as dull as I could have wished to be; but looking at your glowing faces cheerfulness and hope would keep breaking through. Despite the imperfections of your betters we leave you a great inheritance, for which others will one day call you to account. You come of a race of men the very wind of whose name has swept to the ultimate seas. Remember—

Heaven doth with us as we with torches do,
Not light them for themselves. . . .

Mighty are the Universities of Scotland, and they will prevail. But even in your highest exultations never forget that they are not four, but five. The greatest of them is the poor, proud homes you come out of, which said so long ago: "There shall be education in this land." She, not St. Andrews, is the oldest University in Scotland, and all the others are her whelps.

In bidding you good-bye, my last words must be of the lovely virtue. Courage, my children, and "greet the unseen with a cheer." "Fight on, my men," said Sir Andrew Barton. Fight on—you—for the old red gown till the whistle blows.

Invictus

William Ernest Henley
(1849–1903)

OUT OF the night that covers me,
　　Black as the pit from pole to pole,
I thank whatever gods may be,
　　For my unconquerable soul.

In the fell clutch of circumstance
　　I have not winced nor cried aloud.
Under the bludgeonings of chance
　　My head is bloody but unbowed.

Beyond this place of wrath and tears
　　Looms but the horror of the shade,
And yet the menace of the years
　　Finds and shall find me unafraid.

It matters not how strait the gate
　　How charged with punishments the scroll,
I am the master of my fate,
　　I am the captain of my soul.

If

Rudyard Kipling
(1865–1936)

IF YOU can keep your head when all about you
 Are losing theirs and blaming it on you,
If you can trust yourself when all men doubt you,
 But make allowances for their doubting too;
If you can wait and not be tired by waiting,
 Or being lied about, don't deal in lies,
Or being hated, don't give way to hating,
 And yet don't look too good, nor talk too wise:

If you can dream and not make dreams your master;
 If you can think—and not make thoughts your aim;
If you can meet with Triumph and Disaster
 And treat those two imposters just the same;
If you can bear to hear the truth you've spoken
 Twisted by knaves to make a trap for fools,
Or watch the things you gave your life to, broken,
 And stoop and build 'em up with worn-out tools:

If you can make one heap of all your winnings
 And risk it on one turn of pitch-and-toss,
And lose, and start again at your beginnings
 And never breathe a word about your loss;

If you can force your heart and nerve and sinew
    To serve your turn long after they are gone,
And so hold on when there is nothing in you
    Except the Will which says to them: "Hold on!"

If you can talk with crowds and keep your virtue,
    Or walk with Kings—nor lose the common touch,
If neither foes nor loving friends can hurt you;
    If all men count with you, but none too much;
If you can fill the unforgiving minute
    With sixty seconds' worth of distance run,
Yours is the Earth and everything that's in it,
    And—which is more—you'll be a Man, my son!

⚶

The Bridge Builder

Will Allen Dromgoole (d. 1934)

AN OLD MAN going a lone highway
Came at the evening, cold and gray,
To a chasm vast and wide and steep,
With waters rolling cold and deep.

The old man crossed in the twilight dim,
The sullen stream had no fears for him;
But he turned when safe on the other side,
And built a bridge to span the tide.

"Old man," said a fellow pilgrim near,
"You are wasting your strength with building here.
Your journey will end with the ending day,
You never again will pass this way.
You've crossed the chasm, deep and wide,
Why build you this bridge at eventide?"

The builder lifted his old gray head.
"Good friend, in the path I have come," he said,
"There followeth after me today
A youth whose feet must pass this way.
The chasm that was as nought to me
To that fair-haired youth may a pitfall be;
He, too, must cross in the twilight dim—
Good friend, I am building this bridge for him."

"ACRES OF DIAMONDS" is the title of a speech given by Russell H. Conwell in the latter half of the nineteenth century. Records show that it was delivered over six thousand times in all parts of the country.

Full of Yankee sagacity and values, the speech proclaims that opportunity is waiting everywhere and all the time.

Some authorities have suggested that this speech helped create the American free enterprise system. It could very well have had that impact; Dr. Conwell was immensely popular and attracted large crowds.

Following service in the Civil War, Dr. Conwell had a distinguished career as a down-to-earth speaker and preacher in Philadelphia, Pennsylvania. He was the founder and first president of Temple University.

Acres of Diamonds

Russell H. Conwell (1843–1925)

WHEN GOING DOWN the Tigris and Euphrates rivers many years ago with a party of English travelers I found myself under the direction of an Arab guide whom we hired at Baghdad. He thought that it was not only his duty to guide us down those rivers, and do what he was paid for doing, but also to entertain us with stories curious and weird, ancient and modern, strange and familiar. Many of them I have forgotten, but there is one I shall never forget.

"I will tell you a story now which I reserve for my particular friends." When he emphasized the words "particular friends," I listened and I have ever been glad I did. There once lived not far from the River Indus an ancient Persian by the name of Ali Hafed. He said that Ali Hafed owned a very large farm, that he had orchards, grain fields, and gardens; that he had money at interest, and was a wealthy and contented man. He was contented because he was wealthy, and wealthy because he was contented.

One day there visited that old Persian farmer one of those ancient Buddhist priests, one of the wise men of the East. He sat down by the fire and told the old farmer how this world of ours was made. He said that this world was once a mere bank of fog, and that the Almighty thrust His finger into this bank of fog, and began slowly to move His finger around, increasing the speed until at last He whirled this bank of fog into a solid ball of fire. Then it went rolling through the universe, burning its way through other banks of fog, and condensed the moisture without, until it fell in floods of rain upon its hot surface, and cooled the outward crust. Then the internal fires bursting outward through the crust threw up the mountains and hills, the valleys, the plains and prairies of this wonderful world of ours. If this internal molten mass came bursting out and cooled very quickly it became granite; less quickly copper, less quickly silver, less quickly gold, and, after gold, diamonds were made.

Said the old priest, "A diamond is a congealed drop of sunlight." Now that is literally scientifically true, that a diamond is an actual deposit of carbon from the sun. The old priest told Ali Hafed that if he had one diamond the size of his thumb he could purchase the country, and if he had a mine of diamonds he could place his children upon thrones through the influence of their great wealth.

Ali Hafed heard all about diamonds, how much they were worth, and went to his bed that night a poor man. He had not lost anything, but he was poor because he was discontented, and discontented because he feared he was poor. He said, "I want a mine of diamonds," and he lay awake all night.

Early in the morning he sought out the priest. Ali Hafed said to him: "Will you tell me where I can find diamonds?"

"Diamonds! What do you want with diamonds?" "Why, I wish to be immensely rich." "Well, then, go along and find them. That is all you have to do; go and find them, and then you have them." "But I don't know where to go." "Well, if you will find a river that runs through white sands, between high mountains, in those white sands you will always find diamonds." "I don't believe there is any such river." "Oh yes, there are plenty of them. All you have to do is to go and find them, and then you have them." Said Ali Hafed, "I will go."

So he sold his farm, collected his money, left his family in charge of a neighbor, and away he went in search of diamonds. He began his search at the Mountains of the Moon. Afterward he came around into Palestine, then wandered on into Europe, and at last when his money was well spent and he was in rags, wretchedness, and poverty, he stood on the shore of that bay at Barcelona, in Spain, when a great tidal wave came rolling in between the pillars of Hercules, and the poor, afflicted, suffering, dying man could not resist the awful temptation to cast himself into that incoming tide, and he sank beneath its foaming crest, never to rise in this life again.

When that old guide had told me that awfully sad story he stopped the camel I was riding on and went back to fix the baggage that was coming off another camel, and I had an opportunity to muse over his story while he was gone. I remember saying to myself, "Why did he reserve that story for his 'particular friends'?" There seemed to be no beginning, no middle, no end, nothing to it. That was the first story I had ever heard told in my life, and would be the first one I ever read, in which the hero was killed in the first chapter. I had but one chapter of that story, and the hero was dead.

When the guide came back and took up the halter of my camel, he went right ahead with the story, into the second chapter, just as though there had been no break. The man who purchased Ali Hafed's farm one day led his camel into the garden to drink, and as that camel put its nose into the shallow water of that garden brook, Ali Hafed's successor noticed a curious flash of light from the white sands of the stream. He pulled out a black stone having an eye of light reflecting all the hues of the rainbow. He took the pebble into the house and put it on the mantel which covers the central fires, and forgot all about it.

A few days later this same old priest came in to visit Ali Hafed's successor, and the moment he opened that drawing room door he saw that flash of light on the mantel, and he rushed up to it, and shouted: "Here is a diamond! Has Ali Hafed returned?" "Oh no, Ali Hafed has not returned, and that is not a diamond. That is nothing but a stone we found right out here in our own garden." "But," said the priest, "I tell you I know a diamond when I see it. I know positively that is a diamond."

Then together they rushed out into that old garden and stirred up the white sands with their fingers, and lo! there came up other more beautiful and valuable gems than the first. "Thus," said the guide to me, and, friends, it is historically true, "was discovered the most magnificent diamond mine in all the history of mankind, excelling the Kimberly itself. The Kohinoor, and the Orloff of the crown jewels of England and Russia, the largest on earth, came from that mine."

When that old Arab guide told me the second chapter of his story, he then took off his Turkish cap and swung it around in the air again to get my attention to the moral. As he swung his hat, he said, "Had Ali Hafed remained at home and dug in his own cellar, or underneath his own wheat fields, or in his own garden, instead of wretchedness, starvation, and death by suicide in a strange land, he would have had 'acres of diamonds.' For every acre of that old farm, yes, every shovelful, afterward revealed gems which since have decorated the crowns of monarchs."

When he had added the moral to his story I saw why he reserved it for "his particular friends." But I did not tell him I could see it. It was that mean old Arab's way of going around a thing like a lawyer, to say indirectly what he did not dare say directly, that "in his private opinion there was a certain young man then traveling down the Tigris River that might better be at home in America." I did not tell him I could see that, but I told him his story reminded me of one, and I told it to him quick, and I think I will tell it to you.

I told him of a man out in California in 1847, who owned a ranch. He heard they had discovered gold in southern California, and so with a passion for gold he sold his ranch to Colonel Sutter, and away he went, never to come back. Colonel Sutter put a mill upon a stream that ran through that ranch, and one day his little girl brought some wet sand from the raceway into their home and sifted it through her fingers before the fire, and in that falling sand a visitor saw the first shining scales of real gold that were ever discovered in California. The man who had owned the ranch wanted gold, and he could have secured it for the mere taking. Indeed, thirty-eight millions of dollars has been taken out of a very few acres since then. About eight years ago I delivered this lecture in a city that stands on that farm, and they told me that a one-third owner for years and years had been getting one hundred and twenty dollars in gold every fifteen minutes, sleeping or waking.

But a better illustration really than that occurred here in our own Pennsylvania. If there is anything I enjoy above another on the platform, it is to get one of these German audiences in Pennsylvania before me, and fire that at them, and I enjoy it tonight. There was a man living in Pennsylvania, not unlike some Pennsylvanians you have seen who owned a farm, and he did with that farm just what I should do with a farm if I owned one in Pennsylvania—he sold it. But before he sold it he decided to secure employment collecting coal oil for his cousin, who was in the business in Canada, where they first discovered oil on this continent. They dipped it from the running streams at that early time. So this Pennsylvania farmer wrote to his cousin asking for employment. You see, friends, this farmer was not altogether a foolish man. No, he was not. He did not leave his farm until he had something else to do. *Of all the simpletons the stars shine on I don't know of a worse one than the man who leaves one job before he has gotten another.* When he wrote to his cousin for employment, his cousin replied, "I cannot engage you because you know nothing about the oil business."

Well, then the old farmer said, "I will know," and with most commendable zeal he set himself to the study of the whole subject. He began away back at the second day of God's creation when this world was covered thick and deep with that rich vegetation which since has turned to the primitive beds of coal. He studied the subject until he found that the drainings really of those rich beds of coal furnished the coal oil that was worth pumping, and then he found how it came up with the living springs. He studied until he knew what it looked like, smelled like, tasted like, and how to refine it. Now said he in his letter to his cousin, "I understand the oil business." His cousin answered, "All right, come on."

So he sold his farm, according to the county record, for $833 (even money, "no cents"). He had scarcely gone from that place before the man who purchased the spot went out to arrange for the watering of the cattle. He found the previous owner had gone out years before and put a plank across the brook back of the barn, edgewise into the surface of the water just a few inches. The purpose of that plank at that sharp angle across the brook was to throw over to the other bank a dreadful-looking scum through which the cattle would not put their noses. But with that plank there to throw it all over to one side, the cattle would drink below, and thus that man who had gone to Canada had been himself damming back for twenty-three years a flood of coal oil which the state geologists of Pennsylvania declared to us ten years later was even then worth a hundred millions of dollar to our state, and four years ago our geologists declared the discovery to be worth to our state a thousand millions of dollars. The man who owned that territory on which the city of Titusville now stands, and those Pleasantville valleys, had studied the subject from the second day of God's creation clear down to the present time. He studied it until he knew all about it, and yet he is said to have sold the whole of it for $833, and again I say, "no sense."

But I need another illustration. I found it in Massachusetts, and I am sorry I did because that is the state I came from. This young man in Massachusetts furnishes just another phase of my thought. He went to Yale College and studied mines and mining, and became such an adept as a mining engineer that he was employed by the authorities of the university to train students who were behind in their classes. During his senior year he earned $15 a week for doing that work. When he graduated they raised his pay from $15 to $45 a week, and offered him a professorship, and as soon as they did he went right home to his mother. *If they had raised that boy's pay from $15 to $15.60 he would have stayed and been proud of the place, but when they put it up to $45 at one leap, he said, "Mother, I won't work for $45 a week. The idea of man with a brain like mine working for $45 a week!* Let's go to California and stake out gold mines and silver mines, and be immensely rich."

Said his mother, "Now, Charlie, it is just as well to be happy as it is to be rich."

"Yes," said Charlie, "but it is just as well to be rich and happy, too." And they were both right about it. As he was an only son and she a widow, of course he had his way. They always do.

They sold out in Massachusetts, and instead of going to California, they went to Wisconsin, where he went into the employ of the Superior Copper Mining Company at $15 a week again, but with the proviso in his contract that he should have an interest in any mines he should discover for the company.

He had scarcely gotten out of the old homestead before the succeeding owner went out to dig potatoes. The potatoes were already growing in the ground when he bought the farm, and as the old farmer was bringing in a basket of potatoes it hugged very tight to the ends of the stone fence. When that basket hugged so tight he set it down on the ground, and then dragged on one side, and pulled on the other side, and this farmer noticed in the upper and outer corner of that stone wall, right next the gate, a block of native silver eight inches square. That professor of mines, mining, and mineralogy who knew so much about the subject that he would not work for $45 a week, when he sold that homestead in Massachusetts sat right on that silver.

My friends, that mistake is very universally made, and why should we even smile at him. I often wonder what has become of him.

As I come here tonight and look around this audience I am seeing again what through these fifty years I have continually seen—men that are making precisely that same mistake. I say to you that you have "acres of diamonds" in Philadelphia right where you now live. "Oh," but you will say, "you cannot know much about our city if you think there are any 'acres of diamonds' here." But if you do not have the actual diamond mines literally you have all that would be good for you to have.

Again I say that the opportunity to get rich, to attain unto great wealth, is here in Philadelphia now, within the reach of almost every man and woman who hears me speak tonight, and I mean just what I say. I have not come to this platform to recite something to you. I have come to tell you what is in God's sight I believe to be the truth, and if the years of life have been of any value to me in the attainment of common sense, I know I am right; that the men and women sitting here have within their reach "acres of diamonds." There never was a place on earth more adapted than the city of Philadelphia today, and never in the history of the world did a poor man without capital have such an opportunity to get rich quickly and honestly as he has now in our city. I say it is the truth, and I want you to accept it as such; for if you think I have come to simply recite something that happened elsewhere, then I would better not be here. I have no time to waste in any such talk, but to say the things I believe, and unless some of you get richer for what I am saying tonight my time is wasted.

I say that you ought to get rich, and it is your duty to get rich. How many of my pious brethren say to me, "Do you, a Christian minister, spend your time going up and down the country advising young people to get rich, to get money?" "Yes, of course I do." They say, "Isn't that awful! Why don't you preach the gospel instead of preaching about man's making money?" "Because to make money honestly is to preach the gospel." That is the reason. The men who get rich may be the most honest men you find in the community.

"Oh," but says some young man here tonight, "I have been told all my life that if a person has money he is very dishonest and dishonorable and mean and contemptible." My friend, that is the reason why you have none, because you have that idea of people. The foundation of your faith is altogether false. Let me say here clearly, and say it briefly, though subject to discussion which I have not time for here, ninety-eight out of one hundred of the rich men of America are honest. That is why they are rich. That is why they are trusted with money. That is why they carry on great enterprises and find plenty of people to work with them. It is because they are honest men.

My friend, you take and drive me out into the suburbs of Philadelphia, and introduce me to the people who own their homes around this great city, those beautiful homes with gardens and flowers, those magnificent homes so lovely in their art, and I will introduce you to the very best people in character as well as in enterprise in our city, and you know I will.

Money is power, and you ought to be reasonably ambitious to have it. You ought because you can do more good with it than you could without it. Money printed your Bible, money builds your churches, money sends your missionaries, and money pays for preachers, and you would not have many of them, either, if you did not pay them.

I say, then, you ought to have money. If you can honestly attain riches in Philadelphia, it is your Christian and godly duty to do so. It is an awful mistake of these pious people to think you must be awfully poor in order to be pious.

Some men say, "Don't you sympathize with the poor people?" Of course I do, or else I would not have been lecturing these years. I won't give in but what I sympathize with the poor, but the number of poor who are to be sympathized with is very small. To sympathize with a man whom God has punished for his sins, thus to help him when God would still continue to a just punishment, is to do wrong, no doubt about it, and we do that more than we help those who are deserving. While we should sympathize with God's poor—that is, those who cannot help themselves—let us remember there is not a poor person in the United States who was not made poor by his own shortcomings, or by the shortcomings of someone else. It is all wrong to be poor, anyhow. Let us give in to that argument and pass that to one side.

A gentleman gets up back there, and says, "Don't you think there are some things in world that are better than money?" Of course I do. Some things in this world that are higher and sweeter and purer than money. Love is the grandest thing on God's earth, but fortunate the lover who has plenty of money. Money is power, money is force, money will do good as well as harm. In the hands of good men and women it could accomplish, and it has accomplished, good.

I heard a man get up in a prayer meeting in our city and thank the Lord he was "one of God's poor." Well, I wonder what his wife thinks about that? She earns all the money that comes into that house, and he smokes a part of that on the veranda. I don't want to see any more of the Lord's poor of that kind, and I don't believe the Lord does. And yet there are some people who think in order to be pious you must be awfully poor. That does not follow at all. While we sympathize with the poor, let us not teach a doctrine like that.

Yet the age is prejudiced against advising a Christian man from attaining unto wealth. The prejudice is so universal and the years are far enough back, I think, for me to safely mention that years ago up at Temple

University there was a young man in our theological school who thought he was the only pious student in that department. He came into my office one evening and sat down by my desk, and said to me: "Mr. President, I think it is my duty sir, to come in and labor with you." "What has happened now?" Said he, "I heard you say at the Academy, at the Peirce School commencement, that you thought it was an honorable ambition for a young man to desire to have wealth, and that you thought it made him temperate, made him anxious to have a good name, and made him industrious. You spoke about man's ambition to have money helping to make him a good man. Sir, I have come to tell you the Holy Bible says that 'money is the root of all evil.'"

I told him I had never seen it in the Bible, and advised him to go out into the chapel and get the Bible, and show me the place. So out he went, and soon stalked into my office with Bible open, with all the bigoted pride of the narrow sectarian, or of one who founds his Christianity on some misinterpretation of Scripture. He flung the Bible down on my desk, and fairly squealed into my ear: "There it is, Mr. President; you can read it for yourself." I said to him: "Take that Bible and read it yourself, and give the proper emphasis to it."

He took the Bible, and proudly read, "'The love of money is the root of all evil.'"

When he quoted it right, of course he quoted the absolute truth. "The *love* of money is the root of all evil." He who tries to attain unto it too quickly, or dishonestly, will fall into many snares, no doubt about that. The love of money. What is that? It is making an idol of money, and idolatry pure and simple everywhere is condemned by the Holy Scriptures and by man's common sense. The man that worships the dollar instead of thinking of the purposes for which it ought to be used, the man who idolizes simply money, the miser that hoards his money in the cellar, or hides it in his stocking, or refuses to invest it where it will do the world good, that man who hugs the dollar until the eagle squeals has in him the root of all evil.

I think I will leave that behind me now and answer the question of nearly all of you who are asking, "Is there opportunity to get rich in Philadelphia?" Well, now, how simple a thing it is to see where it is, and the instant you see where it is it is yours. Some old gentleman gets up back there and says, "Mr. Conwell, have you lived in Philadelphia for thirty-one years and don't know that the time has gone by when you can make anything in this city?" "No, I don't think it is." "Yes, it is; I have tried it." "What business are you in?" "I kept a store here for twenty years, and never made over a thousand dollars in the whole twenty years."

"Well, then, you can measure the good you have been to this city by what this city has paid you, because a man can judge very well what he is worth by what he received. If you have not made over a thousand dollars in twenty years in Philadelphia, it would have been better for Philadelphia if they had kicked you out of the city nineteen years and nine months ago. A man has no right to keep a store in Philadelphia twenty years and not make at least five hundred thousand dollars, even though it be a corner grocery uptown." You say, "You cannot make five thousand dollars in a store now." Oh, my friends, if you will just take only four blocks around you, and find out what the people want and what you ought to supply and set them down with your pencil, and figure up the profits you would make if you did supply them, you would very soon see it. There is wealth right within the sound of your voice.

Someone says: "You don't know anything about business. A preacher never knows a thing about business." Well, then, I will have to prove that I am an expert. I don't like to do this, but I have to do it because my testimony will not be taken if I am not an expert. My father kept a country store, and if there is any place under the stars where a man gets all sorts of experience in every kind of mercantile transactions, it is in the country store. I am not proud of my experience, but sometimes when my father was away he would leave me in charge of the store, though fortunately for him that was not very often. But this did occur many times, friends: A man would come in the store, and say to me, "Do you keep jackknives?" "No, we don't keep jackknives," and I went off whistling a tune. Why did I care about the man anyhow? Then another farmer would come in and say, "Do you keep jackknives?" "No, we don't keep jackknives." Then I went away and whistled another tune. Then a third man came in the door and said, "Do you keep jackknives?" "No, Why is every one around here asking for jackknives? Do you suppose we are keeping this store to supply the whole neighborhood with jackknives?" Do you carry on your store like that in Philadelphia? The difficulty was I had not then learned that the foundation of godliness and the foundation principle of success in business are both the same precisely. The man who says, "I cannot carry my religion into business" advertises himself either as being an imbecile in business, or on the road to bankruptcy, or a thief, one of the three, sure. He will fail within a very few years. He certainly will if he doesn't carry his religion into business. If I had been carrying on my father's store on a Christian plan, godly plan, I would have had a jackknife for the third man when he called for it. Then I would have actually done him a kindness, and I would have received a reward myself, which it would have been my duty to take.

There are some over-pious people who think if you take a profit on anything you sell that you are an unrighteous man. On the contrary, you would be a criminal to sell goods for less than they cost. You have no right to do that. You cannot trust a man with your money who cannot take care of his own. You cannot trust a man in your family who is not true to his own wife. You cannot trust a man in the world who does not begin with his own heart, his own character, and his own life.

The man over there who said he could not make anything in a store in Philadelphia has been carrying on his store on the wrong principle. Suppose I go into your store tomorrow morning and ask, "Do you know neighbor A, who lives one square away, at house No. 1240?" "Oh yes, I have met him. He deals here at the corner store." "Where did he come from?" "I don't know." "How many does he have in his family?" "I don't know." "What church does he go to?" "I don't know, and don't care. What are you asking all these questions for?"

If you had a store in Philadelphia would you answer me like that? If so, then you are conducting your business just as I carried on my father's business in Worthington, Massachusetts. You don't know where your neighbor came from when he moved to Philadelphia, and you don't care. If you had cared you would be a rich man now. If you had cared enough about him to take an interest in his affairs, to find out what he needed, you would have been rich. But you go through the world saying, "No opportunity to get rich," and there is the fault right at your own door.

But another young man gets up over there and says, "I cannot take up the mercantile business." (While I am talking to trade it applies to every occupation.) "Why can't you go into the mercantile business?" "Because I haven't any capital." Oh, the weak and dudish creature that can't see over its collar! It makes a person weak to see these little dudes standing around the corners and saying, "Oh, if I had plenty of capital, how rich I would get." "Young man, do you think you are going to get rich on capital?" "Certainly." Well, I say, "Certainly not." If your mother has plenty of money, and she will set you up in business, you will "set her up in business," supplying you with capital.

The moment a young man or woman gets more money than he or she has grown to by practical experience, that moment he has gotten a curse. It is no help to a young man or woman to inherit money. It is no help to your children to leave them money, but if you leave them education, if you leave them Christian and noble character, if you leave them a wide circle of friends, if you leave them an honorable name, it is far better than that they should have money. There is no class of people to be pitied so much as the inexperienced sons and daughters of the rich of our generation.

One of the best things in our life is when a young man has earned his own living, and when he becomes engaged to some lovely young woman, and makes up his mind to have a home of his own. Then with that same love comes also that divine inspiration toward better things, and he begins to save his money. He begins to leave off his bad habits and put money in the bank. When he has a few hundred dollars he goes out in the suburbs to look for a home. He goes to the savings bank, perhaps, for half of the value, and then goes for his wife, and when he takes his bride over the threshold of that door for the first time he says in words of eloquence my voice can never touch: "I have earned this home myself. It is all mine, and I divide with thee." That is the grandest moment a human heart may ever know.

But a rich man's son can never know that. He takes his bride into a finer mansion, it may be, but he is obliged to go all the way through it and say to his wife, "My mother gave me that, my mother gave me that, and my mother gave me this," until his wife wishes she had married his mother. I pity the rich man's son.

The statistics of Massachusetts showed that not one rich man's son out of seventeen ever dies rich. I pity the rich man's sons unless they have the good sense of the elder Vanderbilt, which sometimes happens. He went to his father and said, "Did you earn all your money?" "I did, my son. I began to work on a ferry boat for twenty-five cents a day." "Then," said the son, "I will have none of your money," and he, too, tried to get employment on a ferry boat that Saturday night. He could not get one there, but he did get a place for three dollars a week.

Of course, if a rich man's son will do that, he will get the discipline of a poor boy that is worth more than a university education to any man. He would then be able to take care of the millions of his father. But as a rule the rich men will not let their sons do the very thing that made them great. As a rule, the rich man will not allow his son to work—and his mother!

Why, she would think it was a social disgrace if her poor, weak, little lily-fingered, sissy sort of a boy had to earn his living with honest toil. I have no pity for such rich men's sons.

At a banquet here in Philadelphia there sat beside me a kindhearted young man, and he said, "Mr. Conwell, you have been sick for two or three years. When you go out, take my limousine, and it will take you up to your house on Broad Street." I thanked him very much, and perhaps I ought not to mention the incident in this way, but I follow the facts. I got on to the seat with the driver of that limousine, outside, and when we were going up I asked the driver, "How much did this limousine cost?" "Six thousand eight hundred, and he had to pay the duty on it." "Well," I said, "does the owner of this machine ever drive it himself?" At that the chauffeur laughed so heartily that he lost control of his machine. He was so surprised at the question that he ran up on the sidewalk, and around a corner lamppost out into the street again. And when he got out into the street he laughed till the whole machine trembled. He said: "He drive this machine! Oh, he would be lucky if he knew enough to get out when we get there."

I must tell you about a rich man's son at Niagara Falls. I came in from the lecture to the hotel, and as I approached the desk of the clerk there stood a millionaire's son from New York. He was an indescribable specimen of anthropologic potency. He had a skullcap on one side of his head, with a gold tassel in the top of it, and a gold-headed cane under his arm with more in it than in his head. It is a very difficult thing to describe that young man. He wore an eyeglass that he could not see through, patent-

416

leather boots that he could not walk in, and pants that he could not sit down in—dressed like a grasshopper.

This human cricket came up to the clerk's desk just as I entered, adjusted his unseeing eyeglass, and spake in this wise to the clerk. You see, he thought it was "Hinglist, you know," to lisp. "Thir, will you have the kindness to supply me with thome papah and enwelops!" The hotel clerk measured that man quick, and he pulled the envelopes and paper out of a drawer, threw them across the counter toward the young man, and then turned away to his books.

You should have seen that young man when those envelopes came across that counter. He swelled up like a gobbler turkey, adjusted his unseeing eyeglass and yelled: "Come right back here. Now thir, will you order a thervant to take that papah and enwelophs to yondah dethk." Oh, the poor, miserable, contemptible American monkey! He could not carry paper and envelopes twenty feet. I suppose he could not get his arms down to do it. I have no pity for such travesties upon human nature. If you have not capital, young man, I am glad of it. What you need is common sense, not copper cents.

The best thing I can do is to illustrate by actual facts well known to you all. A. T. Stewart, a poor boy in New York, had $1.50 to begin life on. He lost 87$\frac{1}{2}$ cents of that on the very first venture. How fortunate that young man who loses the first time he gambles. That boy said, "I will never gamble again in business," and he never did. How came he to lose 87$\frac{1}{2}$ cents? You probably all know the story how he lost it—because he bought some

417

needles, threads, and buttons to sell which people did not want, and had them left on his hands, a dead loss. Said the boy, "I will not lose any more money in that way." Then he went around first to the doors and asked the people what they did want. Then when he had found out what they wanted he invested his $62^1/2$ cents to supply a known demand.

Study it wherever you choose—in business, in your profession, in your housekeeping, whatever your life, that one thing is the secret of success. You must first know the demand. You must first know what people need, and then invest yourself where you are most needed. A. T. Stewary went on that principle until he was worth what amounted afterward to forty millions of dollars, owning the very store in which Mr. Wanamaker carries on his great work in New York. His fortune was made by his losing something, which taught him the greatest lesson that he must only invest himself or his money in something that people need. When will you salesmen learn it? When will you manufacturers learn that you must know the changing needs of humanity if you would succeed in life? Apply yourselves, all you Christian people, as manufacturers or merchants or workmen to supply that human need. It is a great principle as broad as humanity and as deep as the Scripture itself.

The best illustration I ever heard was of John Jacob Astor. You know that he made the money of the Astor family when he lived in New York. He came across the sea in debt for his fare. But that poor boy with nothing in his pocket made a fortune of the Astor family on one principle. Some young man here tonight will say, "Well, they could make those fortunes over in New York, but they could not do it in Philadelphia!" My friends, did you ever read that wonderful book of Riis (his memory is sweet to us because of his recent death), wherein is given his statistical account of the records taken in 1889 of 107 millionaires of New York? If you read the account you will see that out of the 107 millionaires only seven made their money in New York. Out of the 107 millionaires worth ten million dollars in real estate then, 67 of them made their money in towns of less than 3,500 inhabitants. It makes not so much difference where you are as who you are. But if you cannot get rich in Philadelphia you certainly cannot do it in New York.

Now John Jacob Astor illustrated what can be done anywhere. He had a mortgage once on a millinery store, and they could not sell bonnets enough to pay the interest on his money. So he foreclosed that mortgage, took possession of the store, and went into partnership with the very same people, in the same store, with the same capital. He did not give them a dollar of capital. They had to sell goods to get any money.

Then he left them alone in the store just as they had been before, and he went out and sat down on a bench in the park in the shade. What was John Jacob Astor doing out there, and in partnership with people who had failed on his own hands? He had the most important and, to my mind, the most pleasant part of that partnership on his hands. For as John Jacob Astor sat on that bench he was watching the ladies as they went by; and where is the man who would not get rich at that business? As he sat on the bench if a lady passed him with her shoulders back and head up, and looked straight to the front, as if she did not care if all the world did gaze on her, then he studied her bonnet, and by the time it was out of sight he knew the shape of the frame, the color of the trimmings, and the crinklings in the feather. But in John Jacob Astor's day there was some art about the millinery business, and he went to the millinery store and said to them: "Now put into the show window just such a bonnet as I describe to you, because I have already seen a lady who likes such a bonnet. Don't make up any more until I come back." Then he went out and sat down again, and another lady passed him of a different form, of different complexion, with a different shape and color of bonnet. "Now," said he, "put such a bonnet as that in the show window." He did not fill his show window with a lot of hats and bonnets to drive people away, and then sit on the backstairs and bawl because people went to Wanamaker's to trade. He did not have a hat or a bonnet in that show window but what some lady liked before it was made up.

The tide of custom began immediately to turn in, and that has been the foundation of the greatest store in New York in that line, and still exists as one of three stores. Its fortune was made by John Jacob Astor after they had failed in business, not by giving them any more money, but by finding out what the ladies liked for bonnets before they wasted any material in making them up. I tell you if a man could foresee the millinery business he could foresee anything under heaven!

Suppose I were to go through this audience tonight and ask you in this great manufacturing city if there are not opportunities to get rich in manufacturing. "Oh yes," some young man says, "there are opportunities here still if you build with some trust and if you have two or three millions of dollars to begin with as capital." Young man, the history of the breaking up of the trusts that attach upon "big business" is only illustrating what is now the opportunity of the smaller man. The time never came in the history of the world when you get rich so quickly manufacturing without capital as you can now.

But you will say, "You cannot do anything of the kind. You cannot start without capital." Young man, let me illustrate for a moment. I must do it. It is my duty to every young man and woman, because we are all going into business very soon on the same plan. Young man, remember, if you know what people need you have gotten more knowledge of a fortune than any amount of capital can give you.

There was a poor man out of work living in Hingham, Massachusetts. He lounged around the house until one day his wife told him to get out and work, and, as he lived in Massachusetts, he obeyed his wife. He went out and sat down on the shore of the bay, and whittled a soaked shingle into a wooden chain. His children that evening quarreled over it, and he whittled a second one to keep peace.

While he was whittling the second one a neighbor came in and said: "Why don't you whittle toys and sell them? You could make money at that." "Oh," he said, "I would not know what to make." "Why don't you ask your own children right here in your own house what to make?" "What is the use of trying that?" said the man. "My children are different from other people's children." (I used to see people like that when I taught school.) But he acted upon the hint, and the next morning when Mary came down the stairway, he asked, "What do you want for a toy?" She began to tell him she would like a doll's bed, a doll's washstand, a doll's carriage, a little doll's umbrella, and went on with a list of things that would take him a lifetime to supply. So, consulting his own children, in his own house, he took the firewood, for he had no money to buy lumber, and whittled those strong, unpainted Hingham toys that were for so many years known all over the world.

That man began to make those toys for his own children, and then made copies and sold them through the boot-and-shoe store next door. He began to make a little money, and then a little more, and Mr. Lawson, in his *Frenzied Finance* says that man is the richest man in Massachusetts, and I think it is the truth. And that man is worth a hundred millions of dollars today, and has been only thirty-four years making it on that one principle— that one must judge that what his own children like at home other people's children would like in their homes, too; to judge the human heart by oneself, by one's wife or by one's children. It is the royal road to success in manufacturing. "Oh," but you say, "didn't he have any capital?" Yes, a penknife, but I don't know that he had paid for that.

I spoke thus to an audience in New Britain, Connecticut, and a lady four seats back went home and tried to take off her collar, and the collar button stuck in the buttonhole. She threw it out and said, "I am going to get something better than that to put on collars." Her husband said: "After what Conwell said tonight, you see there is a need of an improved collar fastener that is easier to handle. There is a human need; there is a great fortune. Now, then, get up a collar button and get rich." He made fun of her, and consequently made fun of me.

When her husband ridiculed her, she made up her mind she would make a better collar button, and when a woman makes up her mind "she will," and does not say anything about it, she does it. It was that New England woman who invented the snap button which you find anywhere now. It was first a collar button with a spring cap attached to the outer side. Any of you who wear modern waterproofs know the button that simply pushes together, and when you unbutton it you simply pull it apart. That is the button to which I refer, and which she invented. She afterward invented several other buttons, and then invested in more, and then was taken into partnership with great factories. Now that woman goes over the sea every summer in her private steamship—yes, and takes her husband with her! If her husband were to die, she would have money enough left now to buy a foreign duke or count for some such title as that at the latest quotations.

Now what is my lesson in that incident? It is this: I told her then, though I did not know her, what I now say to you. "Your wealth is too near to you. You are looking right over it"; and she had to look over it because it was right under her chin.

I have read in the newspaper that a woman never invented anything. Well, that newspaper ought to begin again. Of course, I do not refer to gossip—I refer to machines—and if I did I might better include the men. That newspaper could never appear if women had not invented something. Friends, think. Ye women, think! You say you cannot make a fortune because you are in some laundry, or running a sewing machine, it may be, or walking before some loom, and yet you can be a millionaire if you will but follow this almost infallible direction.

When you say a woman doesn't invent anything, I ask, who invented the Jacquard. The printer's roller, the printing press, were invented by farmer's wives. Who invented the cotton gin of the South that enriched our country so amazingly? Mrs. General Greene invented the cotton gin and showed the idea to Mr. Whitney, and he, like a man, seized it. Who was it that invented the sewing machine? If I would go to school tomorrow and ask your children they would say, "Elias Howe."

He was in the Civil War with me, and often in my tent, and I often heard him say that he worked fourteen years to get up that sewing machine. But his wife made up her mind one day that they would starve to death if there wasn't something or other invented pretty soon, and so in two hours she invented the sewing machine. Of course he took out the patent in his name. Men always do that. Who was it that invented the mower and the reaper? According to Mr. McCormick's confidential communications, so recently published, it was a West Virginia woman, who, after his father and he had failed altogether in making a reaper and gave it up, took a lot of shears and nailed them together on the edge of a board, with one shaft of each pair loose, and then wired them so that when she pulled the wire the other way it opened them, and there she had the principle of the mowing machine.

If you look at a mowing machine, you will see it is nothing but a lot of shears. If a woman can invent a mowing machine, if a woman can invent a Jacquard loom, if a woman can invent a cotton gin, if a woman can invent a trolley switch—as she did and made the trolleys possible; if a woman can invent, as Mr. Carnegie said, the great iron squeezers that laid the foundation of all the steel millions of the United States, "we men" can invent anything under the stars! I say that for the encouragement of the men.

Who are the great inventors of the world? Again this lesson comes before us. The great inventor sits next to you, or you are the person yourself. "Oh," but you will say, "I have never invented anything in my life." Neither did the great inventors until they discovered one great secret. Do you think it is a man with a head like a bushel measure or a man like a stroke of lightning? It is neither. The really great man is a plain, straightforward, everyday, common-sense man. You would not dream that he was a great inventor if you did not see something he had actually done. His neighbors do not regard him so great. You never see anything great over your back fence. You say there is no greatness among your neighbors. It is all away off somewhere else. Their greatness is ever so simple, so plain, so earnest, so practical, that the neighbors and friends never recognize it.

True greatness is often unrecognized. That is sure. You do not know anything about the greatest men and women. I went out to write the life of General Garfield, and a neighbor, knowing I was in a hurry, and as there was a great crowd around the front door, took me around to General Garfield's back door and shouted, "Jim! Jim!" And very soon "Jim" came to the door and let me in, and I wrote the biography of one of the grandest men of the nation, and yet he was just some old "Jim" to his neighbor. If you know a great man in Philadelphia and you should meet him tomorrow, you would say, "How are you, Sam?" or "Good morning, Jim." Of course you would. That is just what you would do.

One of my soldiers in the Civil War had been sentenced to death, and I went up to the White House in Washington—went there for the first time in my life—to see the President Abraham Lincoln. I went into the waiting room and sat down with a lot of others on the benches, and the secretary asked one after another to tell him what they wanted. After the secretary had been through the line, he went in, and then came back to the door and motioned for me. I went up to the anteroom, and the secretary said: "That is the President's door right over there. Just rap on it and go right in." I never was so taken aback, friends, in all my life, never. The secretary himself made it worse for me, because he had told me how to go in and then went out another door to the left and shut that.

There I was, in the hallway by myself before the President of the United States of America's door. I had been on fields of battle, where the shells did sometimes shriek and the bullets did sometimes hit me, but I always wanted to run. I have no sympathy with the old man who says, "I would just as soon march up to the cannon's mouth as eat my dinner." I have no faith in a man who doesn't know enough to be afraid when he is being shot at. I never was so afraid when the shells came around us at Antietam as I was when I went into that room that day; but I finally mustered the courage—I don't know how I ever did—and at arm's length tapped on the door. The man inside did not help me at all, but yelled out, "Come in and sit down!"

Well, I went in and sat down on the edge of a chair, and wished I were in Europe, and the man at the table did not look up. He was one of the world's greatest men, and was made great by one single rule. Oh, that all the young people of Philadelphia were before me now and I could say just this one thing, and that they would remember it. I would give a lifetime for the effect it would have on our city and on civilization. Abraham Lincoln's principle for greatness can be adopted by nearly all. This was his rule: Whatsoever he had to do at all, he put his whole mind into it and held it all there until that was all done. That makes men great almost anywhere. He stuck to those papers at that table and did not look up at me, and I sat there trembling.

Finally, when he had put the string around his papers, he pushed them over to one side and looked over to me, and a smile came over his worn face. He said: "I am a very busy man and have only a few minutes to spare. Now tell me in the fewest words what it is you want." I began to tell him, and mentioned the case, and he said: "I have heard all about it and you do not need to say any more. Mr. Stanton, the Secretary of War, was talking to me only a few days ago about that. You can go to the hotel and rest assured that the President never did sign an order to shoot a boy under twenty years of age, and never will. You can say that to his mother anyhow."

Then he said to me, "How is it going in the field?" I said, "We sometimes get discouraged." And he said: "It is all right. We are going to win out now. We are getting very near the light. No man ought to wish to be President of the United States, and I will be glad when I get through; then Tad and I are going out to Springfield, Illinois. I have bought a farm out there and I don't care if I again earn only twenty-five cents a day. Tad has a mule team, and we are going to plant onions."

Then he asked me, "Were you brought up on a farm?" I said, "Yes; in the

427

Berkshire Hills of Massachusetts." He then threw his leg over the corner of the big chair and said, "I have heard many a time, every since I was young, that up there in those hills you have to sharpen the noses of the sheep in order to get down to the grass between the rocks." He was so familiar, so everyday, so farmer-like, that I felt right at home with him at once.

He then took hold of another roll of paper, and looked up at me and said, "Good morning." I took the hint then and got up and went out. After I had gotten out I could not realize I had seen the President of the United States. But a few days later, when still in the city, I saw the crowd pass through the East Room by the coffin of Abraham Lincoln, and when I looked at the upturned face of the murdered President I felt then that the man I had seen such a short time before, who, so simple a man, so plain a man, was one of the greatest men that God ever raised up to lead a nation on to ultimate liberty. Yet he was only "Old Abe" to his neighbors. When they had the second funeral, I was invited among others, and went out to see that same coffin put back in the tomb at Springfield. Around the tomb stood Lincoln's old neighbors, to whom he was just "Old Abe." Of course that is all they would say.

Did you ever see a man who struts around altogether too large to notice an ordinary working mechanic? Do you think he is great? He is nothing but a puffed-up balloon, held down by his big feet. There is no greatness there.

Who are the great men and women? My attention was called the other day to the history of a very little thing that made the fortune of a very poor man. It was an awful thing, and yet because of that experience he—not a

428

great inventor or genius—invented the pin that now is called the safety pin, and out of that safety pin made the fortune of one of the great aristocratic families of this nation.

A poor man in Massachusetts who had worked in the nailworks was injured at thirty-eight, and he could earn but little money. He was employed in the office to rub out the marks on the bills made by pencil memorandums, and he used a rubber until his hand grew tired. He then tied a piece of rubber on the end of a stick and worked it like a plane. His little girl came and said, "Why, you have a patent, haven't you?" The father said afterward, "My daughter told me when I took that stick and put the rubber on the end that there was a patent, and that was the first thought of that." He went to Boston and applied for his patent, and every one of you that has a rubber-tipped pencil in your pocket is now paying tribute to the millionaire. He was once a poor man who thought—just thought.

⁂

A LITTLE BOOK, *I Dare You*, by William H. Danforth, who was founder and chairman of the board of the Ralston-Purina Company, has done me personally no end of good. My own copy is the twenty-ninth edition, privately printed; the book has touched thousands of lives.

To cite one case, *I Dare You* inspired sales of over $5 million worth of insurance in a special day of the Life Underwriters Association. It presents a fourfold program: "Think tall, Stand tall, Smile tall, Live tall." I knew the author personally, and he was a most inspiring person. His book has had huge sales among successful people.

Regretfully I can print here only a few pages of *I Dare You*.

429

What I've dared I've willed;
And what I've willed, I'll do!
Herman Melville (1819–1891)

⚜

You Can Be Bigger Than You Are

William H. Danforth (1870–1955)

As a small boy, before the time of drainage ditches, I lived in the country surrounded by swamp lands. Those were days of chills and fever and malaria. When I came to the city to school, I was sallow-cheeked and hollow-cheated. One of my teachers, George Warren Krall, was what we then called a health crank. We laughed at his ideas. They went in one ear and came out the other. But George Warren Krall never let up. One day he seemed to single me out personally. With flashing eye and in tones that I will never forget, he looked straight at me and said, "I dare you to be the healthiest boy in the class."

That brought me up with a jar. Around me were boys all stronger and more robust than I. To be the healthiest boy in the class when I was thin and sallow and imagined at least that I was full of swamp poisons!—the man was crazy. But I was brought up to take dares. His voice went on. He pointed directly at me. "I dare you to chase those chills and fevers out of your system. I dare you to fill your body with fresh air, pure water, whole-some food, and daily exercise until your cheeks are rosy, your chest full, and your limbs sturdy."

As he talked something seemed to happen inside me. My blood was up. It answered the dare and surged all through my body into tingling finger tips as though itching for battle.

I chased the poisons out of my system. I built a body that has equalled the strongest boys in that class, and has outlived and outlasted most of them. Since that day I haven't lost any time on account of sickness. You can imagine how often I have blessed that teacher who dared a sallow-cheeked boy to be the healthiest in the class.

Several years later, Henry Woods, one of our promising boys, pushed through the door of my office early one morning and stood facing me defi-antly.

"I'm quitting," he said.

"What's the trouble, Henry?"

"Just this, I'm no salesman. I haven't got the nerve. I haven't got the ability, and I'm not worth the money you are paying me."

There was something splendid about the courage of a man who would so frankly admit failure to his boss. He couldn't do that without nerve. Suddenly my mind recalled the boyhood scene when a teacher dared a hollow-cheated youngster to be strong. To Henry's surprise, instead of ac-cepting his resignation, I looked him squarely in the eye and said:

"If I know how to pick men, you have sales stuff in you. *I dare you,*

Henry Woods, to get out of this office, right now, and come back tonight with more orders than you have ever sold in any one day in your whole life."

He looked at me dumbfounded. Then a flash came into his eyes. It must have been the light of battle—the same something that had surged through me years before in answer to the teacher's dare. He turned and walked out of my office.

That night he came back. The defiant look of the early morning was replaced by the glow of victory. He had made the best record of his life. He had beaten his best—and he has been beating his best ever since. Incidentally, I'll give you a secret of his life. In his quiet way he is one of the best helpers of young salesmen I ever knew. He thrives by giving his experience to others. The world is full of men like Henry Woods just waiting for a Dare.

In the American Youth Foundation Camps each summer I come into contact with hundreds of young people who possess qualities of leadership. A few years ago a young fellow, who was working as a mechanic in a large electrical firm, came to me much perplexed. He had been forced to go to work when he had finished high school. Later he saw boys with technical college training outstrip him. Sensing he had ability to be much more than a mechanic, I dared him to leave his job and go back to school. Again I saw that priceless light of battle leap into the eyes of a fighter. He had no money, but, somehow, he got to college, was graduated with honors, and today the might-have-been mechanic is a prominent electrical engineer. I can tell you one of the secrets of his life, too . . . he keeps on growing by sharing, because now he has a mania for helping others get an education.

432

These are brief pages taken from the book of my practical experiences. There are scores of other pages like them. Unfortunately, however, there are many pages that would tell that other story of those who have been dared to do the super thing, but in whose eyes the light of battle failed to gleam. But the "I Dare You" plan *has* worked with thousands. It will work with you.

ARE YOU ONE OF THE PRICELESS FEW?

I am going to unfold a secret power that but few know how to use—the secret power of daring and sharing which carries with it tremendous responsibilities. Once you have it, you can never be the same again. Once it is yours, you can never rest until you have given it to others. And the more you give away the greater becomes your capacity to give. Deep down in the very fire of your being you must light an urge that can never be put out. It will catch this side of your life, then that side. It will widen your horizon. It will light up unknown reserves and discover new capacities for living and growing. It will become, if you don't look out, a mighty conflagration that will consume your every waking hour. And to its blazing glory a thousand other lives will come for light and warmth and power.

It is going to take courage to let this urge possess you. My life in business and my contacts with young people have convinced me that the world is full of unused talents and latent ability. The reason these talents lie buried is that the individual hasn't the courage to dig them up and use them. Everybody should be doing better than he is, but only a few dare. Prospectors for gold tell us that gold is where they find it. It may be in the bed of a river or on the mountain top. And prospectors for courage tell us the same thing. The one who dares may be found in a cottage or in a castle. But wherever you live, whoever you are, whatever you have or have not— if you dare, you are challenged to enlist in a great cause.

H. G. Wells tells how every human being can determine whether he has really succeeded in life. He says: "Wealth, notoriety, place, and power are no measure of success whatever. The only true measure of success is the ratio between what we might have done and what we might have been on the one hand, and the thing we have made and the thing we have made of ourselves on the other."

I want you to start a crusade in your life—to dare to be your best. I maintain that you are a better, more capable person than you have demonstrated so far. The only reason you are not the person you should be is you don't dare to be. Once you dare, once you stop drifting with the crowd and face life courageously, life takes on a new significance. New forces take shape within you. New powers harness themselves for your service.

Who wants to do unimportant and uninteresting things? Who even wants to gratify an ambition that has grown into a passion for fame and fortune? To desire something permanent in life, to develop your gifts to the largest possible use that's your dare. You have a wealth of possibilities, but maybe up to this time you have lacked a definite aim. You have a gun and plenty of ammunition. Now I dare you to aim at something worthy of the best that is in you.

My practical experience has convinced me that inner growth and broadening personality come from daring and sharing. You dare to use the talents you have. You find yourself growing stronger—physically, mentally, socially and spiritually. You multiply your daring a hundred-fold by sharing its fruits. You give your life away and, behold! a richer life comes back to you. This principle works through all of life:

Our most valuable possessions are those which can be shared without lessening: those which, when shared, multiply. Our least valuable possessions are those which, when divided, are diminished.

But how dare, you ask? First, it is necessary to agree that living aggressively changes the whole complexion of life. So many are preys to fear. You fear losing your job. You fear sickness or hard times or failure. But remember, courage is not the absence of fear, it is the conquest of it. Not until you dare to attack will you master your fears.

⁕

Thought Conditioners
Norman Vincent Peale (b. 1898)

THE PLANE FROM New York rolled up to the gate at Chicago's O'Hare Airport, and passengers surged into the aisle. A man in back of me exclaimed, "Hey you," slapping me on my back and saying, "You saved my life." He pulled my booklet called *Thought Conditioners* out of his pocket. "With this!" he added.

435

The booklet was beat-up and frayed, showing much use. Indeed, it was so tattered that I said, "Well, I'm glad it benefited you, but let me send you a fresh copy."

"Nothing doing. This copy saved my life and I'm hanging on to it." So saying, he shook me by the hand vigorously. "Be seeing you," he said, and was lost in the crowd.

The booklet, *Thought Conditioners*, contains my favorite verses from the Bible, verses that have guided me personally through life. I wrote this booklet to share these verses with all who asked for them, and we have distributed free of charge more than five million copies! It's called *Thought Conditioners* for a special reason. Because success and happiness depend on certain kinds of thoughts that habitually pass through our minds, it is vital that we condition the mind with the right kind of mental activity; in other words, the right kind of thinking. One of the wisest men of all time was Marcus Aurelius, who said, "Our life is what our thoughts make of it."

Just as air-conditioning can make the air in a room crisp and healthy, so thought conditioning can make the mind alert and powerful enough to change the thinking that comes up from the subconscious mind, a creative kind of thinking that leads to success and happiness.

The Bible states in the following verse what its thoughts will do: "If ye abide in me, and my words abide in you, ye shall ask what ye will, and it shall be done unto you" (John 15:7).

Thought conditioning is an action technique. You may read these verses and say to yourself, "Yes, I see what is suggested," and simply let it go at that. But then they will make very little difference in your life.

On the other hand, if you take forty days and memorize one statement each day, repeating it morning, noon, and night so it is lodged in your memory, a wonderful thing will happen. When stress or temptation or failure or success comes, your mind will automatically release to your consciousness the appropriate verse to steer your thoughts and action in the right direction. This is called guidance. The way it happens is almost miraculous. I know it works, and millions of others will agree. This is what is meant by an action technique.

I earnestly hope that you will try it. Your thought processes will become strong, healthy, and successful.

I have included here only the Bible verses. The entire booklet contains a paragraph with each verse suggesting how it may be applied in your everyday life with its problems and successes. If you are interested in having the *Thought Conditioners* booklet, you may write for a free copy to Peale Center for Christian Living, 66 East Main Street, Pawling, New York 12564. Ask for booklet no. 15002.

1. Peace I leave with you, my peace I give unto you: not as the world giveth, give I unto you. Let not your heart be troubled, neither let it be afraid. (John 14:27)
2. The things which are impossible with men are possible with God. (Luke 18:27)
3. Renew a right spirit within me. (Psalm 51:10)
4. Come unto Me, all ye that labor and are heavy laden, and I will give you rest. (Matthew 11:28)
5. What things soever ye desire, when ye pray, believe that ye receive them, and ye shall have them. (Mark 11:24)
6. Trust in the Lord with all thine heart; and lean not unto thine own understanding. (Proverbs 3:5)

7. I am come that they might have life, and that they might have it more abundantly. (John 10:10)

8. Confess your faults one to another, and pray one for another, that ye may be healed. The effectual fervent prayer of a righteous man availeth much. (James 5:16)

9. If God be for us, who can be against us? (Romans 8:31)

10. The kingdom of God is within you. (Luke 17:21)

11. For God hath not given us the spirit of fear; but of power, and of love, and of a sound mind. (II Timothy 1:7)

12. Thou shalt guide me with Thy counsel, and afterward receive me to glory. (Psalm 73:24)

13. Wherefore take unto you the whole armor of God, that ye may be able to withstand in the evil day, and having done all to stand. (Ephesians 6:13)

14. God is our refuge and strength, a very present help in trouble. (Psalm 46:1)

15. He that handleth a matter wisely shall find good: and whoso trusteth in the Lord, happy is he. (Proverbs 16:20)

16. Incline your ear, and come unto Me: hear, and your soul shall live. (Isaiah 55:3)

17. Now unto him that is able to do exceeding abundantly above all that we ask or think, according to the power that worketh in us. (Ephesians 3:20)

18. Ask, and it shall be given you; seek, and ye shall find; knock, and it shall be opened unto you. (Matthew 7:7)

19. I have learned, in whatsoever state I am, therewith to be content. (Philippians 4:11)

20. My soul, wait thou only upon God; for my expectation is from Him. (Psalm 62:5)

21. Be strong and of a good courage; be not afraid, neither be thou dismayed: for the Lord thy God is with thee withersoever thou goest. (Joshua 1:9)

22. Be ye transformed by the renewing of your mind. (Romans 12:2)

23. But as many as received Him, to them gave He power. (John 1:12)

24. The thing which I greatly feared is come upon me, and that which I was afraid of is come unto me. (Job 3:25)

25. This one thing I do, forgetting those things which are behind, and reaching forth unto those things where are before, I press toward the mark for the prize of the high calling of God in Christ Jesus. (Philippians 3:13, 14)

26. In all these things we are more than conquerors through Him that loved us. For I am persuaded, that neither death, nor life, nor angels, nor principalities, nor powers, nor things present, nor things to come, nor height, nor depth, nor any other creature, shall be able to separate us from the love of God, which is in Christ Jesus our Lord. (Romans 8:37–39)

27. If any man thirst, let him come unto Me, and drink. (John 7:37)

28. Love your enemies, bless them that curse you, do good to them that hate you, and pray for them which despitefully use you, and persecute you. (Matthew 5:44)

29. I can do all things through Christ which strengtheneth me. (Philippians 4:13)

30. In Him we live, and move, and have our being. (Acts 17:28)

31. If any man be in Christ, he is a new creature: old things are passed away; behold all things are become new. (II Corinthians 5:17)

32. Whosoever shall say unto this mountain, be thou removed, and be thou cast into the sea; and shall not doubt in his heart, but shall believe that those things which he saith shall come to pass; he shall have whatsoever he saith. (Mark 11:23)

33. They that wait upon the Lord shall renew their strength; they shall mount up with wings as eagles; they shall run and not be weary; and they shall walk and not faint. (Isaiah 40:31)

34. Eye hath not seen, nor ear heard, neither have entered into the heart of man, the things which God hath prepared for them that love Him. (I Corinthians 2:9)

35. Cast thy burden upon the Lord, and He shall sustain thee: He shall never suffer the righteous to be moved. (Psalm 55:22)

36. Thou wilt keep him in perfect peace, whose mind is stayed on Thee. (Isaiah 26:3)

37. This is the refreshing. (Isaiah 28:12)

38. I sought the Lord, and He heard me, and delivered me from all my fears. (Psalm 34:4)

39. When ye stand praying, forgive, if ye have ought against any. (Mark 11:25)

40. They shall hunger no more, neither thirst any more; neither shall the sun light on them, nor any heat. For the lamb which is in the midst of the throne shall feed them, and shall lead them unto living fountains of waters: and God shall wipe away all tears from their eyes. (Revelation 7:16–17)

꧁꧂

I CLOSE THIS BOOK with an account of the end of the great war between brothers, called by the North the Civil War and by the South of our long-healed country the War Between the States.

It is from a wonderful book, *A Dual Biography, Lee and Grant,* by Gene Smith. The author wrote of the two opposing generals with utter fairness and admiration for both.

Because I grew up in southern Ohio and used to watch the final defeat by death of the old veterans of the northern army and cherished my many friends of the South, I naturally have a fondness for the classic and heroic story of the Blue and the Gray.

441

Lee and Grant at Appomattox

Gene Smith (b. 1929)

LEE AND GRANT met face to face only four times; once during the Mexican War, when one of them was an illustrious staff officer and the other a lowly lieutenant; twice at the end of the Civil War, when each stood at the head of a great army; once in the White House, when one of them was President of the United States and the other the president of an obscure college. Only four times. Yet their names are linked forever in history—Robert E. Lee and Ulysses S. Grant.

This is the dramatic story of those two towering figures. It is the story of who they were as boys; as ardent young soldiers; as tender suitors of their wives-to-be; as husbands, fathers, generals.

Two men from two very different worlds.

And when their armies clashed, the earth shook and America held its breath. . . .

Off to the west, Grant tracked Robert Lee. To avoid getting entangled in rearguard skirmishes, he pushed his men on a parallel course south of Lee's, artillery horses shouldering the infantry off the roads, wagon trains rocking in the rear, the whole a mass of rushing men and horses running a race in the Virginia springtime.

Lee sped on, heading for the town of Amelia Court House some forty miles away, where trainloads of supplies had been directed. He was arrow-straight in the saddle, his face as calm as though he were watching the dress parade of a victorious army instead of a fleeing horde of smashed formations and broken regiments. He came to Amelia Court House with thirty thousand hungry men and found boxes of ammunition—but nothing to eat. The trainloads of food, mistakenly sent on to Richmond, were now in Federal hands. He took the news with no show of emotion, but from then on there was a haggard look on his face.

Twenty-five miles to the south, Grant was handed a dispatch from Sheridan saying he had intercepted the route Lee would have to take west out of Amelia Court House. The news was read to the troops, who wildly cheered it.

In the morning Sheridan struck Confederate columns on the move at Sayler's Creek and captured three thousand Confederates, including Custis Lee. And aide rode up and told Robert Lee that the wagon train had also been captured. Lee turned to General William Mahone, who was riding with him. "General, I have no other troops. Will you take your division to Sayler's Creek?"

He rode ahead with Mahone, the shrunken division following, and came to a high ridge overlooking the creek. Running up the ridge toward him were teamsters who had lost their wagons, soldiers who had thrown away their rifles—a routed mob.

"My God!" he cried. "Has the army been dissolved?" He went forward, seized a battle flag and, alone, on Traveller, held it up. Some of the men kept running, but others halted and formed with Mahone's division. The bunting blew itself around Lee's motionless figure. "I wish to fight here," he said.

"General Lee! Uncle Robert! Where's the man who won't follow Uncle Robert?" his soldiers shouted back; and they fought.

Ulysses Grant walked up the steps of a hotel in Farmville and wrote a note to General Lee:

> General:
>
> The result of the last week must convince you of the hopelessness of further resistance. I feel it is so, and regard it as my duty to shift from myself the responsibility of any further effusion of blood, by asking of you the surrender of that portion of the C. S. Army known as the Army of Northern Virginia.
>
> Very respectfully, your obedient servant,
>
> U. S. Grant

Under a white flag the note began its journey to Lee's hands. That evening Lee read it and silently handed it to General Longstreet. "Not yet," Longstreet said. Lee wrote back:

> Though not entertaining the opinion you express of the hopelessness of further resistance on the part of the Army of Northern Virginia, I reciprocate your desire to avoid useless effusion of blood, and ask the terms you will offer on condition of its surrender.

In his mind there arose the specter of chained captives, traitors taken in shackles to rows of gibbets. Grant sent a reply saying that the only condition he would insist on was that the men who laid down their arms pledge not to take them up again.

While Grant's reply was on its way to Lee, the Confederates kept their westward course, mules falling dead in the mud, famished men eating wild onions, grass, last year's rotted potatoes, anything.

In the morning Henry Wise, formerly governor of Virginia, now a general, found Lee on the rear portico of the house he was using as headquarters. "General Lee," Wise said, "my poor, brave men are lying on yonder hill more dead than alive. For more than a week they have been fighting day and night without food, and, by God, sir, they shall not move another step until somebody gives them something to eat."

"Come in, General," Lee said soothingly. "They deserve something to eat and shall have it, and you shall share my breakfast."

Lee then asked Wise's opinion of the situation they faced. "Situation!" Wise exploded. "There is no situation! Nothing remains, General Lee, but to put your poor men on your poor mules and send them home in time for spring plowing. This army is hopelessly whipped."

"Oh, General, do not talk so wildly. What would the country think of me if I did what you suggest?"

"Country be damned! There is no country. There has been no country, General, for a year or more. You are the country to these men. They have fought for you. They have shivered through a long winter for you. If you demand the sacrifice, there are still thousands of us who will die for you. That is why I say to you, sir, that the blood of any man killed hereafter is upon your head."

Lee said nothing but stood for some time at an open window, studying the crowd of men fleeing west through the fields.

445

Later that day the Reverend William N. Pendleton, serving as chief of artillery for the Army of Northern Virginia, went to Lee and said that he and several other high officers had agreed that the situation was hopeless. They made their opinions known to their commander, Pendleton said, in order to relieve him of having to take the full responsibility for an offer to surrender.

"I trust it has not come to that!" Lee said. Sooner than accede to a demand by General Grant for unconditional surrender, Lee said, he would die at his post.

Grant's letter saying he asked only that men lay down their arms was delivered. Lee read it and wrote back that in his previous note, "I did not intend to propose surrender but to ask the terms of your proposition." General Lee wrote he would be glad to meet Grant for a discussion of how peace could be restored, and he asked for a meeting at ten the next morning.

His note reached Grant just after midnight on April 9. A courier brought it to the house he was staying in and woke up the staff by calling, "Dispatches for General Grant!" The note went upstairs to Grant, who discussed it with Rawlins. "He did not propose to surrender!" Rawlins said angrily. "That's cool, but a falsehood. He *did* propose, in his heart, to surrender. Now he wants to arrange for peace, something beyond and above the surrender of his army. No, sir. He has to surrender, and nothing else!"

Grant's voice was soft and persuasive. "Some allowance must be made for the trying position in which General Lee is placed. He is compelled to defer somewhat to the wishes of his government. But it all means precisely the same thing. If I meet Lee, he will surrender before I leave."

Grant wrote:

As I have no authority to treat on the subject of peace, the meeting proposed for 10 a.m. today could lead to no good. I will state, however, General, that I am equally anxious for peace with yourself, and the whole North entertains the same feeling. By the South laying down their arms they will hasten that most desirable event.

At that moment John Gordon's men were moving to attack the Yankee cavalry that was blocking the last direction of retreat. "I will strike that man a blow in the morning," Lee had said the previous evening. If Gordon's infantry now encountered only cavalry, the enemy could be pushed aside. If there was infantry behind the cavalry, the problem would be quite different.

Off to the east, the Union infantry rushed through the darkness toward where their cavalry was struggling against Gordon's push. Sometime around nine in the morning they heard heavy firing up ahead. They were put into double-time march, and panting and sweating, they went through woods and out into a field and up a ridge, where their cavalry was falling back. They heard the Confederate artillery fire. A shell crashed into a barn on the ridge, and the building burst into flames. As the Federal cavalry retired, the infantry went forward. Three quarters of a mile away was another ridge, at the foot of which was the Confederate skirmish line, the rifle pits clearly visible.

The Confederate infantry had not opened up, but their artillery was firing. The Union men waited for the Confederates to start shooting, but nothing happened. Then they saw a white flag advancing.

"Tell General Lee," General Gordon said, "I have fought my corps to a frazzle, and I fear I can do nothing unless I am heavily supported by

Longstreet's corps." But Longstreet was holding off thousands of Federals in the rear. The Army of Northern Virginia was caught, surrounded.

Lee heard Gordon's message without a word. Then he spoke as to himself. "There is nothing left me to do but to go and see General Grant, and I would rather die a thousand deaths."

He ordered a flag of truce.

Earlier, away to the west, Grant and Rawlins had set out to join Sheridan at the head of the Union advance. At eleven o'clock they stopped to rest by some burning logs, from which they lighted their cigars. They heard a man shouting and turned to see one of Meade's staff officers on a coal-black stallion that was white with foam. The officer was waving his hat. He jumped off his mount, saluted and handed over a sealed envelope. Rawlins took the envelope and handed it to Grant. Nobody said anything. Grant read the message mechanically, handed it back to Rawlins and said in his usual voice, "You had better read it aloud."

Rawlins took a deep breath and read, "I received your note of this morning with reference to the surrender of this army. I now request an interview for that purpose."

There was silence for a moment. No one looked at anyone else. Then an artillery officer jumped on a log, waved his hat and proposed three cheers. A feeble hurrah came from a few throats and ended brokenly as men began to cry.

Lee lay resting on fence rails covered with blankets, under an apple tree. He was wearing a new uniform with embroidered belt, new gauntlets, high boots with red silk stitchings on their tops and gold spurs at the heels, a sash and a gilded presentation sword whose hilt was formed in the head of a lion. "I have probably to be Grant's prisoner, and I thought I must make my best appearance," he said to one of his generals. The firing had died, and all along the heights appeared noiseless dark blue columns, a great host that looked below on white flags.

A little after midday a Confederate staff officer and a Union colonel came riding up to Lee. "General Lee," said the Confederate officer, "allow me to introduce you to Colonel Babcock."

Grant's aide Orville E. Babcock saluted. Lee stood up. Never had he looked grander. He bowed. Babcock handed over a letter. Under the apple tree, Lee read Grant's acceptance of his offer to meet to arrange the surrender.

He ordered Traveller saddled and asked an aide, Charles Marshall, to go with him on his last mission. They set out with Babcock and a Confederate sergeant, George Tucker, who waved a white handkerchief as they road along—a sign that the truce was in effect. Through silent lines of men they went. Word flew to Grant that they would meet in the little hamlet of Appomattox Court House: two dozen houses, two dirt streets. It was Palm Sunday afternoon, April 9, 1865. Four years less three days had elapsed since the first shell screamed down on Fort Sumter.

As Lee passed, some of his troops broke into cheers. He waved his hand to silence them, in fear that any excitement might bring a shattering of the truce.

The riders came to the outskirts of the hamlet. They halted and waited there while Marshall and Tucker went to find a suitable place where the two commanders could meet.

The first townsman Marshall saw was Wilmer McLean, who offered the use of his house, a substantial dwelling with a well-furnished front parlor. Marshall sent Tucker back to tell Lee. With Babcock at his side, Lee rode to the house, dismounted and went up the stairs. Outside, the street filled up with Union officers.

Half an hour later came Ulysses S. Grant, riding with one hand in his pocket. He had ridden more than thirty-five miles that day over Virginia's muddy springtime roads. He wore the uniform of a private, with lieutenant general's stars sewn on.

Grant got off Cincinnati, who went to munching the spring grass by Traveller's side, and mounted the steps of the McLean house, alone, dirty, no sword, no sash. Mexico came into his mind, he told people later, Mexico and a colonel telling him that General Scott wanted officers to come to headquarters in full uniform. Embarrassment and a strange depression seized him—embarrassment that Lee might now think he had come covered with mud and in a private's crude clothing to rub salt into a wound, depression because of the mission he was on, to demand surrender of a man who had fought so long and hard, so nobly.

"General Lee."

"General Grant."

"I met you once before, General Lee, while we were serving in Mexico.

I have always remembered your appearance, and I think I should have recognized you anywhere."

Seated at small tables ten feet apart, Lee and Grant began talking about Mexico and then the weather in Virginia. Finally Grant signaled Marshall and Babcock to invite in the other gentlemen. Some one dozen Union officers quietly filed in. Then Lee said, "I suppose, General Grant, that the object of our present meeting is fully understood. I asked to see you to ascertain upon what terms you would receive the surrender of my army."

It must have been a relief for Grant to have Lee bring up the subject. Grant had been reluctant, his officers saw, to mention it himself. "The terms I propose," he said, "are those stated substantially in my letter of yesterday—officers and men to be paroled and disqualified from taking up arms again, and all arms, ammunition and supplies to be delivered up as captured property."

"Those are about the conditions I expected would be proposed," Lee said. There would be no triumphal march with prisoners in tow, no hangings.

"Very well, I will write them out." Grant took an order book and started writing in pencil. In the midst of his work he paused and looked at Lee's elegant saber hanging from a gold-braid sword belt. When he was finished, he rose and handed Lee the draft. It struck the watching Federal officers how deliberate Lee's actions were as he placed the order book on the table in front of him, pushed away two candleholders, put a pair of glasses on his nose, crossed his legs and began to read. The room was entirely silent. He came to Grant's final sentences: "The arms, artillery, and private property to be turned over to the officer appointed by me to receive them. This will not embrace the side arms of the officers. This done, each officer and man will be allowed to return to their homes, not to be disturbed by United States authority so long as they observe their paroles."

He looked up at Grant. "This will have a very happy effect on my army," he said. The elegant sword would not have to be handed over in days-of-chivalry display. "There is one thing I would like to mention," Lee said. "The cavalrymen and artillerist own their own horses in our army. I would like to understand whether these men will be permitted to retain their horses."

Grant responded. "I take it that most men in the ranks are small farmers, and as the country has been so raided by the two armies, it is doubtful they will be able to put in a crop to carry themselves and their families through the next winter without the aid of the horses they are now riding, and I will arrange it this way."

"This will have the best possible effect upon the men," Lee said. "It will do much toward conciliating our people."

The letter was given to an officer for copying. Grant signed the copy, and Lee told Marshall how to reply. Marshall wrote:

> Lieut-Gen. U. S. Grant:
> I have received your letter of this date containing the terms of surrender of the Army of Northern Virginia as proposed by you. As they are substantially the same as those expressed in your letter of the 8th instant, they are accepted.
> Very respectfully, your obedient servant

Lee signed, and the letters were exchanged. It was over.

By now it was getting on toward four o'clock. After saying a few polite words to one another, the two generals stood up and shook hands. Lee bowed to other men, then went through the door, carrying his hat and gloves. Some Federal officers sitting on the porch sprang up and saluted. He mechanically returned the honor. He gazed out over the yard, past the village, to the little valley where his army was. He drew on his gloves slowly and then absently banged his fists together several times. Traveller and Sergeant Tucker were out of sight. He roused himself and called, "Orderly! Orderly!"

"Here, General, here!" Tucker cried from around the corner. He brought the horse and Lee mounted. A long sigh came from him—"almost a groan," one officer later wrote. Marshall came down the steps and got on his horse. Behind him came Ulysses Grant and the other Union officers.

Grant stopped and took off his hat. His men followed his example. Lee looked at them, raised his hat in silence, turned Traveller and rode back to what had been his army.

As he approached the Confederate lines, a cheer from the troops along the road greeted him, but it died off very suddenly when they saw Lee's face. The road was crowded with men. More men came running, hats off, to pack themselves about him as he slowly made his way. He tried to go on, but the press of bodies halted the horse.

"General, are we surrendered?" a man asked.

Lee took off his hat. "Men," he said, "we have fought the war together, and I have done the best I could for you." His voice was ragged. "You will all be paroled and go to your homes." Tears came into his eyes. His lips moved and formed a soundless, broken attempt at "good-bye."

He pressed Traveller through them. "Good-bye, General, God bless you," he heard over and over from men weeping and touching the horse and his boots. Hat in hand, tears running down his face, Lee said farewell again and again and in broken phrases told his veterans to go home, plant a crop and obey the law. Victorious generals are always cheered by their men, but history knew no such precedent for a commander defeated.

Grant rode away to where his camp would be that night. Hearing the sound of gun salutes from his lines, he ordered the firing stopped. "The Confederates are our countrymen again," he said. He got to the camp and sat in front of his tent, despite a slight shower coming down. Bands played. "Ingalls," he said to an aide, "do you remember that old white mule—" and he talked about someone's mount back in Mexico.

In the morning, by prearrangement, they met again. Surrounded by Yankee officers, they sat their horses just outside the village. They talked for nearly an hour in a drizzling rain, Grant suggesting that Lee meet with Lincoln. "Whatever you and he agree on will be satisfactory to the reasonable people of the North and South."

"General Grant, you know that I am a soldier of the Confederate Army, and I cannot meet Mr. Lincoln. I do not know what Mr. Davis is going to do, and I cannot undertake to make any terms." They saluted each other, and Grant rode back to his tent to pack for City Point. Lee prepared a last message to his men:

After four years of arduous service marked by unsurpassed courage and fortitude, the Army of Northern Virginia has been compelled to yield to overwhelming numbers and resources.

I need not tell the brave survivors of so many hard fought battles, who have remained steadfast to the last, that I have consented to this result from no distrust of them; but feeling that valor and devotion could accomplish nothing that could compensate for the loss that must have attended the continuance of the contest, I determined to avoid useless sacrifice.

With an unceasing admiration of your constancy and devotion to your Country, and a grateful remembrance of your generous consideration for myself, I bid you all an affectionate farewell.

Grant went to City Point. He had telegraphed Julia he would arrive in time for dinner. She had it prepared in the galley of the dispatch boat and then, dressed to the nines, sat with the wives of two other generals and waited. A telegram arrived saying the general was delayed. At four in the morning Julia lay down in her berth, fully dressed, to awaken in broad daylight with her husband standing over her. The dinner was eaten as breakfast. When it was over, Julia asked if he would be going to Richmond.

"I would not distress these people," Grant said. "They are feeling their defeat bitterly, and you would not add to it by my witnessing their despair, would you?"

Instead they went to Washington. The city was wildly celebrating. Buildings were illuminated, bands were playing, and across the Potomac, a thousand freed slaves gathered on the grounds of what had been Robert E.

Lee's estate and was now the property of the United States of America. The freedmen sang "The Year of Jubilee" as rockets shot into the air. Signs in the city read U.S. Army Navy, U.S. Grant.

Grant sat in at a Cabinet meeting, and the President asked if anything had been heard from Sherman in North Carolina, where it was expected that, following Lee's example, Joe Johnson would shortly surrender his forces. Grant replied he was hourly expecting news, and Lincoln said he had reason to believe it likely. There was a dream he had had several times, he explained; it preceded every great event of the war—Fort Sumter, Bull Run, Antietam, Gettysburg, Vicksburg and other battles. He seemed in his dream to be "in some singular, indescribable vessel" that was moving rapidly "towards an indefinite shore." "I had this strange dream again last night," Lincoln said, "and we shall, judging from the past, have great news shortly."

After the meeting, the President asked Grant if the general and his wife would join him and the First Lady in a visit to the theater that night. Grant tentatively accepted, but Julia Grant told her husband she would not spend an evening in the company of the woman whose behavior had been so upsetting back at City Point when she had insulted Mrs. Ord. The President would have to be told that the Grants were going off to visit their children, who were in school in New Jersey. Grant complied with her wish. Ever after he wondered what would have happened had he been in Ford's Theatre that evening.

General Lee stayed in Appomattox until the last parole was made out for the last Confederate, and the last flag surrendered and the last musket stacked for the conqueror to take home.

It was over. Six hundred and twenty thousand men were dead, more than a quarter million southern, more than three hundred and fifty thousand northern. Robert E. Lee, on Traveller, set off on the road to Richmond, followed by his old headquarters wagon and an ambulance carrying an ill member of his staff. He declined to stay in private homes along the way, but pitched his tent as he had during the war.

News of his journey ran ahead of him. When he got to Richmond, a throng was waiting along the route he would have to take into the city. The people were silent, with hats off, wrote one witness. "There was no excitement, no hurrahing; but as the great chief passed, a deep, loving murmur arose from the very hearts of the crowd. Taking off his hat and simply bowing his head, the great man passed silently to his own door; it closed upon him and his people had seen him for the last time in his battle harness."

In June, two months after the surrender, Grant went to West Point, which he had not seen since leaving it, to attend the graduation ceremonies and to go to the nearby residence of Winfield Scott and receive greetings "from the oldest general to the greatest general." Then he returned to Galena, where thousands of people came out to see him pass under triumphal arches and where a huge sign referred to what he had once said he would do if he were mayor of the town: *General, the sidewalk is built.* A committee of citizens presented him with another house. He went to his parents' place near Cincinnati, and Hannah Grant in her apron said, "Well, Ulysses, you've become a great man, haven't you?" and went back to her household tasks.

❧